THE SOUL OF SCIENCE:

Christian Faith and Natural Philosophy

Nancy R. Pearcey
and
Charles B. Thaxton

CROSSWAY BOOKS • WHEATON, ILLINOIS
A DIVISION OF GOOD NEWS PUBLISHERS

Library of Congress Cataloging-in-Publication Data
Pearcey, Nancy R.
    The soul of science : Christian faith and natural philosophy /
Nancy R. Pearcey and Charles B. Thaxton
       p.   cm. — (Turning point Christian worldview series)
    1. Religion and science—History. I. Thaxton, Charles B.
II. Title. III. Series.
BL245.P43 1994   261.5'5—dc20   93-42580
ISBN 0-89107-766-9

02   01   00
15 14 13 12 11 10 9 8 7 6 5

THE SOUL OF SCIENCE

"In reviewing the contributions of the major scientists from the medieval period to the present day, the authors have a lightness of touch and an honesty of style which is refreshing. I consider *The Soul of Science* to be a most significant book which, in our scientific age, should be required reading for all thinking Christians."
—David Shotton, University of Oxford

"This is a first-rate book—a readable, nicely written, substantive treatment of key aspects of the history and philosophy of science. It would be an excellent text for courses on science and religion."
—J. P. Moreland, Biola University,
author, *Christianity and the Nature of Science*

"Pearcey and Thaxton show that the alliance between atheism and science is a temporary aberration and that, far from being inimical to science, Christian theism has played and will continue to play an important role in the growth of scientific understanding."
—Phillip Johnson, University of California, Berkeley,
author, *Darwin On Trial*

"An eminently readable account of the rise of modern science and its complicated relationship to Christianity. This book should destroy for all time the persistent myth that science and Christianity have always been at war with each other. All thoughtful Christians are in debt to these two excellent scholars. The best book of its kind in a very long while."
—James Sire, Senior Editor, InterVarsity Press

"Excellent historical review of philosophical ideas associated with the growth of science . . . compact education accessible to all comers."
—Walter R. Hearn, Professor of Science and
Christianity, New College, Berkeley

"Pearcey and Thaxton show the rich interplay between scientific thinking and the deeper philosophical and religious notions that have often informed and motivated scientific research. The best book of its kind in print!"
—Stephen C. Meyer, Whitworth College,
author, *Genesis 1 and the Origin of the Earth*

"Covers a lot of material in a way that is readable and insightful. . . . A good contribution to the current discussion."
—Christopher B. Kaiser, author,
Creation and the History of Science

"A marvelously clear exposition. It's one of the best nontechnical explanations of relativity I've ever seen."
—Roy Clouser, author, *The Myth of Religious Neutrality*

TURNING POINT Christian Worldview Series
Marvin Olasky, General Editor

Science, philosophy, even theology, are, all of them,
legitimately interested in questions about the nature of space,
structure of matter, patterns of action and, last but not least, about the
nature, structure, and value of human thinking and of human science.
Thus it is that science, philosophy, and theology, represented as often
as not by the very same men—Kepler and Newton, Descartes and
Leibniz—join and take part in the great debate.

—Alexandre Koyré
*From the Closed World to
the Infinite Universe*

TABLE OF

CONTENTS

ACKNOWLEDGMENTS

We are grateful to the Fieldstead Institute for a grant that enabled us to devote time to this project. Special thanks likewise to Marvin Olasky, series editor, for his excellent suggestions and his patience in shepherding the book over rocky terrain. We also want to express our appreciation to Byron Borger, owner of Hearts and Minds bookstore, who tenaciously hunted down books needed for research and alerted us to important new works as they came out.

We would like to thank the following people for giving generously of their time to review various parts of the manuscript in draft form: Jeff Boersema, Robert Brabenec, Gene Chase, Roy Clouser, Frederick Gregory, Christopher Kaiser, David Lindberg, Donald McNally, Steve Meyer, J. P. Moreland, Paul Nelson, Jim Neidhardt, Jitse van der Meer, Ted Plantinga, Robert Newman, Del Ratzsch, Kim Robbins, Karen Scantlin, David Shotton, Frederick Skiff, Paul Thigpen, Thaddeus Trenn, Peter Vibert, Jonathan Wells. We also thank J. Richard Pearcey for excellent editorial assistance.

INTRODUCTION

*I*saac Newton—a Christian? I never learned *that* in school." The young woman's jaw dropped in surprise. She had recently earned a master's degree in an honors program at a major university. She had been a leader in Christian campus groups. Yet not once in her educational career had she learned that key figures in the history of science operated within a Christian framework, that their science was inspired and motivated by their religious convictions.

Those of us who work in the sciences may be so familiar with these historical facts that we forget how remote they are to the average Christian in the pew. The typical science textbook is narrowly designed to acquaint students with major scientific discoveries. It presents little of the scientists' underlying philosophical or religious motivations. The sole exceptions to that rule seem to be instances when philosophical or religious beliefs were *rejected*—such as Copernicus's rejection of Ptolemaic geocentric cosmology or Galileo's rejection of Aristotelian physics. This selective textbook presentation tends to create in the student an implicitly positivist impression of science—that progress in science consists in its "emancipation" from the confining fetters of religion and metaphysics. Typically the student also assumes, at least unconsciously, that the historical characters who led this emancipation must have shared the same derogatory view of religion and philosophy.

Nothing could be further from the truth. In recent decades, the positivist view of science has been assailed for both logical difficulties and historical inaccuracies. As a result, science historians have developed a new sensitivity to the role played by extra-scientific factors in the development of modern science. Historians have broadened their interest beyond the textbook presentation, with its simple chronology of discoveries, to the scientist as a human being—to the complex of beliefs, assumptions, and socio-political forces that motivated his scientific research. The result has been a much more interesting and colorful tapestry of the past and ultimately a more accurate portrayal of the progress of science.

The new approach more readily recognizes the influence of Christianity on science. Up to the turn of the century, Christianity was the dominant intellectual force in most areas of life and culture in the West. Christians were not a marginalized minority; they were the majority. The truth is that we cannot really understand a Newton, a Descartes, or a Cuvier without delving into the religious and philosophical ideas that drove their scientific work.

We speak advisedly of both religious *and* philosophical ideas. For while orthodox Christians have held certain fundamental theological convictions in common, they have often differed in their understanding of how to express and apply their theology in areas such as science. Christians begin with Scripture and creation—God's Word and God's world. But the way we relate the two is through the intermediary of philosophy—a philosophy of nature and of God's relationship to it, an abstract conception informed by Scripture but not uniquely determined by Scripture. Christians who share theological orthodoxy may embrace different philosophies of nature.

In this book, we will identify and track some of the more significant philosophical streams of thought since the scientific revolution. As we proceed, it will become clear that the progress of science was a far cry from the simple "emancipation" from religion. On the contrary, science has been shaped largely by debates *among Christians* over which philosophy of nature gives the best way to conceptualize the kind of world God created and the nature of His relationship to it. Even after philosophical materialism began to penetrate scientific thought, Christian influences remained vibrant. References to God in public discourse were common. Not until the late nineteenth to early twentieth century did Christian faith lose its hold as a shared, public commitment and retreat to the realm of private, individual belief.

Our goal in this book is to describe highlights in the growth of science both before and after this change took place. Roughly the first half of the book covers the history of science in its formative stages when Christianity was the backdrop to virtually all scientific discussion, when disagreements took place primarily among Christians over how to best express God's relationship to the natural world. The second half of the book describes key controversies that have changed the face of science since Christianity declined as a public and communal faith—the revolution in mathematics brought on by non-Euclidean geometry, the revolution in physics triggered by relativity theory and quantum mechanics, and the revolution still taking place in biology through the discovery of DNA and the rise of molecular biology. We will outline some of the challenges these revolutions raised to a Christian understanding of nature.

In a survey book of this type, directed at a semi-popular audience, we paint necessarily with broad strokes. We can only hope we have highlighted and simplified without oversimplifying. Furthermore, our goal is to be historical and descriptive rather than analytical or polemical, which means we describe historical controversies and debates without necessarily coming down on any particular side. Finally, we do not seek to give a comprehensive treatment of the subject matter of various disciplines. Instead, we point out highlights in each field, themes and ideas that we find significant for a Christian understanding of science and its historical development.

Our main purpose in this book is to reintroduce Christians to a part of our rich intellectual heritage. Like the young woman described earlier, many Christians live on the thin edge of contemporary life with only a tenuous connection to the past. This ahistorical perspective tends to reinforce a pietistic attitude toward faith and culture. If all we know is today—and no one can deny that today Christianity is on the margins of the intellectual and cultural world—then we have no model for breaking out of that pattern.

By acquainting ourselves with forerunners in the faith, however, we discover a different model. We learn that until comparatively recent times, Christians have actively worked out the implications of their faith in all areas of life and scholarship—from philosophy to mathematics to physics to biology. Christian faith has not been a purely private matter. Nor has it been shut off in a separate part of life, as though it were relevant to worship but not to work.

In this book we introduce readers to people whose "secular" accomplishments flowed from a deep commitment to their faith, who understood that Christianity is meant to be developed into a complete worldview. May their example rekindle the same vision in us and inspire us to go and do likewise.

PART ONE

THE NEW HISTORY
OF SCIENCE

ONE

AN INVENTED INSTITUTION:
Christianity and the Scientific Revolution

The most curious aspect of the scientific world we live in, says science writer Loren Eiseley, is that it exists at all. Westerners often unconsciously assume a doctrine of Inexorable Progress, as though the mere passage of time leads inevitably to increased knowledge as surely as an acorn becomes an oak. "Yet the archaeologist would be forced to tell us," says Eiseley, "that several great civilizations have arisen and vanished without the benefit of a scientific philosophy." The type of thinking known today as scientific, with its emphasis upon experiment and mathematical formulation, arose in one culture—Western Europe—and in no other.

Science, Eiseley concludes, is not "natural" to mankind at all. Inquisitiveness about the world is indeed a natural attitude, but institutional science is more than that. "It has rules which have to be learned, and practices and techniques which have to be transmitted from generation to generation by the formal process of education," Eiseley notes. In short, it is "an *invented* cultural institution, an institution not present in all societies, and not one that may be counted upon to arise from human instinct." Science "demands some kind of unique soil in which to flourish." Deprived of that soil, it is "as capable of decay and death as any other human activity, such as a religion or a system of government."[1]

What is that unique soil? Eiseley identifies it, somewhat reluctantly, as the Christian faith. "In one of those strange permutations of which history yields occasional rare examples," he says, "it is the Christian world which finally gave birth in a clear, articulate fashion to the experimental method of science itself."[2]

Eiseley is not alone in observing that the Christian faith in many ways inspired the birth of modern science. Science historians have developed a renewed respect for the Middle Ages, including a renewed respect for the Christian worldview culturally and intellectually dominant during that period. Today a wide range of scholars recognize that Christianity provided both intellectual presuppositions and moral sanction for the development of modern science.

REHABILITATION OF THE MIDDLE AGES

From the Enlightenment until the early twentieth century, scholars generally divided history into three stages—the ancient world, regarded as brilliant though limited in its scientific understanding; the medieval world, dismissed as a time of intellectual and cultural desolation (the "dark ages"); and the modern age, heralded as a time when reason and enlightenment arose to dispel the mists of medieval superstition. But in recent years that simple schema has been challenged, particularly its negative characterization of the medieval period.

The rehabilitation of the Middle Ages began with the work of French physicist and philosopher Pierre Duhem (1861-1916). Searching for historical examples to illustrate his philosophy of science, Duhem investigated the history of statics (a branch of mechanics dealing with masses or forces at rest). At the outset of his research, he adopted the common assumption that the Middle Ages had contributed nothing to science. He anticipated that his story would begin with the ancient Greeks (Archimedes) and proceed directly to Leonardo da Vinci, vaulting over all intervening history.

But digging into historical sources, Duhem uncovered the work of a thirteenth-century scientist named Jordanus de Nemore, who had anticipated Leonardo and Galileo in his work on the foundations of statics. Duhem then uncovered fourteenth-century scientists such as Albert of Saxon, Jean Buridan, and Nicole Oresme, who had likewise done important work in the field. He became convinced that the roots of modern science reached back to the work of these medieval scientists—and that far from being a period of stagnation, the Middle Ages actually laid the foundations for the flowering of science.

Duhem was a Catholic, and some have dismissed his conclusions as an attempt to cast a more favorable light on the Middle Ages, dominated as it was by the Catholic church. But as historian David Lindberg argues, Duhem seems to have been genuinely surprised by the scientific fertility of the medieval mind.[3] This is not to say, however, that he was insensitive to the religious implications of his discoveries. Duhem was quick to see apologetical value in the fact that Christianized medieval Europe was not hostile to scientific learning after all—that, on the contrary, it was the womb that gave birth to the scientific enterprise.

Images of War

Duhem's work inspired other historians to probe the various ways Christianity provided an intellectual environment conducive to scientific endeavor. That such questions are even entertained indicates a dramatic turnaround in thinking about the relation between science and Christian faith. The image most of us grew up with was one of conflict and hostility. Phrases such as "the war between science and religion" are so familiar many people don't even challenge them.

Yet this conception of warfare is actually a *mis*conception, and one of recent lineage. Over some three centuries, the relationship between faith and science can best be described as an alliance. The scientist living between 1500 and the late 1800s inhabited a very different universe from that of the scientist living today. The earlier scientist was very likely to be a believer who did not think scientific inquiry and religious devotion incompatible. On the contrary, his motivation for studying the wonders of nature was a religious impulse to glorify the God who had created them. Indeed, though he studied the physical creation, he was unlikely to be a scientist per se (the term "scientist" was not coined until 1834) but a churchman. Especially in the English countryside, the parson-naturalist was a common figure.

As Colin Russell tells it in his book *Cross-Currents: Interactions Between Science and Faith,*[4] the idea of a war between science and religion is a relatively recent invention—one carefully nurtured by those who hope the victor in the conflict will be science. In late nineteenth-century England, several small groups of scientists and scholars organized under the leadership of Thomas H. Huxley to overthrow the cultural dominance of Christianity—particularly the intellectual dominance of the Anglican church. Their goal was to secularize society, replacing the Christian worldview with scientific naturalism, a worldview that recognizes the existence of nature alone. Though secularists, they understood very well that they were replacing one religion by another, for they described their goal as the establishment of the "church scientific." Huxley even referred to his scientific lectures as "lay sermons."

It was during this period that a whole new literature emerged purporting to reveal the hostility religion has shown toward science throughout history. The most virulent were works by John William Draper (1811-1882) and Andrew Dickson White (1832-1918)—works regarded by most historians today as severely distorted because of the authors' polemical purposes.

Draper's *History of the Conflict Between Religion and Science* portrayed the history of science as "a narrative of the conflict of two contending powers, the expansive force of the human intellect on one side, and the compression arising from traditionary faith and human interests on the other." The faith Draper has in mind is primarily that of the Catholic church, and he uses the language of "antagonism" and "struggle"—"a bitter, a mortal animosity." He accuses the Catholic church of "ferociously suppressing by the stake and the sword every attempt at progress" and of having hands "steeped in blood!"[5]

Draper's dramatic scenario of a great battle between theologians and scientists attracted a wide readership, but its anti-Catholicism eventually dated the book. White's *A History of the Warfare of Science with Theology* had a more lasting influence. As late as 1955, Harvard historian of science George Sarton was still praising White for writing "an instructive book."[6] In 1965, in an abridged edition of White's book, historian Bruce Mazlish praised White for establishing his thesis "beyond any reasonable doubt."[7] And in 1991, a well-known science writer, on hearing that we were composing a book on the history of science and Christian faith, took the time to write us and recommend White's book as an important treatment of the subject.

White states his central thesis in these words:

> In all modern history, interference with science in the supposed interest of religion, no matter how conscientious such interference may have been, has resulted in the direst evils both to religion and to science.[8]

Heaping up quotation upon quotation, laced with heavy sarcasm and irony, White purported to prove the pernicious effects of Christianity upon the advance of science. White's themes were picked up by several lesser writers, all telling the same story, etching into Western consciousness a mythology of fierce combat between science and Christian faith.

Even as the warfare image spread, however, it began to be challenged. Scientists and historians such as Alfred North Whitehead and Michael B. Foster became convinced that, far from impeding the progress of science, Christianity had actually encouraged it—that the Christian culture within which science arose was not a menace but a midwife to science.

THE NATURE OF NATURE

It should not be terribly surprising that Christianity was an important ally of the scientific enterprise. After all, modern science arose within a culture saturated with Christian faith. That historical fact alone is suggestive. It was Christianized Europe that became the birthplace of modern science—there and nowhere else.

Through sheer practical know-how and rules-of-thumb, several cultures in antiquity—from the Chinese to the Arabs—produced a higher level of learning and technology than medieval Europe did. Yet it was Christianized Europe and not these more advanced cultures that gave birth to modern science as a systematic, self-correcting discipline. The historian is bound to ask why this should be so. Why did Christianity form the matrix within which this novel approach to the natural world developed?

Of course, many factors other than Christian faith contributed to making science possible—the growth of trade and commerce, technological advances, the founding of scientific institutions such as the Royal Society, increased circulation of journals, and so on. Yet these were not so much the sources of the scientific revolution as the avenues by which it spread. The source itself seems to have been a tacit attitude toward nature, a flowering forth of assumptions whose roots had been deepening and strengthening for centuries.[9]

Scientific investigation depends upon certain assumptions about the world—and science is impossible until those assumptions are in place. As Foster argues, Western thinkers had to ascribe to nature the character and attributes that made it a possible object of scientific study *in advance of* the actual establishment of science.[10] As Whitehead puts it, "faith in the possibility of science" came *antecedently* to the development of actual scientific theory.

This faith, Whitehead explains, rested on certain habits of thought, such as the lawfulness of nature—which in turn, he maintains, came from the Christian doctrine of the world as a divine creation. Whitehead did not mean that everyone living in Europe at the time of the scientific revolution was a committed Christian. But even those who rejected orthodox Biblical doctrines continued to live and think within the intellectual framework of the Biblical worldview. "I am not talking of the explicit beliefs of a few individuals," Whitehead says, but rather "the impress on the European mind arising from the unquestioned faith of centuries"—the "instinctive tone of thought and not a mere creed of words."[11]

What is this "tone of thought"? Christian conceptions of reality are woven so extensively into the fabric of the Western mind that it takes an effort of the historical imagination to perceive their originality. Indeed, throughout much of Western history, Christian scholars have been so receptive to external philosophical ideas—so willing to formulate their positions in terms derived from Aristotelianism or neo-Platonism (as we shall see in following chapters)—that the uniqueness of the Christian perspective was nearly obscured. Yet unique it was, and the best way to perceive its novelty is to set it alongside contrasting views common in the ancient world.

Here Today, Here Tomorrow

Science is the study of nature, and the possibility of science depends upon one's attitude toward nature. Biblical religion gave to Western culture several of its fundamental assumptions about the natural world.

To begin with, the Bible teaches that nature is real. If this seems too obvious to mention, recall that many belief systems regard nature as unreal. Various forms of pantheism and idealism teach that finite, particular things are merely "appearances" of the One, the Absolute, the Infinite. Individuality and separateness are illusions. Hinduism, for instance, teaches that the everyday world of material objects is *maya*, illusion. It is doubtful whether a philosophy that so denigrates the material world would be capable of inspiring the careful attention to it that is necessary for science.

The Christian doctrine of creation, on the other hand, teaches that finite objects are not mere appearances of the Infinite. God made them; they have a real existence. In the words of Langdon Gilkey, professor of theology at the University of Chicago School of Divinity, the doctrine of creation implies that the world is not illusory; it is "a realm of definable structures and real relations, and so is a possible object both for scientific and for philosophical study."[12]

God Made It Good

Science rests not only on metaphysical convictions but also on convictions about value. A society must be persuaded that nature is of great value, and hence an object worthy of study. The ancient Greeks lacked this conviction. The ancient world often equated the material world with evil and disorder; hence, it denigrated anything to do with material things. Manual labor was relegated to slaves, while philosophers sought a life of leisure in order to pursue the "higher things." Many historians believe this is one reason the Greeks did not develop an empirical science, which requires practical, hands-on observation and experimentation.

Against the surrounding Greek culture, the early church defended a high view of the material world.[13] Christianity teaches that the world has great value as God's creation. Genesis repeats the joyful refrain again and again: "And God saw that it was good." In the words of Mary Hesse, a British philosopher of science, "there has never been room in the Hebrew or Christian tradition for the idea that the material world is something to be escaped from, and that work in it is degrading. Material things are to be *used* to the glory of God and for the good of men." As a result, "in western Europe in the Christian era there was never the same derogation of manual work. There was no slave class to do the work, and craftsmen were respected."[14]

The dignity of work became an even more prominent theme in the Reformation. The concept of "calling" was extended from church vocations to secular vocations. According to theologian Ian Barbour, Protestants believed that "man should serve God not by withdrawing to a monastic life but by carrying out any honest and useful job with integrity and diligence." This general enhancement of the dignity of work, Barbour says, served to endorse scientific work as well.[15]

John Calvin, for example, did not call merely for the devotional contemplation of creation; he also called for active labor in creation, both practically and intellectually. In Calvin's words, "there is need of art and more exacting toil in order to investigate the motion of the stars, to determine their assigned stations, to measure their intervals, to note their properties."[16]

In the spirit of the Reformation, the astronomer Johannes Kepler wrote of being "called" by God to use his talents in his work as an astronomer. In one of his notebooks, Kepler broke spontaneously into prayer:

I give you thanks, Creator and God, that you have given me this joy in thy creation, and I rejoice in the works of your hands. See I have now completed the work to which I was called. In it I have used all the talents you have lent to my spirit.[17]

In the same spirit, the early chemist Jean-Baptiste van Helmont insisted that the pursuit of science is "a good gift," given by God. This broad concept of calling lent spiritual and moral sanction to science as a legitimate way of serving God.

A Garden, Not a God

In Biblical teaching, nature is good, but it is not a god. It is merely a creature. The Bible stands firmly against any deification of the creation.

Pagan religions are typically animistic or pantheistic, treating the natural world either as the abode of the divine or as an emanation of God's own essence. The most familiar form of animism holds that spirits or gods reside in nature. In the words of Harvey Cox, a Baptist theologian, pagan man "lives in an enchanted forest." Glens and groves, rocks and streams are alive with spirits, sprites, demons. Nature teems with sun gods, river goddesses, astral deities. Totemism rests on the idea that the creatures of the natural world are tied to human beings in a bond of spiritual kinship.[18]

The Biblical doctrine of creation rules out all this. God does not inhabit the world the way a dryad inhabits a tree; He is not the personalization of natural forces. He is not the world's "soul"; He is its Creator. It is the work of His hands, as a vase is the work of the potter. The opening lines of Genesis 1 stand in stark contrast to most ancient religions in rejecting any religious status to the sun, moon, and stars. In Genesis the heavenly bodies are not divine; they are merely "light-bearers," placed in the sky to serve God's purposes, the way a woman hangs a lantern to light the porch.

Dutch historian of science R. Hooykaas describes this as the "de-deification" of nature.[19] Natural phenomena—sun, moon, forests, rivers—are no longer seen as the locus of deity, no longer objects of religious awe and reverence. They are creations of God, placed in the world to serve His purposes and contribute to human welfare.

The de-deification of nature was a crucial precondition for science. As long as nature commands religious worship, dissecting her is judged impious. As long as the world is charged with divine beings and powers, the only appropriate response is to supplicate them or ward them off. In the words of seventeenth-century chemist Robert Boyle, the tendency to regard nature as sacred "has been a discouraging impediment" to science.[20]

Science is not merely a method of inquiry; it begins with an intellectual stance vis-a-vis the natural world. As Cox writes, "however highly developed a culture's powers of observation, however refined its equipment for measuring, no real scientific breakthrough is possible until man can face the natural world unafraid."[21] The monotheism of the Bible exorcised the gods of nature, freeing humanity to enjoy and investigate it without fear. When the world was no longer an object of worship, then—and only then—could it become an object of study.

A Rational God, an Orderly World

To become an object of study the world must be regarded as a place where events occur in a reliable, predictable fashion. This, too, was a legacy of Christianity. Whereas paganism taught a multitude of immanent gods, Christianity taught a single transcendent Creator, whose handiwork is a unified, coherent universe.

Presbyterian theologian Thomas Derr expresses the idea in these words:

> Man did not face a world full of ambiguous and capricious gods who were alive in the objects of the natural world. He had to do with one supreme creator God whose will was steadfast. Nature was thus abruptly desacralized, stripped of many of its arbitrary, unpredictable, and doubtless terrifying aspects.[22]

In a similar vein, Nobel Prize-winning biochemist Melvin Calvin muses on the fundamental conviction in science that the universe is ordered:

> As I try to discern the origin of that conviction, I seem to find it in a basic notion discovered 2000 or 3000 years ago, and enunciated first in the Western world by the ancient Hebrews: namely, that the universe is governed by a single God, and is not the product of the whims of many gods, each governing his own province according to his own laws. This monotheistic view seems to be the historical foundation for modern science.[23]

Of course, the idea of order in nature rests not simply on the *existence* of a single God but also on the *character* of that God. The God revealed in the Bible is trustworthy and dependable; the creation of such a God must likewise be dependable. Derr explains:

> As the creation of a trustworthy God, nature exhibited regularity, dependability, and orderliness. It was intelligible and could be studied. It displayed a knowable order.[24]

The work of Copernicus provides a historical example. Copernicus tells us that, in his search for a better cosmology than that of Aristotle and Ptolemy, he first went back to the writings of other ancient philosophers. But he uncovered significant disagreement among the ancients regarding the structure of the universe. This inconsistency disturbed him, Copernicus said, for he knew the universe was "wrought for us by a supremely good and orderly Creator." His own scientific work became a quest for a better cosmology—one that would, in the words of theologian Christopher Kaiser, "uphold the regularity, uniformity, and symmetry that befitted the work of God."[25]

Another historical example comes from the eighteenth century when an explosive increase in knowledge of new life forms threatened to destroy belief in an underlying order in the organic world. Zoologist

Ernst Mayr describes the near-bewilderment among natural historians of the time:

> When viewing the almost chaotic mountains of new species, how could one avoid asking, "Where is that harmony of nature of which every naturalist is dreaming? What are the laws that control diversity? What plan did the father of all things have when he designed little creatures and big ones?"

Yet those committed to the doctrine of creation held firmly to belief in a divine plan even in the face of apparent chaos. "It was simply inconceivable, in a period so strongly dominated by natural theology," Mayr writes, "that organic diversity could be totally without rhyme or reason, that it could be simply the result of 'accident.'" This dogged faith spurred naturalists on in the hope of discovering "the plan of creation."[26] They trusted that because God had made the world, in the end it would reveal an underlying order.

Follow the Law

Belief in an orderly universe came to be summed up in the concept of natural law. The phrase "laws of nature" is so familiar to the modern mind that we are generally unaware of its uniqueness. People in pagan cultures who see nature as alive and moved by mysterious forces are not likely to develop the conviction that all natural occurrences are lawful and intelligible.

In every culture, of course, craftsmen have developed rough-and-ready rules of procedure. But when they encounter an irregularity or anomaly, they simply accept it as part of the inscrutable nature of things. As historian A. R. Hall points out, the concept of natural law was unknown to both the ancient Western world and the Asian world. When the concept finally arose in the Middle Ages, Hall says, it signified "a notable departure" from anything that had gone before.

The source of this departure Hall identifies as the Biblical teaching of a Creator. As he puts it, the use of the word *law* in the context of natural events "would have been unintelligible in antiquity, whereas the Hebraic and Christian belief in a deity who was at once Creator and Law-giver rendered it valid."[27] The Biblical God is the Divine Legislator who governs nature by decrees set down in the beginning. We see that conviction, for example, in the writings of seventeenth-century mathematician and philosopher René Descartes, who said the mathematical laws sought by science were legislated by God in the same manner as a king ordains laws in his realm.

The order of the reasoning here is important. The early scientists did not argue that the world was lawfully ordered, and *therefore* there must be a rational God. Instead, they argued that there was a rational God, and *therefore* the world must be lawfully ordered. They had greater confidence in the existence and character of God than in the lawfulness of nature.

As historian Carl Becker explains, until the scientific revolution was well under way, nature simply did not strike most people as either lawful or rational. Nature "seemed to common sense intractable, even mysterious and dangerous, at best inharmonious to man." The deep conviction that nature is intelligible came from Biblical principles. In Becker's words, theologians

> argued that, since God is goodness and reason, his creation must somehow be, even if not evidently so to finite minds, good and reasonable. Design in nature was thus derived *a priori* from the character which the Creator was assumed to have.

The idea of natural law, Becker concludes, was not derived from observations; it was derived *prior* to observations from belief in the Biblical God.[28] It was not a fact of experience but an article of faith.

Precisely So

One of the most distinctive aspects of modern science is its use of mathematics—the conviction not only that nature is lawful but also that those laws can be stated in precise mathematical formulas. This conviction, too, historians have traced to the Biblical teaching on creation.

The Biblical God created the universe *ex nihilo* and hence has absolute control over it. Genesis paints a picture of a Workman completely in charge of His materials. Hence in its essential structure the universe is precisely what God wants it to be.

This idea was alien to the ancient world. In all other religions, the creation of the world begins with some kind of pre-existing substance with its own inherent nature. As a result, the creator is not absolute and does not have the freedom to mold the world exactly as he wills.

For example, in Greek philosophy the world consists of eternal matter structured by eternal rational universals called Ideas or Forms. In Plato's creation myth, the creator (demiurge) is an inferior deity who did not create from nothing; he merely injected reason (Ideas) into reason-less matter. And even that he did imperfectly because matter was stubborn stuff, capable of resisting the rational structure imparted by the Ideas. In short, this is a creator whose hands are tied, as Hooykaas writes, in two respects:

He had to follow not his own design but the model of the eternal Ideas; and second, he had to put the stamp of the Ideas on a chaotic, recalcitrant matter which he had not created himself.[29]

As a result, the Greeks expected a level of imprecision in nature, a certain fuzziness at the edges. If some facts did not fit their theories, well, that was to be expected in an imperfect world. Individual things were, after all, only rough approximations to the rational Ideas or Forms. As historian Dudley Shapere explains, in Greek thought the physical world "contains an essentially irrational element: nothing in it can be described *exactly* by reason, and in particular by mathematical concepts and laws."[30]

By contrast, the Christian doctrine of creation *ex nihilo* means there is no pre-existing substance with its own independent properties to limit what God can do. God creates the world exactly as He wills. For a Platonist, if a line in nature is not quite circular, that is because nature is an only partially successful approximation to geometrical Ideas. But for a Christian, if God had wanted the line to be circular, He would have made it that way. If it is not exactly a circle, it must be exactly something else—perhaps an ellipse. The scientist can be confident that it is exactly *something*, and not mere capricious variation from the ideal.

A striking example can be found in the work of Kepler, who struggled for years with the slight difference of eight minutes between observation and calculation of the orbit of the planet Mars. Eventually this slight imprecision drove him to abandon the idea of circular orbits and to postulate elliptical orbits. If Kepler had not maintained the conviction that nature must be precise, he would not have agonized over those eight minutes and would not have broken through a traditional belief in circular orbits that had held sway for two thousand years. Kepler spoke gratefully of those eight minutes as a "gift of God."

Thus the application of geometry and mathematics to the analysis of physical motion rests on the Christian doctrine of creation *ex nihilo*. The implication is that God is omnipotent; there is no recalcitrant matter to resist His will. In the words of physicist C. F. von Weizsacker:

> Matter in the Platonic sense, which must be 'prevailed upon' by reason, will not obey mathematical laws exactly: matter which God has created from nothing may well strictly follow the rules which its Creator has laid down for it. In this sense I called modern science a legacy, I might even have said a child, of Christianity.[31]

Historian R. G. Collingwood expresses the argument most succinctly . He writes: "The possibility of an applied mathematics is an expression, in terms of natural science, of the Christian belief that nature is the creation of an omnipotent God."[32]

The Spitting Image

Belief in a rational order in nature would have no practical benefit for science were it not accompanied by the belief that humans can discover that order. Historically, Eiseley says, science stemmed from "the sheer act of faith that the universe possessed order *and could be interpreted by rational minds.*"[33] The latter is just as important as the former. It signifies that science cannot proceed without an epistemology, or theory of knowledge, guaranteeing that the human mind is equipped to gain genuine knowledge of the world. Historically, this guarantee came from the doctrine that humanity was created in the image of God.

A cross-cultural comparison can help clarify the point. Joseph Needham, a student of Chinese culture, asks in his book *The Grand Titration* why the Chinese never developed modern science. The reason, he said, is that the Chinese had no belief either in an intelligible order in nature nor in the human ability to decode an order should it exist. As Needham writes:

> There was no confidence that the code of Nature's laws could be unveiled and read, because there was no assurance that a divine being, even more rational than ourselves, had ever formulated such a code capable of being read.

The Chinese did sense some order in nature, but they conceived of it as an inherent necessity inscrutable to the human mind. "It was not an order ordained by a rational personal being," Needham explains, "and hence there was no guarantee that other rational personal beings would be able to spell out in their own earthly languages the pre-existing divine code of laws which he had previously formulated."[34]

In Europe, by contrast, there *was* such a "guarantee"—namely, belief that a rational Creator made both the world and also "rational personal beings." The implication is that the two kinds of rationality—divine and human—are in some measure similar. As a result, humans can "think God's thoughts after Him." As Kaiser explains, it is because humans reflect the same rationality by which God ordered creation that they can understand that order. Stated briefly, the natural world is comprehensible because "the same Logos that is responsible for its ordering is also reflected in human reason."[35]

We find historical evidence for this confidence in human reason in a study of science and religion in Elizabethan England by historian Paul Kocher. During that period, Kocher says, people generally believed that natural science was a gift of God to humanity. This was not taken to mean that science had been implanted ready-made in the human mind; rather God had created humans with the powers of observation and reasoning necessary to gain reliable knowledge about the natural world. Confidence in human reason was tempered by the doctrine of the Fall, which taught that the human intellect is marred by sin and open to error and distortion. In the main, however, Christian faith undergirded the conviction that humans had been given the capacity to know truth. In Kocher's words, the theory of knowledge tacitly accepted by Elizabethan scientists "rested on the faith that God, having placed man here on earth, could not have been so wasteful or so ironic as to blind him to the real nature of the surrounding world."[36]

Look and See

To say that the order of creation can be grasped by human intelligence is to say that it is intelligible. Yet there may be differing ideas of what *kind* of order and what kind of intelligibility the world exhibits. Throughout Western history, various conceptions of intelligibility have vied for acceptance.

Consider first the Aristotelian concept of intelligibility. Aristotelian logic understood natural objects on the model of man-made artifacts. An artifact like a chair or a saucepan can be analyzed as a material substratum arranged according to the guiding principle of a rational goal or purpose (the Aristotelian Form). Indeed, what *defines* the object is not the material base but the purpose. It does not matter, for example, whether a saucepan is made of aluminum or cast iron, just so long as it is an object in which liquids may be heated.

Moreover, once we understand the purpose of the saucepan, we may then deduce by rigorous logic many of its properties—that its shape must be such that it can contain liquid, that it must not melt when heated, that it must not dissolve in certain liquids, and so on. In Aristotelian logic, these properties belong to its essence or Form.

The same logic was applied to nature. For the Aristotelian, nature consists of matter structured by purposes, essences, Forms. The scientist best understands a natural object by asking what it is for. Once the purpose of the object has been uncovered, in Aristotle's view, the scientist knows all that is really necessary. He has penetrated to the heart of reality. He does not need to make detailed observations of the object because, with its purpose in mind, he can deduce what its essential properties must be, just as we deduced the properties of a saucepan.[37]

This pattern of reasoning was taken from geometry. Once we

know that a triangle is a three-sided figure, we can deduce many of its other properties. Thus Aristotelian science tended to stress rational intuition of purposes or Forms followed by deduction, rather than observation and experiment.

In the thirteenth century, Thomas Aquinas adapted Aristotelian philosophy to Christian belief in a hybrid system of thought that came to be called scholasticism. The scholastics reinterpreted the Forms as God's purposes in nature, injected by God at creation. In the Christianized version, the Forms became created powers that act as God's lieutenants or vice-regents to order nature. As a result, science continued to emphasize rational intuition of the Forms rather than experimentation. Experimental science had to await a shift away from Aristotelianism.

The shift began when some Christians became troubled by the Aristotelian concept of Forms. The concept appeared to limit God's creative activity, as though God had to make do with the prescribed properties of matter. For example, some Christian Aristotelians argued that the "nature" of the heavens demanded circular motion by its inner law of rational necessity—as though God's hand were restrained by some inherent necessity in the structure of things.

In 1277 Etienne Tempier, Bishop of Paris, issued a condemnation of several theses derived from Aristotelianism—that God could not allow any form of planetary motion other than circular, that He could not make a vacuum, and many more. The condemnation of 1277 helped inspire a form of theology known as voluntarism, which admitted no limitations on God's power. It regarded natural law not as Forms inherent *within* nature but as divine commands imposed from *outside* nature. Voluntarism insisted that the structure of the universe—indeed, its very existence—is not rationally necessary but is contingent upon the free and transcendent will of God.

Voluntarist theology eventually inspired the Reformers who emphasized the passive impotence of sinners in salvation and the freedom and sovereignty of God. As Gary Deason shows, these theological ideas eventually trickled over into science. The view of sinners as passive inspired a parallel view of matter as passive. Matter was driven not by internal rational Forms but by the sovereign commands of God. The freedom of God in bestowing salvation inspired a parallel view of His freedom in creation and providence. God was not restricted by any inherent necessity; He freely bestowed order according to His own will and design.[38]

As historian A. C. Crombie explains, the problem with Christian Aristotelianism was that it viewed the universe as "a necessarily determined emanation from God's reason, instead of a free creation of His

will, as Christian theology taught." In its extreme form, Aristotelianism
held

> that the ultimate rational causes of things in God's mind could be
> discovered by the human reason; and that Aristotle had in fact dis-
> covered those causes, so that the universe *must necessarily* be con-
> stituted as he had described it, and *could not* be otherwise.[39]

It was this notion of necessity constraining even God Himself that the
voluntarists objected to. In contrast, they emphasized God's omnipotence and His freedom to create the world according to His own purposes, by His sovereign commands.

   As a historical example, consider van Helmont, an early chemist.
Van Helmont was adamantly opposed to the Aristotelian concept of
final cause, and equated natural law with divine command. He wrote:

> I believe that Nature is the command of God, whereby a thing is
> that which it is, and doth that which it is commanded to do or act.

This, he wrote, is "a Christian definition, taken out of the Holy
Scripture," as opposed to an Aristotelian definition.[40] In fact, van
Helmont's intense opposition to Aristotle won him an appearance
before the Spanish Inquisition and a stint in prison.

   Robert Boyle echoed the themes of voluntarist theology as well,
referring to God as the "free establisher of the laws of motion" and
noting that these laws "depend perfectly on his will." He spoke of
God's creatures as "the limited and arbitrary productions of his power
and will," formed not by any independent rational agency within creation but by "God's immediate fiat."[41]

   Isaac Newton's commitment to voluntarism is evident in the following quotation from an unpublished manuscript: "The world might
have been otherwise than it is (because there may be worlds otherwise
framed than this). Twas therefore noe necessary but a voluntary & free
determination yt should bee thus."[42]

   One of the most important consequences of voluntarist theology
for science is that it helped to inspire and justify an experimental
methodology. For if God created freely rather than by logical necessity,
then we cannot gain knowledge of it by logical deduction (which traces
necessary connections). Instead, we have to go out and look, to observe
and experiment. As Barbour puts it:

> The world is orderly and dependable because God is trustworthy
> and not capricious; but the details of the world must be found by

observation rather than rational deduction because God is free and did not have to create any particular kind of universe.[43]

For example, Aristotle had argued that the earth must be at the center of the cosmos because it is "natural" for the heaviest element to gravitate towards the geometric center. In other words, he appealed to an innate tendency in matter. Copernicus, on the other hand, argued that there can be many centers of gravity because gravity is "*bestowed* on the parts of bodies by the Creator"—and obviously the Creator can bestow such powers wherever He chooses. As Kaiser explains, for Copernicus "the laws of nature are not intrinsic and cannot be deduced *a priori*: rather they are imposed or infused by God"[44] and can only be known *a posteriori*, through empirical investigation.

The clearest statement of the connection between voluntarist theology and experimental method is in Roger Cotes's Preface to the second edition of Newton's *Principia*. Cotes argued that the world "could arise from nothing but the perfectly free will of God directing and presiding over all." In all of creation, Cotes wrote, there is "not the least shadow" of logical necessity—and "*therefore*," he concluded, we must learn "from observations and experiments."[45]

We see that the conviction that the world is contingent—its order imposed rather than inherent—provided a powerful justification for the experimental method of science. As historian John Hedley Brooke puts it, "If the workings of nature reflected the free agency of a divine will, then the only way to uncover them was by empirical investigation. No armchair science, premised on how God *must* have organized things, was permissible."[46] Science must observe and experiment.

Not Our Ways

The idea that the creation is contingent is sometimes taken to mean it is chaotic and unpredictable. But in its Christian form, contingency does not mean that at all. The goal of voluntarist theology was to emphasize that God is not bound by anything outside Himself; He *is*, however, bound by His own nature. As theologian Thomas Torrance writes, "The contingency of the creation as it derives from God is inseparably bound up with its orderliness, for it is the product not merely of his almighty will but of his eternal reason."[47] The world does not have its own inherent rationality, but it is intelligible because it reflects God's rationality.

Yet because it is God's rationality we are talking about and not our own, we cannot always anticipate how it will reveal itself in creation. As theologian John Baillie puts it, "While everything in nature observes a rational pattern, and is therefore in principle intelligible by us, we cannot know in advance *which* rational pattern it is going to follow."[48] In science that means we cannot merely intuit what seems reasonable. Instead, we must observe how nature operates. We must look and see.

The implication again is that science must be experimental. A prime historical example is Galileo. He did not follow the typical method of inquiry in his day and ask whether it was "reasonable" to suppose that a ten-pound weight would fall to the ground more quickly than a one-pound weight, based on the "nature" of weight. Instead, he dropped two balls from the leaning tower of Pisa and watched what happened. We cannot presume to know how God thinks, Galileo argued; we must go out and look at the world He created.[49]

Roger Cotes gives this argument its clearest expression. "He who is presumptuous enough to think that he can find the true principles of physics and the laws of natural things by the force alone of his own mind, and the internal light of his reason," Cotes wrote, must suppose "that himself, a miserable reptile, can tell what is fittest to be done." These words are taken from the same passage quoted above where Cotes recommends that instead of relying on "the internal light" of our own reason, we ought to rely on observation and experiment. Hence the Christian conviction that God's ways are not our ways was another powerful inspiration in the new experimental approach to science.

The Glory of God and the Benefit of Mankind

Modern science has given birth to modern technology, as we all know. Yet the transition from science to technology itself required certain presuppositions about the world. It required a set of beliefs that sanctioned active intervention in natural processes to advance human purposes.

In animism and pantheism, the divine is immanent in the universe, whether conceived as several deities inhabiting the woods and rivers or as a single spirit permeating all things. The universe is the sole all-encompassing reality.

In this context, the individual is an expression of nature, incapable of transcending his environment. The intellectual stance vis-a-vis nature is passive. The human mind is thoroughly embedded in nature; it does not transcend it as subject over against object. As a consequence, humans are interested in knowing nature only in order to adapt and conform to it, not in order to harness its forces for practical ends.

By contrast, the Biblical view begins with a transcendent God and with the creation of humanity in His image. Humans find their essential kinship not with nature—as expressed in totems and idols—but with God. The human mind is thus capable of transcending nature and confronting it as subject. In this context, the individual is active vis-a-vis nature. Humans do not merely conform to nature but are free to manipulate it, both theoretically in mathematical formulas and practically by experiment.[50] In this way, Christianity provided both an intellectual framework and a motive for developing technology. Borrowing a favorite phrase of the early scientists, the goal of science was the glory of God and the benefit of mankind.

Christians found Biblical justification for an active use of nature in the creation account (Genesis 1:28), where God gives human beings "dominion" over the earth. Dominion was understood not as license to exploit nature ruthlessly but as responsibility to cultivate it, care for it, and harness its forces for human benefit.

In Genesis we also learn that God brought the animals to Adam to be named (2:19-20). It was idiomatic in Hebrew that to name something is to assert mastery over it; hence this account gives additional sanction for human dominion over nature. It was also idiomatic in Hebrew that a name should express the essential nature of a thing. Hence naming the animals required careful investigation to determine what sort of things they were—a task involving detailed observation, description, and classification. Thus Genesis appeared to give divine justification to the study and analysis of the natural world. Science came to be understood as one aspect of the "cultural mandate," the Christian duty to investigate and develop the powers of creation through human culture. John Cotton, a Puritan divine who emigrated to America, wrote in 1654 that "to study the nature and course and use of all God's works is a duty imposed by God."[51]

That modern science owes something to the Christian notion of duty was first suggested by sociologist R. K. Merton in the 1930s.[52] Since that time, several critics have assailed the so-called "Merton thesis," many arguing that his focus was overly narrow. (He treated primarily Puritanism.) Nevertheless, as science historian P. M. Rattansi argues, it is now generally accepted that the Christian concept of moral obligation played an important role in attracting people to the study of nature. It was by necessity a strong attraction, since at the time scientific study had to be carried on "outside the traditional framework of higher education and, indeed, [had] to oppose the natural philosophy taught at the universities." Hence the enduring truth in the Merton thesis, Rattansi argues, is that the Christian religion provided "a powerful religious motive" for engaging in experimental science. In his words, Protestant principles encouraged a commitment to the study of God's "Book of Nature" as complementing the study of the book of God's word. They imposed a religious obligation to make such study serve the twin ends of glorifying God and benefiting fellow-men.[53]

The second part of that phrase—"benefiting fellow-men"—justified not only science but also technology. The early scientists regarded technology as a means of alleviating the destructive effects of the curse recorded in Genesis 3. As Francis Bacon (1561-1626) expressed it, man "fell at the same time from his state of innocency and from his dominion over creation." Yet, "both of these losses can, even in this life, be in some part repaired; the former by religion and faith, the latter by arts and sciences." As humans used the sciences to restore their dominion over creation, they could alleviate the suffering imposed by the Fall.

Thus science was permeated with religious concern for the poor and the sick, with humanitarian efforts to alleviate toil and tedium. As historian Lynn White explains, the "spiritual egalitarianism" of Biblical religion "ascribes infinite worth to even the lowliest of human beings as potentially children of God"—a conviction that bore fruit in humanitarian efforts to raise them up from their lowly estate. Biblical faith thus engendered "a religious urge to substitute a power machine for a man where the required motion is so severe and monotonous that it seems unworthy of a child of God."[54]

The very idea that the conditions of human life could be ameliorated was itself revolutionary—and was rooted in Biblical doctrine. As Cox points out, the idea of improving one's life cannot occur to people trapped in a cyclic, fatalistic, or deterministic view of history.[55] But the Biblical view of history is linear, open to divine activity. In the course of time, God can create something genuinely new. So can human beings, who are made in His image. Both God and humans are first causes who can set in motion a new chain of secondary causes. Thus the Biblical view of history inspired the use of science and technology to improve the human condition.

It might be helpful to summarize this chapter so far by using John Hedley Brooke's taxonomy of the ways Christianity has influenced the development of science. To begin with, Christian teachings have served as *presuppositions* for the scientific enterprise (e.g., the conviction that nature is lawful was inferred from its creation by a rational God). Second, Christian teachings have *sanctioned* science (e.g., science was justified as a means of alleviating toil and suffering). Third, Christian teachings supplied *motives* for pursuing science (e.g., to show the glory and wisdom of the Creator). And fourth, Christianity played a role in *regulating* scientific methodology (e.g., voluntarist theology was invoked to justify an empirical approach in science).[56]

Among professional historians the image of warfare between faith and science has shattered. Replacing it is a widespread recognition of Christianity's positive contributions to modern science.

CONTROVERSIES BETWEEN CHURCH AND SCIENCE

Tell the proverbial man on the street that Christianity exerted a positive influence on the rise of modern science, and you are likely to elicit astonishment and disbelief. The new appreciation for religion has not filtered down from the academy to popular culture—or to the church pew. When we told Christian friends that we were writing a book on the contributions of Christianity to science, the typical response was skepticism. To counter that skepticism, we need to debunk some common misconceptions.

Anti-religious polemics have often exaggerated the church's opposition to science. For example, Andrew Dickson White offers the sweeping statement that "all branches of the Protestant Church— Lutheran, Calvinist, Anglican—vied with each other in denouncing the Copernican doctrine as contrary to Scripture."[57] But the reality is that the Reformers largely ignored the Copernican controversy, apart from a few scattered remarks recorded from a table talk by Martin Luther and a sermon by John Calvin. And even these are historically questionable. In the case of Luther, the table talks were not recorded until several years later, culled from the memory of participants. Some historians doubt whether Luther actually made the disparaging comment about Copernicus attributed to him.

In the case of Calvin, White tells us Calvin took the lead in opposing Copernicanism, citing Psalm 93:1 ("The world is firmly established, it cannot be moved") and then asking, "Who will venture to place the authority of Copernicus above that of the Holy Spirit?" But historians point out that Calvin said no such thing and never attacked Copernicus in any way in print.[58]

The truth is that theologians had little reason to concern themselves with Copernicanism. Modern historians often write as though Copernican theory represented a grave threat to the Christian view of human significance. Copernicus demoted mankind, it is said, from his exalted place on the center stage of the universe. For example, in *The Making of the Modern Mind* historian John Herman Randall writes that the Copernican revolution "swept man out of his proud position as the central figure and end of the universe, and made him a tiny speck on a third-rate planet revolving about a tenth-rate sun drifting in an endless cosmic ocean."[59]

The implication is that Christians mobilized against Copernicanism to resist this shattering of their cozy cosmology. But the literature of the day does little to support this portrayal. It is true that medieval cosmology, adapted from Aristotelian philosophy, placed the earth at the center of the universe. But in medieval cosmology the center of the universe was not a place of special significance. Quite the contrary, it was the locus of evil. At the very center of the universe was Hell, then the earth, then (moving outward from the center) the progressively nobler spheres of the heavens.

In this scheme of things, humanity's central location was no compliment, nor was its loss a demotion. In fact, in Copernicus's own day a common objection to his theory was that it elevated mankind *above* his true station.[60] In medieval cosmology, human significance was rooted not in the earth's central location but in the regard God shows toward it. Hence the idea that Copernican theory threatened the Christian teaching of human significance is an anachronism. It reads back into history the *angst* of our own age.

The Galileo Controversy

Christian support for the scientific enterprise is revealed more clearly when we draw a distinction between the church and individual believers. Several of the early scientists were at odds with ecclesiastical politics while holding fervently to personal religious beliefs.

The textbook case of religious persecution is the story of Galileo. The standard account was told in Jacob Bronowski's popular television series the "Ascent of Man," which portrayed Galileo before the Inquisition as a simple confrontation between good and evil. But historian Martin Rudwick[61] condemns the television series as an example of "scientific triumphalism" unworthy of a scientist of Bronowski's stature. Bronowski's treatment of Galileo's trial was a "travesty," Rudwick says, that could result only from a deliberate choice "to ignore the historical research" available.

The historical research Rudwick refers to is a body of evidence showing that considerably more was involved than a simple confrontation between science and religion. Giorgio de Santillana, whose book *The Crime of Galileo* is widely considered the best modern account, argues that the Galileo affair was not a confrontation between "the scientist" and a religious credo at all. Ironically "the major part of the Church intellectuals were on the side of Galileo," de Santillana notes, "while the clearest opposition to him came from secular ideas" (i.e., from the academic philosophers). Even the Pope who ordered Galileo's return to Rome, in chains if necessary, to answer charges before the Inquisition had once been one of the "Galileisti" (Galileo's circle of followers).[62]

The truth is that, on the whole, the Catholic church had no argument with Galileo's theories as science. Their objection had to do with Galileo's attack on Aristotelian philosophy—and all the metaphysical, spiritual, and social consequences they associated with it. As philosopher of science Philipp Frank explains, the reason Galileo's attack on Aristotle was treated so seriously was that to many people at the time Aristotle's philosophy was "regarded as necessary for the formulation of religious and moral laws."[63]

Aristotle viewed each object as a quasi-organic entity propelled by an inner striving to fulfill its ideal nature—its purpose or Form— just as human beings are motivated by a sense of moral obligation to fulfill their highest nature. In Aristotelian philosophy, objects are moved by inherent tendencies more akin to moral striving than to push-pull mechanical forces.

One of those inner tendencies was an impulse toward a "natural place" in the universe. In Aristotelian physics, a flame goes up and a rock falls down because every object has a tendency to strive for its "natural place." Physical place was, moreover, associated with degrees of nobility (the center of the universe being the lowliest and the higher realms being the noblest). Thus the physical hierarchy studied by science reflected social and political hierarchies; the order in the physical world was related to the order in human society.

The reason some churchmen resisted giving up Aristotelian physics and cosmology was because these were intimately tied to an overall vision of moral and social life. If that tie were broken, they feared morality itself would be destroyed. Hence Galileo seemed to promote doctrines that were not only wrong but dangerous.[64]

Moreover, these new and dangerous ideas were put forward, as Mary Hesse points out, "dogmatically without sufficient evidence to support them" at the time. (Not until Newton was heliocentrism given a physical mechanism.) And when the evidence available at the time does not support a theory, resistance is neither unscientific nor irrational. Hesse concludes:

> . . . for all their shortsightedness, the representatives of the Church had some reason on their side; theirs were the reactions of men who found, as they thought, the whole structure of their world being threatened by irresponsible speculations which did not at that time even have an adequate body of evidence in their support.[65]

A full understanding of the confrontation between Galileo and the Roman church, suggests philosopher of science Jerome Ravetz,[66] must take account of sociological factors as well. The Catholic hierarchy had recently reaffirmed its commitment to Aristotelianism in response to the challenge posed by Protestantism. Hence, Galileo's attack on Aristotle could be interpreted as giving ammunition to the enemy. In addition, a lively struggle was taking place between an older elite in the universities and churches and the newer, more pragmatically oriented elite to which Galileo belonged. Galileo's decision to publish his works in the vernacular was a deliberate affront to the established elites, part of a broad strategy to transfer intellectual leadership to the wider reading public.[67]

In the course of the debate, both sides stooped to ugly tactics. The church used nasty methods and personal spite in a campaign to cut Galileo down to size. Galileo fought back with deliberately provocative and propagandistic writings. His parable *Dialogue Concerning the Two Principal Systems of the World* includes a dim-witted buffoon named Simplicio, a thinly disguised caricature of the Pope who had once been Galileo's friend and follower.[68]

In spite of all this, Galileo never repudiated his faith. The typical retelling of the controversy suggests that since Galileo stood up to the church, he must have been a closet atheist or at least an agnostic. But to be true to history, we must take seriously Galileo's own protestations that he was a genuine Christian believer who had no intention of questioning religious doctrine per se but only the scientific framework inherited from Aristotelian philosophy.

The positivist approach dismisses Galileo's religious defense of his ideas as mere expediency, forced on him by the authorities. But Galileo's behavior cannot be understood unless we accept his own claim that he was a believer and that he placed religion alongside science as a source of genuine information about the world. "Only Galileo's determination to remain within his religious tradition," writes Rudwick, "seems an adequate explanation of why he tried so hard to persuade everyone from the Pope downwards, and why he declined all chances to escape to the safety of the Venetian republic."[69]

Children of Their Time

Let us be the first to acknowledge that Christians have often opposed new ideas in science. But let us also point out that this is not some perverse failing of religious people but a universal human tendency. *All* people tend to resist new ideas. Nor is that necessarily a failing. After all, as long as an idea remains new, its supporters generally have not yet mustered the necessary evidence for it.

As a case in point, critics often castigate the Reformers for not accepting Copernican cosmology—ignoring the fact that at the time the culture *as a whole* did not yet accept Copernicus. The Reformers were not being churlishly anti-intellectual; they were merely reflecting what were generally considered to be well-founded beliefs in their time. As John Dillenberger notes, "The classical Reformation figures, including Luther, Calvin, and Melanchthon, belong to the period in which there was no compelling reason for accepting the Copernican system."[70] In short, the Reformers were geocentric for exactly the same reason that later Protestants were Newtonian and then Einsteinian—namely, that they accepted the scientific theories current in their day.[71]

Altering fundamental concepts about the world is never an easy process. Scientific concepts that appear obvious to moderns because we have been taught them since we were young—concepts such as heliocentricity, elliptical orbits, the circulation of the blood—were exceedingly difficult to hit upon originally. As historian Mark Graubard comments, if the solution to a scientific problem takes generations or even centuries to arrive at, and possibly just as long to become widely accepted, "then it seems more intelligent to believe that the solution is difficult, rather than to blame Aristotle, authoritarianism, human stupidity, vested interests, the Church, or any other scapegoat, for the delay."[72]

If Christian belief were truly a barrier to science, it is difficult to explain why so many founders of modern science were believers. Paracelsus, Boyle, and Newton wrote extensively on theology as well as on science. Others—Kepler and van Helmont—filled their scientific notebooks with prayers, praise, and theological musings.

A common device among historians has been to dismiss these theological interests as irritating distractions from purely scientific work. Yet this reaction is shortsighted, for the religious interest often provided the *motivation* for the scientific work. Many of the early scientists studied creation in an effort to know the Creator. Later, when religious skepticism was on the rise, many scientists hoped to use scientific discoveries to buttress religious belief. Newton wanted his work used for apologetics, as we shall see in later chapters. Mersenne and Descartes, Rattansi points out, "were actively concerned to furnish new weapons to defend religion at a time when the old arguments seemed to have been discredited."[73] Descartes is best remembered for his method of radical doubt; we generally forget that his purpose in doubting everything was to clear the way for a more substantial support for faith. To omit or dismiss these religious motivations is to misunderstand the true nature of science.

Whither Science?

As we conclude this chapter, we cannot avoid a haunting question: If science received much of its impetus from Christian assumptions, what will happen now that those assumptions have eroded—now that Christianity is no longer a public faith undergirding science but merely a private belief held by individual scientists? What will happen to science as the Christian motivation and intellectual scaffolding wither away? Contemporary science still lives off the accumulated capital of centuries of Christian faith. But how long will that capital last? And what will take its place?

"The experimental method succeeded beyond men's wildest dreams," notes Eiseley, "but the faith that brought it into being owes something to the Christian conception of the nature of God." Belief in a trustworthy, rational God led to the assumption of an ordered, rational universe. "And science today," says Eiseley, is still "sustained by that assumption."[74] The question is: How long will that assumption *continue* to sustain science?

It may turn out that science is detachable from the Biblical presuppositions and motivations that sustained its initial development. Science may prove itself to be self-sustaining, driven by sheer intellectual curiosity and technological success.

Yet, once separated from the teaching of divine creation, science has no philosophical ground for its most basic assumption—the lawfulness of nature. "Since the time of Hume," Whitehead says, "fashionable scientific philosophy has been such as to deny the rationality of science." Hume demonstrated that pure empiricism gives no grounds for belief in even such fundamental principles as cause and effect. As a result, Whitehead concludes, scientists today maintain a "scientific faith" in the order of nature while lacking any rational basis for it.[75] And without a rational basis, it is an open question whether that "scientific faith" can long survive.

THE HISTORY OF SCIENCE AND THE SCIENCE OF HISTORY:
Contemporary Approaches and Their Intellectual Roots

*I*n 1964 Frances Yates published a book that dramatically changed the study of science history. She brought into the hallowed domain of science a whole host of things previously shunned as unworthy of serious attention—mysticism, magic, religion. Titled *Giordano Bruno and the Hermetic Tradition*,[1] Yates's book argued that the Renaissance philosopher Bruno (1548-1600), often portrayed as a martyr for the sake of science, was in reality no such thing. Instead, he was a magus who traveled across Europe preaching a pagan gospel rooted in mystical hermetic texts.

Bruno was, it is true, an early advocate of Copernican astronomy—hence his standard portrayal as a hero of science. He is frequently treated as a representative of rationality, a ray of truth in a dogma-darkened world. For example, in *The Making of the Modern Mind*, historian John Herman Randall describes Bruno as "the great martyr of the new science . . . a man whose soul was set on fire by the Copernican discoveries."[2]

But this stirring picture ignores most of what Bruno actually wrote and said. His soul, it turns out, was set on fire less by Copernicanism than by pagan religion. He regarded himself as a missionary for the hermetic tradition, a movement based on the writing of Hermes Trismegistus, erroneously thought to be an Egyptian sage from the time of Moses. The hermetic writings frequently treat the sun as a god, and the rest of the universe as moving and hence alive. This, it turns out, was the real reason Bruno was attracted to Copernicus's heliocentrism. The divinity of the sun seemed compatible with an astronomy that granted it an honored position at the center of the planetary system.

Although Bruno also had some acquaintance with the scientific and mathematical basis of Copernican theory, it was not on those grounds that he defended the theory but rather on religious grounds.[3] In the words of historian Hugh Kearney, "Bruno transformed a mathematical synthesis into a religious doctrine."[4] Eventually, in the Inquisition Bruno was burned at the stake—not because he courageously promulgated a better scientific theory, as is often maintained, but because he claimed to offer a better religion. He argued that the Egyptian pantheism described in the hermetic writings was superior to Christianity.

Bruno was not the only thinker of his generation to plumb ancient mystical texts for inspiration. Renaissance thinkers often sought wisdom from the ancients, which they hoped to present as an alternative to Aristotle's philosophy, then the ruling orthodoxy in theology, philosophy, and science. Among the alternatives that emerged was neo-Platonism, a mystical philosophy from the third century that made extensive use of the hermetic writings. Bruno participated in this broader revival of neo-Platonism.

The new interpretation of Bruno as a neo-Platonic mystic did not come easily to Frances Yates. Originally, she says, she had simply intended to make an English translation of one of Bruno's writings "with an introduction emphasizing the boldness with which this advanced philosopher of the Renaissance accepted the Copernican theory."[5] Yet as she read his works, Yates was puzzled by a sense that what really concerned Bruno was not Copernicanism per se but something else. So thoroughly was she primed by the standard historical interpretation that it took several years of study to recognize that the interpretative key to Bruno's thought was hermeticism.

By treating seriously the philosophical and religious context of the historical debate over heliocentrism, Yates helped spur a new trend among science historians. She was among the first to suggest that mysticism had exerted a positive impact on the origin of the scientific outlook and was therefore a proper object of study for the historian. The Yates thesis, as it came to be called, did not merely hold that science had emerged from a world permeated with magic and mysticism; *that* was already widely known. Her novel interpretation was that mysticism produced a frame of mind that actually *fostered* the rise of modern science.

Standard histories of science treat magic and mysticism as the antithesis of science—as superstitions that hindered the emergence of the modern scientific outlook. For example, Sir James Jeans denounces the "dismal ages" of the medieval period as a time concerned with alchemy, astrology, and magic—"wholly unprofitable quests."[6] Yet this interpretation of history, Yates argues, has limited explanatory power. It can

> explain and follow the various stages leading to the emergence of modern science in the seventeenth century, but it does not explain *why* this happened at this time, why there was this intense new interest in the world of nature and its workings.[7]

The "new interest" in nature had to come from outside science. In fact, it often came from neo-Platonic and hermetic notions of natural magic. As Yates says, magic promoted a new conception of humanity as an active controller of natural forces and inspired an effort to understand nature's mysterious workings.

The Yates thesis sparked extensive polemical debate and helped inspire a new generation of historians who began to work on topics previously deemed marginal and insignificant. Charles Webster exemplifies the new attitude when he argues that the worldview of the scientific revolution was

> the result of the dynamic interplay of forces from many different directions. All of these forces contributed to the process of creativity and change, and none of them deserves to be written off *a priori* as a useless intellectual encumbrance from a discredited magical past.[8]

In the new approach, it became legitimate for historians to examine all the historical antecedents of science, including hermeticism, alchemy, astrology, natural magic, and religion.

HISTORY WITH AN AGENDA

To understand why the Yates thesis garnered such attention, we must back up and trace even earlier trends in the historiography of science. For Yates benefitted from a relatively new willingness to "contextualize" scientific figures, to consider the historical and intellectual matrix in which they worked. This broader movement to contextualize scientific knowledge had its roots in philosophical idealism.

Broadly speaking, there are two approaches to the history of science—positivist and idealist.[9] It was the positivist approach that gave
us the traditional, sanitized picture of Bruno as a scientific hero. It
depicts science as the gradual accumulation of positive knowledge, of
empirically verifiable facts about the world.

Roots of the positivist approach go back to the eighteenth-century Enlightenment philosophers, who were the first generation of self-
consciously anti-Christian scholars. Their goal was to frame a
comprehensive vision of life to replace the Christian vision that had
dominated Western culture since the beginning of the Middle Ages. To
accomplish that goal, they needed something more than an abstract
system of reason; they also needed to make that system concrete, intimately bound to human experience. Their solution was to write histories of Western culture. History itself would demonstrate the superior
nature of Enlightenment philosophy and persuade people that it alone
offered the path to progress. History would serve as a morality tale of
scientific progress.

Their primary tactic was to portray the Middle Ages, the time of
Christian cultural dominance, as a backward and superstitious era.
Take, for example, Voltaire (1694-1778), often considered the first
modern historian. Voltaire described the Middle Ages as a time of
darkness and ignorance, when Western culture was dominated by an
oppressive church and exploited by an opportunistic clergy. "True"
philosophy did not appear until science arose to shake off the shackles of religion and superstition.

The most enthusiastic proponent of progress, however, was the
Marquis de Condorcet (1743-1794), who rhapsodized over the
advance of the human race from barbaric and superstitious origins to
the pinnacle of reason and enlightenment. The villain in Condorcet's
account of Western history was, again, the medieval church with its
dogmas and delusions; the hero, predictably, was science. Condorcet
proposed a doctrine of the infinite perfectibility of human nature
through science.[10]

In *The Heavenly City of the Eighteenth-Century Philosophers*
Carl Becker argues that the histories written in the eighteenth century
(not only by Voltaire and Condorcet but also by Hume, Montesquieu,
and Gibbon) were designed with one purpose in mind—to discredit
Christianity. Enlightenment philosophers knew they were engaged in
a cultural battle for people's hearts and minds. In Becker's words, they
felt themselves "engaged in a life-and-death struggle with Christian
philosophy and the infamous things that support it—superstition,
intolerance, tyranny." Their historical accounts were intended as
weapons in the struggle.

These histories would generally open with the Greco-Roman

world, praised as a golden age of reason; move to the Middle Ages, denounced as a dreary period of ignorance and oppression; and end with the contemporary age, the Enlightenment, heralded as a revival of ancient wisdom and rationality. Clearly, this was no attempt at objective, fact-based history. The "function of the new history," writes Becker, was to demonstrate that human experience confirms what reason had (in the authors' minds) already decreed—namely, that Christian philosophy is "inimical to the welfare of mankind."[11] The Enlightenment historians were not objective researchers; they were polemicists for secularism.

The same theme was picked up in the next century by Auguste Comte (1798-1857), the founder of positivism. All knowledge, Comte said, passes through three stages—the theological or "fictitious" stage, in which the world is explained by supernatural and divine action; the metaphysical stage, in which divine action is replaced by abstract ideas and forces; and the positive stage, in which abstract ideas are replaced by natural laws. Positivism as a philosophy was intricately bound up with the positivist schema of history.

SCIENCE ACCORDING TO POSITIVISM

When specialized histories of science began to appear, most adopted the same positivist perspective. They portrayed the development of science as the inevitable "march of mind" from darkness and superstition into the light of reason—with "reason" defined by the modern secular mind. Anything that anticipated the historian's own outlook was praised as a courageous insight. Anything incompatible with modern secularism was dismissed as superstition or blind dogma.

Positivist accounts of science were written not primarily for descriptive but for normative purposes—to illustrate the dangers of superstition and the glories of true philosophy and science based on reason. They did not merely chronicle events but were intended as persuasive tracts, promoting reason as the source and final arbiter of truth. As physicist and philosopher Thomas Kuhn puts it, they were "hortatory in intent," their aim to teach that positivism, with its complete rejection of religion and metaphysics in favor of reason, was the highest mode of human thought.[12]

Positivism is an example of what historian Herbert Butterfield called "the Whig interpretation of history"—history written from the victors' point of view. Positivist authors measure past thinkers by the yardstick of current knowledge as embodied in the up-to-date textbook. Ideas that coincide with the contemporary textbook are described as courageous, bold, and innovative—regardless of whether it actually *was* courageous or even justified to hold such a position given the knowledge and assumptions of the historical period. Conversely, ideas that contemporary science disapproves are attributed to fear, conformity, and irrationality—regardless of how reasonable such a position may have been in light of the prevailing knowledge and beliefs of the time.

One of the most egregious examples of the Whig interpretation of history is Andrew Dickson White's two-volume *History of the Warfare of Science with Theology* (1896).[13] White combs through Western history for examples of Christians who resisted scientific concepts later accepted by mainstream science, chalking up their resistance to fear and dogmatism while lavishing praise on any historical figures lucky enough to have anticipated modern concepts.

What such an approach lacks, remarks philosopher of science Mary Hesse, is "historical imagination"—the ability to imaginatively reconstruct the past and understand it on its own terms.[14] Science historian Robert Westman dubs it the "Vulgar Triumphalist" approach, in which history is divided into heroes and villains, progressives and reactionaries.[15]

It is, moreover, says Kuhn, profoundly unhistorical.[16] Consider a specific historical problem—the long-lived popularity of the idea of circular orbits, an idea that retained a hold on astronomical thought even after Kepler had demonstrated the mathematical superiority of elliptical orbits. (Galileo, for example, rejected Kepler's theory and retained a commitment to circular orbits.) Whiggish historians dismiss the enduring appeal of circular orbits as the result of the Platonic infatuation with geometric perfection, perpetuated by medieval dogmatism.

But the problem cannot be dismissed in such a cavalier manner. "What is missing" in the positivist explanation, says Kuhn, "is any reference to the elegant and predictively successful astronomical systems built from circles, an achievement on which Copernicus did not himself improve." In other words, circular orbits *fit well* with the empirical evidence available at the time. To hold such a theory was both reasonable and scientific, regardless of the fact that its initial impulse came from Platonic philosophy.

In another example, Kuhn says, positivist historians tend to dismiss the biological concept of fixed species as rising merely from "an excessively literal reading of Genesis." But the truth is that the fixity of species is a pervasive common-sense observation. Even philosopher Antony Flew—certainly no friend of Christianity—comments on the "enormous initial plausibility of what we might label the Genesis view of the nature and presuppositions of biological classification." A strong inclination to this view, Flew continues, "is by no means peculiar to way-out fundamentalist Bible bigots. On the contrary, it seems to be supported by all the most immediate everyday experience."[17] And not only by everyday experience but also by biology itself. The science of taxonomy (the classification of living things) depends on our ability to identify discrete groupings (species, genera, families, etc.). The existence of such discrete groups, Kuhn points out, "becomes extremely difficult to understand unless the current members of each descend from some original pair." Indeed, Kuhn continues, "since Darwin the definition of basic taxonomic categories like species and genus have [sic] necessarily become and remained relatively arbitrary and extraordinarily problematic." In short, a theory of discrete, stable groupings within the organic world can be both reasonable and scientific, regardless of the fact that its initial impulse came from a commitment to Genesis.

Despite its failings, positivism has shaped most people's understanding of science history, especially on the popular level. We all grew up reading science textbooks that painted a broadly positivist picture. The standard textbook treatment generally does no more than chronicle discoveries—who discovered what and when. Rarely is there any mention of the philosophical and religious roots of scientific ideas, rarely any acknowledgement that science often wanders through mistakes and misconceptions, through back alleys and dead-ends. The textbook style presents the history of science only through its finished products, as though they appeared ready-made in the brains of fate-favored geniuses. What emerges is a triumphalist mural of scientific progress from humble beginnings to rational enlightenment.

HISTORY OF SCIENCE AS HISTORY OF IDEAS

It is precisely this historical snobbery that the idealist approach seeks to avoid. Idealism rejects the definition of science as the mere accumulation of positive knowledge. Instead it sees scientific change as a result of conceptual change—of new ideas, concepts, and worldviews. In the past three or four decades, since Yates stirred things up with her new interpretation of Bruno, the idealist approach to the history of science has become remarkably popular. But its intellectual roots reach back much further, to the nineteenth century when the philosophy of history first developed as a separate discipline.

Separating history from the natural sciences required a fierce struggle. From the days of the scientific revolution, philosophers strove for a "unity of knowledge." They hoped that a single method would uncover truth in all fields of inquiry. Francis Bacon argued for the unity of subject areas based on the fact that a "common logic" (the syllogism) applies to them all. Descartes and Leibniz called for a universal method based on mathematics. After Isaac Newton's impressive successes, many held up mathematical physics as the pattern for all knowledge.[18]

But the application of the physics model to all fields of scholarship led inevitably to reductionism. Newtonian physics rested on the assumption that the physical world operates like a huge, interrelated machine. The extension of that paradigm into the social sciences fostered the view that human society is likewise a kind of mechanism—that man himself is a machine, as la Mettrie declared in his book L'homme machine. By the second half of the nineteenth century a doctrinaire materialism had emerged that was aggressively reductionistic.

It was in this intellectual environment that the philosophy of history first became a specialized pursuit. Launching a vigorous effort to stave off reductionist tendencies, philosophers of history such as Wilhelm Dilthey (1833-1911), Heinrich Rickert (1863-1936), and Wilhelm Windelband (1848-1915) appealed to Hegelian idealism. Hegel had distinguished between Nature and Mind (or Spirit, Geist). The idealist historians revived that distinction, differentiating between the sciences that take nature as their subject matter (Naturwissenschaften) and those that take the human mind as their subject matter (Geisteswissenschaften). The former were the natural sciences and the latter were labeled "history." The term included what we call the humanities: religion, ethics, art, literature, psychology, sociology, political theory, education.

Idealist historians argued that these two kinds of science must be pursued via different methodologies, appropriate to the different nature of their subject matter. Natural science focuses on universal regularities; history focuses on the particular and individual. Natural science explains events in terms of causal connections; history explains events in terms of individual motivations, goals, purposes, beliefs. The natural scientist strives for objective, detached observation; the historian must try to understand his subject as a human being—entering into his thought processes and empathizing with his motivations.[19]

In short, the idealists rejected the classic ideal of a unity of knowledge. There are, they argued, two levels of reality—one material and the other mental. Knowledge is likewise twofold. By outlining a distinctive methodology, a distinctive logic, for the humanities, the idealist historians hoped to liberate them from the reductionism of the natural sciences.[20]

The idealist approach to history began to have an impact on the study of science through the writings of E. A. Burtt (The Metaphysical Foundations of Modern Science, 1924), R. G. Collingwood (The Idea of Nature, 1944), and Alexandre Koyré (From the Closed World to the Infinite Universe, 1957). These scholars were guided by the idealist dictum that the historian must get "inside the skin" of his subject and understand his thoughts and beliefs. They sought to enter into the minds of previous generations and understand their scientific ideas on their own terms. Their approach is expressed nicely by British philosopher Bertrand Russell, who says that in studying a historical figure, "the right attitude is neither reverence nor contempt, but first a kind of hypothetical sympathy, until it is possible to know what it feels like to believe in his theories."[21] Instead of judging the work of a historical figure against the standard of a modern textbook, idealists seek to judge his accomplishments within his own historical context.

Conceptual Conversion

One of the best-known historians of the new school is Thomas Kuhn. A physicist who switched to history, Kuhn experienced what we might call a conversion to the idealist methodology.[22] As he tells the story, his "enlightenment" began when he sought to understand the background to the physics of Galileo and Newton—which in turn meant researching Aristotelian physics.

Kuhn discovered that the early scientists had scrapped Aristotle's physical theories entirely and started over from scratch. In other words, the scientific revolution did not represent a gradual, cumulative building of knowledge—for there was nothing in Aristotle's physics for Galileo to build upon. Instead Galileo had to start over and create the science of mechanics (the study of motion) from the bottom up.

This complete inadequacy of Aristotelian physics puzzled Kuhn. In dealing with other subjects, Aristotle was an astute observer. He made penetrating studies in biology and politics. Why did his talents of observation fail him so miserably in physics? How did he come up with views that strike the modern mind as absurd? And why were his strange views taken seriously for so many centuries?

To answer these questions, Kuhn says, he had to undergo a kind of Gestalt switch—a sudden turn to a whole new way of looking at things. In examining Aristotle's overall philosophy, he suddenly understood that for Aristotle all forms of change were outworkings of a single process, from the fall of a stone (mechanics) to the artist's creation of a sculpture (aesthetics) to the growth of an embryo to adulthood (biology).

It was biology, moreover, that provided the basic paradigm of change. Just as embryonic development has a natural end point or goal (namely, the adult form), so the motion of physical objects must have a natural goal. This was the source of the concept of natural place. In Aristotelian physics, light bodies (like smoke) have a natural tendency to move upward; heavy bodies tend to move toward the center of the universe (identified with the center of the earth).

Only after he had stepped into Aristotle's conceptual universe, says Kuhn, did he grasp how *within that context* the philosopher's views on motion made excellent sense. In Aristotelian physics, objects were endowed with dispositions, aspirations (such as the urge to move toward their natural place). To understand Aristotle we have to shift mentally from the type of cause familiar to us today to a completely different type—not a mechanical force but a personalistic striving. As a result of this Gestalt switch, "I did not become an Aristotelian physicist," Kuhn says, "but I had to some extent learned to think like one." Suddenly strained metaphors became straightforward descriptions; apparent absurdities made sense. Kuhn had learned to enter empathetically into the ancient Greek mind.

This is the idealist approach to science history. It seeks to understand the Gestalts—the overall worldviews—that have shaped science. Science does not consist simply in positive discoveries; it consists, above all, in ideas.

Ironically, at the same time that positivists such as Ernst Mach were seeking to eradicate all metaphysics from science—denouncing it as a hangover from a prescientific stage—idealists such as E. A. Burtt were bringing it back in. Even more galling for the positivist, metaphysics was being placed at the very heart of modern science. Hence the significance of the title of Burtt's book, *The Metaphysical Foundations of Modern Science.* He was throwing down the gauntlet to positivism.

Idealist historians argue that historical figures such as Copernicus, Galileo, Descartes, and Newton were not just making scientific investigations; they were responding to and contributing to metaphysical views of the world. "Nor was this ascribed to the 'backwardness' of [their] minds, as a remnant of their prescientific training," notes historian Marx Wartofsky. "It was seen as essential to the theory-formation of classical physics itself."[23]

No "Dark" Ages

In the hands of the idealists, the contours of history changed dramatically. Just as positivism drew support from historical accounts denigrating the Middle Ages, so idealism drew support from a rehabilitation of the Middle Ages.

The first person to recognize the positive medieval contributions to modern science was the French physicist and philosopher Pierre Duhem (1861-1916). Duhem was one of the first scholars to use history as a tool for understanding scientific concepts. To his surprise, he discovered much of scientific value in the late Middle Ages. Duhem found, for example, that Jean Buridan (1300-1360) and Nicole Oresme (+1382) had anticipated Galileo in their physical theories. Yet they had never been credited for it. Duhem concluded that "the mechanics and physics of which modern times are justifiably proud proceed, by an uninterrupted series of scarcely perceptible improvements, from doctrines professed in the heart of the medieval schools."[24]

The simplistic demarcation of the Middle Ages as a time of intellectual and cultural desolation turned out to be grossly inaccurate. Today historians treat the ideas of the Middle Ages seriously as the base from which the "new science" sprang—and not only the ideas of the Middle Ages but of earlier periods as well. During the Renaissance even older philosophies and teachings were revived, notably neo-Platonism, hermeticism, alchemy, and natural magic. Just note the titles of the following works: *A History of Magic and Experimental Science; Occult and Scientific Mentalities in the Renaissance; Reason, Experiment, and Mysticism in the Scientific Revolution;* and *Religion, Science, and Worldview.*[25]

If these titles are any indication, interest in the religious and philosophical roots of scientific thought is alive and well today as never before. The study of the history of science has moved far from its positivist beginnings. Most historians today have embraced an idealist approach, summed up aptly in the words of Alexandre Koyré: "History must grasp the real unity of the scientific activity . . . linked, in its development, with the societies which gave it birth."[26]

WHICH WAY THE HISTORY OF SCIENCE?

As an independent academic discipline, the history of science is still a relatively young field. Most writers on the subject started out either as philosophers or scientists. Only since 1950 has the majority of practitioners in science history been trained for a full-time career in the field. Of these, most subscribe to the new idealist or contextualist approach to the history of science.

How do we as Christians evaluate these new developments in the history and philosophy of science? As a counter to positivism, the idealist approach has been beneficial. Positivism treats history as the gradual emancipation of human thought from the chains of religion and metaphysics. By contrast, idealism treats science as a single thread woven inextricably into the larger tapestry of human thought—along with religion, philosophy, and the social and political milieu. Surely this is a more realistic understanding of the scientific enterprise.

But the new approach harbors its own dangers. Historical sensitivity may give way to historical relativism, in which all cultures and beliefs are regarded as equally true or valid. When that happens, the study of history merges into historicism—the belief that there is no transhistorical truth and that all knowledge is caught up in a continual process of historical change.

Many scholars in the history, philosophy, and sociology of science today in fact display a marked tendency toward historicism. They dismiss the idea that science is a search for truth and instead reduce scientific theories to constructions of the intellectual, economic, or political conditions of a particular society and period. The history of science even has its *enfants terribles*, such as Paul Feyerabend, who go so far as to argue that the accumulation of knowledge we call science is a limited, culture-bound worldview not to be prized more highly than any other worldview, be it pagan myth or medieval witchcraft.[27]

To account for this sometimes extreme historicism, we must return to the ideal of the unity of knowledge. Idealist historians such as Dilthey proposed that there is not one kind of knowledge but two—of Nature and of Mind—each with its own methodology. This distinction has been remarkably fruitful in freeing the human sciences from domination by the physical sciences and in overthrowing Whiggish approaches to history.

Today this bifurcation of knowledge into two streams is being reversed and the unity of knowledge is being reasserted. But this time it is not the physical sciences that are taking over and asserting dominance but rather the human sciences. Dilthey's intellectual offspring in history and sociology are reverting to the unity of knowledge—but the unity is being reestablished from the other side of the divide. All knowledge is being recast into the relativistic pattern that Dilthey had reserved for the human sciences.

Dilthey argued that the difference in methodology between the natural and the human sciences leads to a difference in the type of knowledge obtained. The natural sciences yield objective, unchanging knowledge, whereas the human sciences—history, religion, ethics, politics—yield only subjective, evolving knowledge. In these fields, Dilthey said, we deal not with universal truths but with products of the human mind, and hence with individual perspectives and beliefs emerging under particular conditions.

But contemporary historians reject this distinction. After all, they argue, science too is a product of the human mind. It too deals with individual perspectives emerging under particular historical conditions. Why should scientific knowledge be placed in a different category from all other forms of knowledge? Why should it be treated as absolute, atemporal truth? Contemporary historians argue that science, like the humanities, should be regarded as merely the limited perspective of a particular culture.[28]

A New Form of Reductionism

Because of this looming historicism, the discipline of science history is in some disarray today. Some erstwhile supporters of the idealistic approach are now backpedaling as they see the relativistic implications being drawn from it. For example, Paolo Rossi's book *Francis Bacon: From Magic to Science* was a pioneering work in unveiling the mystical sources of the scientific revolution. But today Rossi feels that the emphasis on mystical sources has gone too far. He complains that "the image of Bacon as the 'father' or 'founder' of modern science is giving way to that of Bacon as the 'transformer of hermetic dreams.'"

What has happened, Rossi says, is that a movement that "started out as a useful corrective to the conception of the history of science as a triumphant progress" has itself turned into a new form of reductionism—one in which the great achievements of a Bacon or a Copernicus are explained away by references to their metaphysical or mystical sources. It is one thing to recognize that the early scientists received inspiration from ancient beliefs; it is another thing to reduce their work to a simple outgrowth of those beliefs. After all, the greatness of the early scientists, Rossi argues, was precisely their ability to take existing beliefs and alter them or make new use of them.[29]

Attention to the metaphysical and social context of scientific knowledge does not lead necessarily to reductionism or relativism. But the fact is that it often does. A study of the mystical neo-Platonic roots of a Bruno or a Copernicus can lead to a greater appreciation of the rich interconnectedness of human thought; but it can also be interpreted to mean that science is at its foundations nothing but mysticism in a new guise. A study of ideological conflicts in science can serve as a corrective to simplistic chronicles of factual discoveries; but it can also lead to a denial of the possibility of objective facts apart from ideology. A historically sensitive treatment can help moderns realize that what sounds irrational and alien to us was genuinely rational in an earlier period, given the current state of knowledge; but it can also lead to a denial of any universal standard of rationality. Considering the relativistic, anti-Western, deconstructionist climate in American universities today, perhaps it should come as no surprise that the latter set of interpretations is fast becoming dominant. Many historians have come to question whether it is proper to evaluate earlier thought-forms by any categories of truth and rationality at all. Indeed, many have embraced what Rossi calls "the absolute *equivalence* . . . of all possible world-pictures," even the most primitive and irrational.[30]

Ironically, while these developments have been taking place in the history and philosophy of science, most practicing scientists have remained cheerfully oblivious to it all. The majority continue to be naive realists, blithely assuming that science yields reliable "facts." And given that the number of working scientists far exceeds the number of science historians, that makes realism the dominant view in science today. It is a view, moreover, that appears to be buttressed by the everyday experience of the bountiful practical benefits of science. When science works so well, it is difficult not to conclude that it bears at least some relation to a world that really exists.

As we close this chapter, a question inevitably lingers in the mind. Which of these two trends will ultimately direct the future of science: the subjective relativism so widespread in history and philosophy faculties or the pragmatic realism of practicing scientists? Each position represents a form of reductionism; each poses a different challenge to Christians.

Old-fashioned realism, usually with a positivist flavor, has long been used in arguing that science is the only reliable source of truth. Religion is relegated to the realm of private feeling and experience. The newer historicism undermines *all* claims to transcendent and universal truth—and hence likewise relegates Christianity to the realm of private opinion. Christians need to have an answer for both positions. And though this is not a book on apologetics, it serves as a reminder that we all need to be prepared to defend our faith—to be prepared, as Peter says, to give an answer to anyone who asks us.

THE FIRST SCIENTIFIC REVOLUTION

A NEW "THINKING CAP":
Three Little Sciences and
How They Grew

What is science about? "Facts," says the proverbial man on the street. Science establishes the facts of nature. Yet the truth is that when stripped of all interpretation, facts don't really tell us very much. Bare facts can nearly always be reinterpreted in different ways within different theoretical frameworks.

As a result, surprisingly enough, scientific advance rarely comes solely through the accumulation of new facts. It comes most often through the construction of new theoretical frameworks. If we trace the course of science from its inception, says historian Herbert Butterfield, we see that scientific change was brought about not primarily by new facts or observations "but by transpositions that were taking place inside the minds of the scientists themselves." Scientific progress, Butterfield concludes, results from "putting on a different kind of thinking-cap."[1] To understand scientific development, it is not enough merely to chronicle new discoveries and inventions. We must also trace the succession of worldviews.

Intellectually speaking, modern science emerged through a complex interplay of Christian and Greek thought. Christianity formed the comprehensive intellectual milieu of the early scientists, the stage upon which all their ideas were acted out. But those ideas were shaped in crucial ways by interaction with Greek philosophy. Hence, an understanding of the origins of science requires a knowledge of both Biblical teaching and Greek science. In chapter 1 we discussed the influence of

Biblical teaching; in this chapter we home in on the influence of Greek philosophy.

Greek science was not all of one piece, nor was it assimilated into Western culture all at once. From the twelfth century on, the Western mind was stimulated by a progressive recovery of ancient texts. The first to become available was Aristotle's philosophy, which theologians struggled masterfully to incorporate into Christian philosophy. The hybrid was later called scholasticism. Its most influential representative was Thomas Aquinas.

By 1500 the scholastics had assimilated the ideas of Galen and Ptolemy. At about that time, Plato's work became available, largely in the form of neo-Platonism, a mystical vision of the world as a series of emanations from the Divine Mind. Pythagorean mathematics often had a prominent place in neo-Platonism. The technical treatises of Archimedes did not become known until the Renaissance.

These varied and often conflicting streams of Greek thought created an enormous intellectual challenge for Western thinkers, a challenge intensified by the religious upheaval of the Reformation. The scientific revolution took place in the midst of this intellectual ferment. It was inspired by, and contributed to, the surrounding interplay of philosophies and theologies. To sort out the complex intellectual strands influencing science, we will identify three main categories of thought—Aristotelian, neo-Platonic, and mechanistic.[2]

THE WORLD ACCORDING TO ARISTOTLE

Philosophers typically describe all of reality in metaphors derived from a single aspect of the world—whatever aspect the philosopher himself finds most interesting or significant. The three worldviews that influenced the development of modern science each centered on a different metaphor. The Aristotelian worldview pictured the world as a vast organism.

Not only a philosopher but also a biologist, Aristotle analyzed all processes of change in categories borrowed from the growth and development of living organisms. Even prior to modern genetics, it was obvious that the development of living organisms must be directed by some internal pattern that ensures that acorns always grow into oaks, not maples, and that chicks always grow into hens, not horses. Based on this observation, Aristotle concluded that all forms of motion or change (all natural processes, as we would say) are directed by a built-in goal or purpose—a so-called final cause, which he also called an object's Form. To intuit the Form and encapsulate it within a concise, logical definition constituted, for Aristotle, scientific knowledge.

In the high Middle Ages, the scholastics adapted the Aristotelian heritage to Christian teachings, translating the notion of final causes or Forms into divine purposes. Christian Aristotelians viewed God primarily in terms of a rational Mind whose thoughts are known by logical analysis. During much of the sixteenth and seventeenth centuries, scholasticism was the dominant teaching in all Catholic and most Protestant universities.

As Ptolemy's astronomy and Galen's anatomy became available, these were absorbed into the Aristotelian framework. By the end of the Middle Ages, Aristotelianism had become a comprehensive worldview. It taught that the earth is located at the center of the universe. Around it revolve the planets and the sun, each in its own circular orbit. Earth is the realm of imperfection, populated by bodies composed of the four elements—earth, air, fire, and water. Heaven is the realm of perfection, populated by bodies composed of an incorruptible element—the "quintessence," or fifth essence.

When the scientific revolution began, many elements of the Aristotelian worldview were challenged, especially in astronomy and in physics. Yet Aristotelianism made lasting contributions to biology— which is not surprising considering that biology was the source of its fundamental concepts and hence the field where those concepts fit best. Key figures in the scientific revolution such as Andreas Vesalius (1514-1564), the father of modern anatomy, and William Harvey (1578-1657), who discovered the circulation of the blood, worked within the Aristotelian and Galenic tradition.

Positivist historians would lead us to believe that progress in science came through a repudiation of the ancients. Vesalius and Harvey are interpreted as figures in a line of revolts against Aristotle and Galen. In the words of historian Mark Graubard, the standard picture is "that Harvey rose up against [Galen] in scientific rebellion and established the reign of truth by evidence and test, thus ushering in modern science." Indeed, "hundreds of books and essays have been issued on Harvey as the brave destroyer of the Galenic Tradition."[3]

But this standard picture is badly out of focus. It results, Graubard argues, from a Whiggish interpretation of the history of science that fails to appreciate the extent to which Vesalius and Harvey remained firmly within the Aristotelian and Galenist tradition. From the fifteenth century through the early part of the seventeenth century, the medical school in Padua achieved prominence precisely because it revived the work of Galen. It was here that Vesalius taught. Here too Harvey was educated. Harvey himself attributed much of his inspiration to the Aristotelian tradition, always speaking of both Aristotle and Galen with reverence and awe. He even insisted that his own great discovery, the circulation of the blood, "does not shake but much rather confirms the ancient medicine."[4]

Harvey's very mode of reasoning was Aristotelian. To describe the heart, he used analogies derived not from machines (the heart as a pump) but from living things. He wrote, "I began to think whether there might not be *a motion as it were in a circle*" that nourishes the body in much the same way as the water cycle: The rain comes down to nourish the earth and returns to the sky, and "by this arrangement are generations of living things produced."[5] As historian Hugh Kearney comments, Harvey is clearly operating within "the Aristotelian world picture, in which final causes and organic growth and decay are regarded as the key to understanding nature."[6]

Harvey's writings are rich in analogies from human society as well. He writes that the blood

> returns to its sovereign, the heart, as if to its source, or to the inmost home of the body, there to recover its state of excellence or perfection. . . . [it becomes] a kind of treasury of life. . . . The heart, consequently, is the beginning of life, the sun of the microcosm. . . . it is the household divinity which, discharging its function, nourishes, cherishes, quickens the whole body, and is indeed the foundation of life, the source of all action.[7]

Notice that none of Harvey's analogies are mechanical. Instead they are political ("the sovereign"), domestic ("its inmost home"), economic (a "treasury"), and religious ("a household divinity"). Though the language of this passage strikes us as poetic, Harvey included it in the formal reports of his experiments; to him such concepts were a proper part of science itself.

And science was part of a larger worldview. Harvey illustrates the way Christian Aristotelianism was used in defending orthodox religion against rising skepticism. He stood against the atomists and materialists of his day, who held that living things are reducible to material forces acting by chance. Such a view, Harvey argued, derogates "from the honour of the Divine Architect," who created all things with consummate skill "for a certain purpose, and to some good end."

"On all points," Kearney remarks, Harvey was "making a religious stand as much as a scientific discovery."[8] Clearly, any account of the rise of science that portrays it as a process of throwing off the oppression of the past is simplistic.

THE NEO-PLATONIC WORLDVIEW

Whereas the Christian Aristotelian tradition stressed God's rationality, the neo-Platonic tradition stressed His indwelling spirit working in and through matter. A favorite metaphor was God as an artisan—"the best and most orderly Artisan of all," in the words of Copernicus. In the sixteenth and seventeenth centuries, art was treated as emblematic or symbolic. To see creation as a work of art therefore meant treating it as "an intricate language of metaphors, symbols, and emblems"⁹—a code which, properly interpreted, would unlock the secrets of nature. Reading the clues built by God into creation was a matter of mystical insight more than logical reasoning.

Neo-Platonism had its roots in the third century when Plotinus blended various streams of Greek thought into a unified philosophy. Plotinus taught a form of animism or panpsychism—that everything is imbued with life or a soul. This philosophy viewed the universe as a self-creative being with a passive element (matter) and an active element (a rational World Soul) animating and directing natural processes. Like Aristotelianism, neo-Platonism saw the world as an organism but with a different emphasis: In explaining natural processes it appealed not to rational Forms but to the creative power of spiritual forces. These forces were often regarded as divine, or at least as avenues of divine activity in the world.

Neo-Platonism contained two somewhat distinct streams of thought. One stream can be traced in astronomy; it contained a strong Pythagorean element with a profound and even mystical respect for mathematics. The other stream can be traced in medicine and early chemistry; it focused on immanent, quasi-spiritual forces in nature— "active principles," as they were called. Let's look more closely at each of these in turn.

THE EARLY ASTRONOMERS

Pythagorean philosophy regarded mathematics with near-religious awe as the key to understanding ultimate reality. In contrast, Aristotelianism ranked mathematics quite low on the scale of intellectual skills, and accorded it no religious connotations. Through the revival of neo-Platonism, many early scientists came under the spell of Pythagorean philosophy, which they promptly reinterpreted in Christian categories. The secrets of the cosmos, they said, were written by God in mathematical language. As Kearney puts it, for neo-Platonists "the pursuit of mathematics was not a secular activity. It was akin to religious contemplation."¹⁰

Copernicus

The work of Nicolaus Copernicus (1473-1543) is widely used as the peg upon which to hang the beginning of the scientific revolution. His heliocentric theory of the planetary system challenged the reigning geocentric astronomy inherited from Aristotle and Ptolemy. But where did Copernicus's inspiration come from? Not from any new empirical data, the records show, but from his commitment to neo-Platonism.

Copernicus came under the influence of neo-Platonism while studying in Italy. Kearney describes the encounter as "the equivalent of a religious conversion."[11] In neo-Platonism, immaterial mathematical Ideas act as causes of everything in the material world. Adapted by Christians, these were translated as "ideas in the mind of God."

Many neo-Platonists felt that the most appropriate symbol of God's creative ability was the sun, whose light and warmth enable all living things on earth to exist. Neo-Platonism thus became linked to a kind of sun mysticism. Whereas Aristotle taught that the earth was the center of the universe, some neo-Platonist writers argued that the sun must be the center of the universe, as only that position was compatible with its dignity as a divine symbol.

This mystical view of the sun seems to have inspired Copernicus's scientific studies. Certainly his words in the following passage reveal a touch of neo-Platonic sun mysticism:

> In the middle of all sits the Sun enthroned. In this most beautiful temple could we place this luminary in any better position from which he can illuminate the whole at once? He is rightly called the Lamp, the Mind, the Ruler of the Universe. . . . So the sun sits upon a royal throne ruling his children the planets which circle round him.

In the same passage, Copernicus quotes Hermetic literature referring to the sun as "the Visible God."[12]

Historians are uncertain whether neo-Platonism actually spurred Copernicus's conception of a sun-centered planetary system, or whether it merely gave him a set of arguments ready at hand to support his new system against the old geocentric system. It is quite certain, however, that neo-Platonism played a crucial role in shaping contemporary reactions to his theory. Throughout the sixteenth century, the only people who accepted the Copernican theory without reserve were other neo-Platonists.

Aristotelians raised the obvious empirical objections that the earth is a dark, inert, heavy, mass which—as anyone can see—does not move. The heavenly bodies, on the other hand, are points of light and therefore must be constituted of some light, fiery substance. In the face of these obvious everyday observations, to say that the earth is actually a heavenly body just like the planets, orbiting and rotating around the sun, seemed patently absurd.

Heliocentric theory encountered other common-sense objections.

For instance, it was argued that an object thrown into the air should land in a slightly different spot, since while it was in the air the earth would have rotated slightly. Curiously, this argument is valid; the earth's rotation produces what is known as the Coriolis force, which is demonstrated by the Foucault pendulum. The famous Danish astronomer Tycho Brahe argued that a cannonball ought to travel much farther if fired in the same direction the earth is moving (since it would benefit from the added momentum of the earth's movement). Again a valid argument, and not until Galileo developed an early form of relativity theory was it answered (see chapter 8). Opponents also argued that if the earth moved in a colossal orbit around the sun, then the fixed stars ought to show a slight change of position when seen from opposite sides of the orbit (parallax). This argument is valid as well, though the change is so slight that it wasn't observed until 1838.[13]

Not only were the objections to Copernicanism both numerous and logical, but the positive evidence *for* it at the time was nil. As historian A. R. Hall puts it, "to be a Copernican did not add one item to a man's factual knowledge of the heavens."[14] Indeed, the arguments advanced in favor of heliocentrism were not factual at all but philosophical. On neo-Platonic assumptions, Kearney says, "the central place of the sun in the universe seemed axiomatic because it was 'fitting.'" That was hardly a convincing argument, however, since "on Aristotelian assumptions, the earth was the central point of the universe for exactly the same reasons."[15]

Beyond that, the only argument Copernicus could muster was that his system was mathematically simpler. It reduced the number of epicycles needed to explain the planetary orbits from more than eighty to thirty-four. Not a weighty accomplishment, it appealed at the time only to thinkers within the neo-Platonic tradition—to Pythagoreans and Hermeticists—who believed that mathematics provided the key to the truths of nature.

Positivist interpretations of history present every scientific advance as a triumph of rationality over religion and mysticism. But in this case, religion and mysticism were clearly in evidence on the side of the Copernicans. Copernicus himself was not adverse to associating his astronomical theory with the mystical doctrines of neo-Platonism, and among his followers many were positively enthusiastic. (Recall the discussion of Giordano Bruno in chapter 2.)

Nor was opposition to the heliocentric theory due to dogma and obscurantism; instead it was due to its inclusion within a neo-Platonic philosophy at a time when the prevailing philosophy was Aristotelian. Not until Galileo a hundred years later was heliocentrism embraced by any major scientist outside the neo-Platonic tradition. And not until

Newton was heliocentrism given a physical mechanism. Until then the controversy rested entirely on religious and philosophical grounds.

Kepler

Johannes Kepler (1571-1630) was the first important astronomer to follow Copernicus; he too came deeply under the influence of Pythagorean philosophy. Kepler's first major book sought to demonstrate that the planetary system could be inscribed within a series of three-dimensional geometrical shapes. Although he later had to abandon the schema, it reveals his Pythagorean conviction that numbers and geometry are the key to unlocking the secrets of the universe. As Kearney puts it, Kepler believed "God created the cosmos upon the basis of the divinely inspired laws of geometry."[16] In fact, it was his intense commitment to mathematical precision that led Kepler through failure after failure until he finally hit upon elliptical orbits for the planets.

Like Copernicus, Kepler was attracted to a heliocentric astronomy at least in part because he attached religious significance to the sun. He appears to have thought of the sun as the physical seat of God's presence in the world. The sun alone, he says, "we should judge worthy of the most High God, should he be pleased with a material domicile and choose a place in which to dwell with the blessed angels." Again: The sun "alone appears, by virtue of his dignity and power, suited for this motive duty and worthy to become the home of God himself."[17]

Influenced by Gilbert's work on magnetism (see below), Kepler regarded the earth as a great magnet. Indeed, he went further and applied the concept of magnetic attraction to the planetary system as a whole, with the sun as the great central magnet—ideas that prefigure Newton's work on gravity. According to physicist Gerald Holton, the sun thus fulfilled three roles in Kepler's system. It was the mathematical center in describing the motions of the planets; it was the physical center in its exertion of force upon the planets to keep them in their orbits; and it was the metaphysical center as the temple of the deity. These three roles, Holton insists, are inseparable. Kepler's scientific achievement cannot be understood apart from his metaphysical and religious commitments.[18]

Gilbert

William Gilbert (1540-1603) was not an astronomer, but his ideas exerted a profound influence on astronomy. Gilbert produced the first scientific study of magnetism based on precise and carefully recorded experiments. Within the neo-Platonic tradition, magnetism was regarded with special awe as the paradigm of mystical affinity. Just as magnetism mysteriously attracts objects without even touching them, so the world was thought to be filled with spirits or souls that work from afar by attractions and sympathies.

Gilbert was the first to discover that the world itself is a great magnet. Since magnetism orders and arranges things (by north and south), Gilbert regarded it as a rational force. Indeed, he saw magnetism as the soul of the world.[19] Citing the ancients, Gilbert held that the stars and planets likewise have intelligent souls. He wrote:

> We consider that the whole universe is animated, and that all the globes, all the stars, and also the noble earth, have been governed since the beginning by their own appointed souls.[20]

This animistic belief in "souls" in matter strikes modern readers as terribly unscientific. Yet, as Kearney argues, it did not make Gilbert any less a scientist. Indeed, Kearney goes on, it was Gilbert's mystical beliefs that inspired his scientific contributions: "it was precisely his belief in the earth soul which led him to seek an explanation for magnetic phenomena, which within the Aristotelian paradigm remained merely a curiosity."[21]

THE EARLY CHEMISTS

The study of magnetism forms a bridge to the second stream within neo-Platonism, which was enamored with mystical affinities and souls and such. This stream involved the practice of alchemy and natural magic, out of which arose medicine and chemistry. The early chemists regarded nature as a realm of symbol and allegory; their work was to seek after esoteric knowledge to decode those symbols. As Butterfield explains:

> Causes were sought by hunting out analogies and mystical correspondences between things—imagining the stars as male or female, or as hot or cold, and giving them special affinities with minerals or with parts of the human body, so that the whole universe seemed sometimes to be a universe of symbols.

There was a search, Butterfield says, "for secret magical sympathies between objects" that allowed one body to affect another even though they were not in contact.[22] For example, when the Elizabethan doctor Robert Fludd (1574-1637) wished to heal a wound, he applied the ointment not to the patient but to the weapon that had hurt him.

(The healing was thought to be affected by a sympathetic power transmitted from the blood on the weapon to the blood of the wounded patient.) The German doctor Paracelsus (1493-1547) taught that in creating herbs God had inserted magical signs into their structure as a clue to their efficacy—so that the thistle, for example, was designed to relieve a prickly cough.

Paracelsus

Paracelsus used to be banished from the halls of science, dismissed as a mystical alchemist. But today he is honored as one of the founders of modern medicine, pioneering the use of chemistry in medicine. He was also a devout Christian. As historian Allen Debus explains, Paracelsus took a strong stand against the teachings of Aristotle and Galen, arguing that "Aristotle was a heathen author whose philosophy and system of nature was inconsistent with Christianity." Paracelsus and his followers hoped to replace Aristotelianism with a Christian form of neo-Platonism.[23]

Paracelsus viewed each natural substance as a combination of a passive principle (matter) with an active principle (a "virtue" or "spirit") that determined its distinctive character. He sometimes described the latter as "seminal" principles, a term adapted from Augustine's concept of "seeds" implanted by God in creation to unfold over time.[24] Active principles were discovered, it was thought, by heating and distillation—so that alcohol was referred to as "spirit of wine" and nitric acid as "spirit of nitre." Even today we use the Paracelsian word *spirits* to describe the products of certain organic distillations.

Van Helmont

Jean-Baptiste van Helmont (1579-1644), credited with the discovery of gas, was a Paracelsian. He regarded every object as a result of active or "seminal" principles working in and through matter. Van Helmont believed that when an object is burned, its active principle emerges in the form of a characteristic "fume"—what we call a gas.

Like Paracelsus, van Helmont was trained in medicine and his work was motivated by a Christian impulse to alleviate suffering and reverse the effects of the Fall. As historian Walter Pagel comments, "We say that the discovery of gas and pneumatic chemistry was due to the observations of Van Helmont," as though what counted foremost were his careful scientific observations. "We forget, however," Pagel goes on, "that this discovery was a rather incidental part of a religious and vitalistic system of natural philosophy."[25]

In summary, neo-Platonism exerted an enormous influence upon the intellectual world of the sixteenth and seventeenth centuries. It had great appeal for those who revolted against the arid rationalism of Aristotelianism, not unlike the appeal of romanticism two centuries later for those who revolted against the arid materialism of the Enlightenment. Indeed, the two are connected, since a revival of neo-Platonism helped inspire romanticism. But that is a subject for chapter 5.

THE WORLD AS MACHINE

Despite their differences, the Aristotelian and neo-Platonist traditions held in common a view of nature as a living organism. As historian R. G. Collingwood explains:

> No difference of principle was recognized between the seasonal rotation of the heavens and the seasonal growth and fall of leaves on a tree, or between the movements of a planet in the sky and the movements of a fish in the water.[26]

The third tradition that inspired the scientific revolution represents an abrupt rejection of the organic metaphor. The dominant metaphor in the mechanistic worldview is the machine.

Scientists working within the mechanistic tradition were struck by the regularity, permanence, and predictability of the universe. God was seen as the "Great Engineer" (in the words of Mersenne) who had created the universe as a giant clock. Whereas the neo-Platonists regarded nature as an interplay between the passive force of matter and active spiritual forces, mechanistic philosophy rejected the latter, regarding nature as purely passive. The laws of motion were imposed on nature from the outside by God.

Like neo-Platonism, the mechanistic tradition embraced the mathematical treatment of nature—not from any number mysticism, however, but from a conviction that mathematics expresses measurability, analyzability, and clockwork regularity. Among the ancient Greek philosophers, the mechanistic tradition sought inspiration in the writings of the atomist philosophers (e.g., Democritus and Lucretius) and especially the engineer Archimedes. With the translation of his writings into Latin in 1543, an Archimedean revival began in Europe.

The outlook Archimedes seemed to embody was the detached intellectual curiosity of a mechanical engineer. It was practical and unmetaphysical. It had none of the systematizing logic of Aristotelianism, none of the mystical or religious fervor of neo-Platonism. Its fundamental assumption was that the universe operates on the basis of mechanical forces. The task of the scientist is to show how the parts of the universe fit together like the parts of a machine.

Natural phenomena were explained as the result of the size, shape, and
motions of material particles impinging upon one another.

If Aristotelianism portrayed God as the Great Logician, and neo-
Platonism as the Great Magus, then mechanistic philosophy portrayed
Him as the Great Mechanical Engineer. In later centuries, mechanistic
philosophy would be used in polemics against belief in God. Yet most
of its initial supporters were Christians. By conceiving of matter as
completely passive, they sought to attribute all creative and spiritual
power to God. What impels natural processes is not any inherent purposes or Forms (contra Aristotelianism), nor any inherent active forces
(contra neo-Platonism), but God alone. God created the laws by which
the universe operates, just as a clockmaker constructs a clock and sets
its gears in motion.

Galileo

The first important representative of the mechanistic tradition is
Galileo Galilei (1564-1642). His reverence for Archimedes is obvious
in his frequent references to him, often in such adoring terms as "the
most divine Archimedes." By contrast, he took a belligerently hostile
stand against the followers of both Aristotle and Plato. He rejected
Aristotelian final causes and the concept of motion by "natural" tendencies; he had none of the neo-Platonists' sun mysticism or panpsychism. He conceived of God as a Divine Craftsman or Architect who
created the world as an intricate mechanism, following the propositions of geometry and arithmetic.

Descartes

The French philosopher and mathematician René Descartes (1596-
1650) is best known for his insistence that the physical world is a vast
mechanism, that even plants and animals are automatons. What is not
as well known is that he embraced mechanistic philosophy as a strategy for refuting the religious skeptics of his day.

By drawing a sharp distinction between the mechanical universe
and the human spirit, Descartes sought to preserve belief in the latter—
and then to springboard to belief in God. His famous "Cogito, ergo
sum" ("I think, therefore I am") was a religious affirmation. Since
thought is a spiritual activity, the Cogito served as a reply to those who
denied the existence of the human spirit. And from the Cogito,
Descartes moved immediately to the existence of God. It is ironic that
what survived of Cartesian philosophy was not his proof for the existence of the human spirit or of God but only his mechanistic conception of the universe—the universe as a vast, impersonal machine.

The spread of mechanistic philosophy was boosted by the formation of scientific societies. In Italy Galileo's followers formed a group. In France a group formed around the friar Marin de Mersenne (1588-1648) who translated Galileo's works into French. In England Robert Boyle (1627-1691) was instrumental in founding a group that became known as the Royal Society.

Surrounded and outnumbered by supporters of Aristotelian orthodoxy and neo-Platonism, these groups often promoted mechanistic philosophy with missionary zeal. Not infrequently, they combined it with religious apologetics. For instance, Robert Hooke (1635-1703), a member of the Royal Society, argued that nature works mechanically by such "stupendous contrivances" that it is foolish "to think all these things the production of chance." Clear reasoning, Hooke argued, should lead to the conclusion that such excellent mechanisms are "the works of the Almighty."[27]

STRADDLING TWO TRADITIONS

Over time the three traditions outlined here intermingled and influenced each other, producing hybrids. For example, at first glance, Isaac Newton (1642-1727) may appear to be a mechanist. Certainly later generations came to regard his physics as the epitome of the mechanistic approach to science. And his own work gives some justification for that impression.

Newton saw God as a great engineer; he wrote that the Creator of the planetary system must be "very well skilled in mechanics and geometry." Newton's law of universal gravitation applied the same mechanical laws to both earthly and heavenly bodies (which astounded his contemporaries, trained by Aristotle to think that earthly and heavenly bodies were composed of contrasting substances). His experiments with light showed that it acts according to mechanical laws when passed through various media (thus undermining the neo-Platonic view of light as a spiritual symbol). He interpreted light as a stream of particles, a view akin to Boyle's particulate view of chemistry.

Moreover, Newton strongly opposed the neo-Platonic notion of a World Soul, which, when regarded as divine, verged on pantheism. He wrote in the *General Scholium*:

This Being governs all things, not as the soul of the world, but as Lord over all; . . . and *Deity* is the dominion of God, not over his own body, as those imagine who fancy God to be the soul of the world, but over servants.

Eventually, Voltaire and other Enlightenment figures would

use Newton's scientific work to promote a completely mechanistic view of the world—a view that reduced the Biblical Creator to a deistic watchmaker who wound up the universe and then left it to run on its own. In the words of economist John Maynard Keynes, Newton "came to be thought of as the first and greatest of the modern age of scientists . . . who taught us to think on the lines of cold and untinctured reason."[28]

Yet Newton himself was neither a deist nor a rationalist. He saw in the mechanical order of the world evidence for something *beyond* the mechanical world—a living and intelligent Creator. In *General Scholium*, he argues that "this most beautiful system of sun, planets, and comets could only proceed from the counsel and dominion of an intelligent and powerful Being." And in *Opticks*, he writes that the business of science is to "deduce causes from effects, till we come to the very first cause, which certainly is not mechanical." In Newton's eyes, the major benefit of science is religious and moral. It shows us "what is the first cause, what power he has over us, and what benefits we receive from him," so that "our duty towards him, as well as that towards one another will appear to us by the light of nature."

Moreover, the motive for much of Newton's scientific work was apologetical, a fact widely recognized in his own day. Roger Cotes, in his preface to the second edition of Newton's *Principia*, wrote that the book "will be the safest protection against the attacks of atheists, and nowhere more surely than from this quiver can one draw forth missiles against the band of godless men."[29]

So was Newton a mechanist? In recent years much scholarly ink has been spilled in attempts to pin down his philosophical orientation. Keynes studied Newton's manuscripts and concluded that, in contrast to the standard conception, Newton stood within the neo-Platonic tradition with its fascination for symbols and magic. "Why do I call him a magician?" Keynes asks.

Because he looked on the whole universe and all that is in it *as a riddle*, as a secret which could be read by applying pure thought to certain evidence, certain mystic clues which God had laid about the world. . . . He regarded the universe as a cryptogram set by the Almighty.

"Newton was not the first of the age of reason," Keynes concludes. "He was the last of the magicians."[30]

Historian P. M. Rattansi likewise places Newton in the neo-Platonist tradition. Newton adopted the neo-Platonic concept of active principles, regarding them as avenues of divine action in the world. He regarded his own discovery of gravity as a prime example of just such an active principle. Hence Rattansi writes that the concept of force "served for Newton as a manifestation of the divine in the sensible world."[31]

Richard Westfall amasses evidence to show that Newton was preoccupied with alchemy throughout much of his career and that the alchemical concept of attraction contributed significantly to his concept of gravitational attraction (which explains why the mechanists of his day rejected it).[32] E. A. Burtt points out that Newton's concepts of absolute space and time had religious significance. They were intended to represent God's presence within the world, the locus of His perception and control of the physical universe.[33]

Perhaps the best way to make sense of these conflicting streams within Newton's thought is to say that he straddles two traditions. His view of the physical world was inspired partly by mechanistic philosophy; yet he had an urgent desire to defend the realm of spirit against the completely materialistic form of mechanism gaining ground in the intellectual world in his day. To accomplish that, he turned to the neo-Platonic tradition and adopted its concept of active principles. The sheer fact that Newton revived the work of Kepler, who by then was half-forgotten and whose scientific insights were buried in pages of neo-Platonic speculation, reveals his interest in that tradition.

Indeed, when Newton's *Principia* was first published, the Cartesian mechanists dismissed it as just another expression of the mystical philosophy they were trying so hard to expunge from science. They readily recognized in gravity the neo-Platonist idea that the sun exerts an occult power of attraction over the planets (all the worse because the idea was generalized into a law of universal mutual attraction of masses). Not until Voltaire championed his work did Newton receive a sympathetic hearing on the continent.

In the process, however, Voltaire and other Enlightenment philosophers spruced up Newton's image to make it more acceptable to the Enlightenment mentality. They stripped Newton of his religious and mystical views to fit the positivist picture of scientific reason—the picture most of us absorb today from our science and history textbooks.

Newton himself kept his theological and alchemical interests secret during his lifetime. After his death, historians who had access to his papers regarded it as an embarrassment to admit that anyone of Newton's scientific genius could also have seriously entertained views they themselves deemed irrational. As a result, they extracted his scientific results from their theological and neo-Platonic setting, leaving only the mechanistic concepts intact.

AN INTERWOVEN TAPESTRY

The approach to science history presented here is holistic. It places historical figures firmly within their philosophical and religious context, even if that context is one judged by moderns to be superstitious or irrational.

Indeed, many contemporary science historians question the very meaning of the term "rational." Rationality was once thought to include the actual content of beliefs. Moreover, the only belief judged "rational" was materialism—which, by definition, relegated any form of religion or metaphysics to the realm of the "irrational."

But this definition placed historians in a bind. If it is irrational to hold, say, Aristotelian metaphysics or Biblical religion, then a good deal of what the pioneers of modern science believed must be dismissed as irrational and unscientific. Such a conclusion puts the historian in the awkward position of simply ignoring or dismissing a good portion of the history of science.

The problem can be resolved by redefining rationality as that which follows logically from a given set of assumptions. By this definition, it is quite rational for a neo-Platonist to seek for numerical harmonies in the world or for a Christian to seek to know God better by searching out His creation. These activities are not irrational; they are rational extensions from a given set of premises. Today most historians of science have accepted this latter definition of rationality. Hence they can acknowledge that historical figures within science behaved perfectly rationally, given the beliefs they held at the time, even though their ideas may not conform to present-day conceptions.

Moreover, contemporary historians argue that it is impossible to neatly separate out something called "pure" science from the "external" religious and metaphysical influences that supposedly "contaminate" it. Fundamental decisions within science are necessarily affected by extra-scientific commitments. The facts that a researcher considers scientifically interesting in the first place, the kind of research he undertakes, the hypotheses he is willing to entertain, the way he interprets his results, and the extrapolations he draws to other fields—all depend upon prior conceptions of what the world is like.

This is obvious from the historical period we have just covered. During the scientific revolution the Aristotelians enjoyed their greatest successes in biology and medicine. And understandably so, for their philosophical orientation was particularly suited to the study of living things. Hence this tradition gave the world Vesalius and Harvey, but made few contributions to, say, chemistry. Chemical cures did not fit within the Aristotelian framework.

Similarly, the neo-Platonic tradition, with its mystical interest in the sun and in mathematics, was particularly well suited to the study of astronomy. Hence this tradition gave the world Copernicus and Kepler. But it did not give rise to the science of mechanics because that requires a practical interest in mathematics as a tool for measurement. The mechanistic philosophy used concepts quite suited to the study of local motion and gave the world Galileo, Descartes, and Boyle. Its most glaring shortcomings were in biology and medicine. As philosopher of science Philipp Frank comments, Aristotle once said the motion of an animal is easier to understand than the motion of a stone—which given his organic worldview was quite true. But in the mechanistic worldview the situation was reversed. The fall of a stone became straightforward but the motion of animals became difficult to explain.[34] Each philosophical tradition inspired particular kinds of research and supplied an interpretative framework for understanding the results.

Facts and Philosophy

The positivist approach sought to sift out any premodern elements in the early stages of science and preserve only what matches the "facts" as defined by the modern up-to-date textbook. But the contemporary historian treats the entire historical context as important. The early scientists' philosophical and religious convictions were precisely what inspired much of their scientific work.

Take the example of Copernicus. He was not driven to his heliocentric theory by any new facts. As Kuhn writes, "No fundamental astronomical discovery, no new sort of astronomical observation, persuaded Copernicus of ancient astronomy's inadequacy or of the necessity for change." Kuhn concludes:

Any possible understanding of the [Copernican] Revolution's timing and of the factors that called it forth must, therefore, be sought principally *outside of* astronomy, within the larger intellectual milieu inhabited by astronomy's practitioners."[35]

Similarly, Burtt maintains that both Copernicus and Kepler accepted the heliocentric hypothesis "*in advance of* any empirical confirmation." For "the motions of the heavenly bodies could be charted according to Ptolemy just as correctly as according to Copernicus." What motivated Copernicus and Kepler in their science was not primarily any new facts but a philosophical conviction fostered by neo-Platonism—the conviction that the universe is fundamentally mathematical in structure.[36]

In a similar vein, Kearney concludes his study of Kepler with these words:

What the historian cannot do is separate Kepler the "scientist" from Kepler the neo-Platonist mystic. Kepler would not have been moved to question the basis of existing cosmological theories unless he had been a neo-Platonist in the beginning.[37]

It is true that Kepler had access to the best astronomical observations available in his day through the work of Tycho Brahe (whose data collection, incidentally, was motivated in large part by his avid interest in astrology). But Kepler's *interpretation* of those observations to favor heliocentrism was due to his sympathy for the neo-Platonic context in which heliocentric ideas were embedded at the time.

The same argument applies to Newton. We cannot separate Newton the scientist from Newton the religious believer. He wrote extensive volumes on Biblical prophecy, which most historians have ignored, treating his interest in religion as entirely superfluous to his scientific accomplishments. But as Burtt reminds us, "religion was something quite basic to him and in no sense a mere appendage to his science or an accidental addition to his metaphysics."[38] Instead, the driving impulse of Newton's scientific work was, as we have seen, to defend Christian faith against what he saw as an encroaching mechanistic materialism.

"It is important," writes historian Allen Debus, "not to try to separate the 'mystical' and the 'scientific' when they are both present in the work of a single author. To do so would be to distort the intellectual climate of the period."[39] The philosophical, religious, and scientific convictions of the early scientists formed a rich and complex tapestry that cannot be unraveled without destroying the fabric.

Clash of Worldviews

An understanding of this complex tapestry sheds new light on the nature of scientific controversy. Opposition to a new theory is not necessarily due to stupidity, fear, or blind dogmatism. In most cases, it is due to disagreement over the philosophical and religious context in which the new theory appears—and which it is being used to support.

For example, as we saw earlier, the only people to welcome Copernicanism initially were neo-Platonists. Those who rejected heliocentrism did so not because they were closed-minded obscurantists but because they were Aristotelians, who disagreed with the accompanying mystical hermetic philosophy. With its ties to neo-Platonism, says theologian John Dillenberger, Copernicus's system "looked like the revival of an ancient and already discredited philosophical view." Hence the choice between Copernicus and Ptolemy did not appear at the time as a choice between science and philosophy, between rationality and irrationality. Rather, it appeared as a choice between an Aristotelian philosophy that had already been assimilated to a Christian frame of meaning (scholasticism) and a neo-Platonic philosophy that had *not* yet been so assimilated.[40]

Moreover, some advocates of heliocentrism (e.g., Bruno) had stepped outside the Christian frame of meaning entirely and were promoting pantheism, a strategy sure to arouse theological opposition from orthodox believers. Historically, most opposition to new scientific theories among Christians must be understood as opposition not to science per se but to the pagan doctrines and mysticisms associated with it.[41]

The showcase piece supposedly demonstrating the hostility between science and religion is, of course, the story of Galileo, whose attack on Ptolemaic astronomy in favor of Copernicanism brought him into conflict with the Catholic hierarchy. Again, an understanding of worldviews clarifies what was at stake. The Counter-Reformation had inspired a revival of Aristotelianism within the Catholic church. Galileo attacked Aristotelianism, using Copernicanism as a tool and writing brilliant polemical pieces directed against the clerical establishment. This was not a simple matter of bigotry versus intellectual freedom. It was a clash between two traditions, two paradigms—the Aristotelian and the mechanistic.[42]

CONCLUSION

The three general approaches outlined here—the Aristotelian, the neo-Platonic, and the mechanistic—are rough groupings. Individual scientists sometimes straddled more than one tradition, as Newton did. Sometimes they belonged to one tradition while adopting the vocabulary or concepts of another.[43] For example, it is commonly accepted that Galileo was a pragmatic Archimedean standing within the mechanistic tradition. Yet historian William Shea notes that Galileo remained profoundly influenced by Aristotle's model of scientific explanation. His "lifelong passion was to show that the Copernican system could be demonstrated with all the rigour demanded by the Aristotelian canons."[44]

Similarly, Kepler is generally regarded as a mystical neo-Platonist, yet at times he used language more characteristic of the mechanistic tradition, speaking of the heavens as "the celestial machine" and likening it to "a clockwork." As a result, historians sometimes disagree on how to categorize him. Rossi insists that Kepler's ideas were "imbued with Pythagorean mysticism" whereas Debus groups Kepler with the mechanistic philosophers Mersennes and Gassendi.[45] Perhaps the best interpretation is that Kepler moved from one tradition to the other over the course of his life.

Another source of confusion, says philosopher of science Mary Hesse,[46] is the variety of ways scientists use terms. The use of characteristic terminology may not always indicate full-blooded adherence to the philosophy from which the terms derive. Terms may also be used as pious archaisms, as expressions of Christian piety (as was often the case in the Christian use of neo-Platonic terms, such as "soul"), or as familiar labels to appeal to a particular audience. For example, Westman argues that Copernicus's use of neo-Platonic language does not necessarily indicate a philosophical commitment on his part; it may merely indicate his desire to win the patronage of Pope Paul III.[47]

Taking these qualifications into account, the three categories outlined in this chapter help make sense of the varied streams of thought influencing science in its nascent period. Each intellectual tradition inspired the formation of concepts and motivated discoveries of enduring value to science. And, as we shall see in the following chapters, they have continued to exercise an enduring influence on science up to contemporary times.

THE NEWTONIAN WORLD MACHINE: How Does God Relate to the World?

Newtonian physics. To the modern mind, the phrase evokes an image of the universe as a vast machine, with human beings trapped in a mesh of inexorable physical laws. To put a philosophical label on it, Newtonian physics tends to be identified as materialistic and deterministic.

Yet Newton himself was neither a materialist nor a determinist. In fact, he explicitly rejected the clockwork image of the world, arguing that it led to materialism.[1] A highly religious man, Newton even used his physical theories in the service of apologetics, to persuade his contemporaries of the existence of God. How then did his name come to be attached to a philosophy so antithetical to his personal beliefs?

To answer that question, we will trace the development of classical physics from Galileo through Newton and beyond. Standard historical accounts paint a picture of perpetual warfare between science and religion. But as we shall see, the scientists who developed classical physics were mostly Christians seeking to make sense of the way God interacts with His creation—the way He gives order and coherence to the natural world.

The question of how God orders the creation was, of course, the same question that split the three worldviews described in chapter 3. The Aristotelian, neo-Platonic, and mechanistic traditions were each attempts to conceptualize the way God structures the world. Galileo so effectively discredited Aristotelian astronomy and physics, however, that in those fields Aristotelian influence declined, and the battle for intellectual dominance in physics was played out between the mechanistic and neo-Platonic traditions.[2]

Christians in the mechanistic tradition stressed God's transcendent power over creation. Matter was defined as completely passive, without any inherent activating forces, in order to leave room for God's free creative activity. Gradually, however, it became more and more difficult to understand how God could act in a purely mechanical order. The creation was pictured as a giant clockwork, ticking away autonomously. Mechanistically minded Christians came to rely more heavily on extraordinary events such as miracles as signs of God's presence.

Christians in the neo-Platonic tradition tended to stress God's immanent presence in creation. Scientifically, that idea often translated into a notion of spiritual forces as the active power in natural processes. Gradually, those forces came to be seen as semi-autonomous—implanted in creation by God at the beginning and thereafter capable of functioning on their own. Yet they still represented manifestations of divine power working in and through the created order.

The rise of classical physics can be understood as an ongoing debate between these two perspectives—a debate that continues even today in some Christian circles.

CONTINGENT ORDER

In the days of the church fathers, the conception of God's transcendent power *over* and His immanent power *in* creation was balanced and complementary. It was understood that God had transcendent power to act in the world at His will and pleasure; but He had also created the natural world to proceed in regular, consistent patterns that He set up in the beginning and upholds through His immanent presence. This was sometimes described in the language of primary and secondary causes. As Anglican theologian E. L. Mascall says, "The main tradition of classical Christian philosophy, while it insisted upon the universal *primary causality* of God in all the events of the world's history, maintained with equal emphasis the reality and the authenticity of *secondary causes.*"[3]

Theologian Thomas Torrance sums up this balanced view as the "contingent order" of creation. Contingency means the creation is not autonomous. It is not self-originating or self-sustaining; it was created by God and depends continually upon Him. On the other hand, God does not work in the world by perpetual miracle. He has set up a network of secondary causes that act in a regular and consistent pattern. That is, creation has a real order. Hence the phrase, contingent order.[4]

The contingent order of creation is expressed in Scripture from the opening chapters of Genesis. God establishes day and night in Genesis 1:5, and from then on they follow one another in regular sequence. God establishes the processes of biological reproduction in Genesis 1:11-12 (for plants) and 1:20-25 (for animals), and from then on living things reproduce after their kind in a predictable pattern. Genesis 8:22 describes the regular cycle of the seasons. Psalm 148 talks about God's decree governing the regular sequences of the heavens. Likewise, Jeremiah 31:35 says the Lord "appoints the sun to shine by day, who decrees the moon and stars to shine by night." In Jeremiah 33:25 God compares the reliability of His covenant with His people to the reliability of His "covenant with day and night and the fixed laws of heaven and earth." Proverbs 8 describes God marking out the boundaries of land and ocean in terms reminiscent of a surveyor.

The scriptural concept of lawfulness is clearly quite different from the later materialistic concept of natural law as deterministic, impersonal, amoral. In Scripture law is like an executive decree—"subject," in the words of Christopher Kaiser, "to the regular ratification of God."[5] The implication is that the natural world responds in obedience to God just as humans do, though on its own level. The weather is said to obey God; the animals receive their food from Him (Job 28 and 38, Psalm 148). The dominant image of creation is not that of a machine, operating mechanically when a switch is flicked, but that of an obedient subject. Moreover, the order of nature is not closed but open to new events injected by the Creator, like a theater improvisation where the director injects new themes to which the actors all respond.

Medieval Naturalism

In the eleventh and twelfth centuries, this balanced conception of natural law began to split into two divergent streams, which eventually came to be seen as mutually exclusive—a split between God's transcendent will imposed upon the world and His immanent will working in and through the world. The distinction appears in scholastic literature as an opposition between God's transcendent, absolute power (*potentia absoluta*), reflected in His ability to create and to alter the patterns of nature, and His immanent, regular power (*potentia ordinata*), reflected in the normal patterns of cause and effect.

This split was played out in the late Middle Ages between Aristotelianism and voluntarism (discussed in chapters 1 and 2). By incorporating Aristotelian philosophy into Christian thought, Thomas

Aquinas shifted the emphasis sharply to God's immanent power(*potentia ordinata*). Aquinas adopted Aristotelian final causes (Forms that direct all natural processes), translating them into divine purposes in the world. Later Thomists came to regard the Aristotelian Forms as quasi-independent powers, delegated to creation from the beginning and capable of acting independently. They spoke of the Forms as God's vice-regents for ordering and operating the world.

In Aristotelian philosophy, the Forms are logically necessary. But in that case, they constrain even the hand of God Himself, restricting what He can and cannot do in creation. For example, some Christian Aristotelians argued that the planetary orbits *must* be circular–that God Himself could not make them otherwise. Nature began to be personified, spelled with a capital *N*, as though it were an independent entity. This was out-and-out naturalism, where God was no longer necessary for the everyday operation of the creation. The Biblical image of God as Cosmic Legislator gave way to the idea of God as First Mover, who does nothing more than set things in motion at the beginning.[6] The delicate balance of contingent order was lost; the order of creation was becoming increasingly autonomous.

In 1277 Etienne Tempier, Bishop of Paris, issued a condemnation of several theses derived from Aristotelianism. The condemnation represented a reaction against Aristotelian naturalism and a renewed concern for God's absolute power (*potentia absoluta*). Tempier rejected the idea of an inherent necessity in created things, stressing God's freedom to create the world entirely according to His will. This inspired a stream of theology known as voluntarism, which emphasized the contingency of creation as dependent on God's will. The order in creation was not due to immanent Forms; it was imposed externally by God. The world did not have to operate the way it does; God could very well have made it differently had He chosen to. Natural law was regarded not as some inherent order in the world but as an expression of divine commands.

This basic theological division surfaced repeatedly in various forms over the following centuries—controversies that were different in terminology but the same in essence. It was a split between Christians who stressed the transcendent power of God over creation and Christians who stressed the immanent power of God within creation.

Immanent or Transcendent?

Classical physics developed through a debate among Christians over precisely this split—with neo-Platonists on one side and mechanists on the other. As science progressed, the universe was beginning to be conceived as a giant clockwork, and Christians found it increasingly difficult to understand how to "fit God in." The neo-Platonic tradition stressed God's immanence—His power at work in and through the forces of creation. They viewed the world as an interplay of passive forces (matter) and active forces (souls, spirits, or vital forces). Active forces were regarded as creative and hence divine, or at least avenues of divine activity in the world. They were identified with processes that appeared to defy mechanistic explanation—such as chemical reactions, magnetism, electricity, the growth of living things.

Scientists within this tradition were apprehensive that the mechanistic worldview would turn the world into a completely self-sufficient clockwork machine, with no room for spirit or for God. Hence they focused on nonmechanical phenomena as manifestations of divine power in the world.

On the other side, the mechanists stressed God's transcendent power over creation. They were afraid that the neo-Platonic tradition would lead to a form of naturalism, just as Aristotelianism had. The active principles implanted in nature might come to be interpreted as independent powers ordering the world, eliminating the need for God's direct interaction with His creation. For the active principles in matter were often referred to as souls or spirits; they were endowed with psychic characteristics such as rationality and intelligence. If matter contained within itself such powers, what need was there for God?

As a result, the mechanists defined matter as completely inert and passive, believing that this would leave more room for God as the sole animating and ordering impulse in the world. The idea that matter has no inherent powers of its own would lead, the mechanists hoped, to the inference that the lawful behavior we observe requires the continual exercise of divine power. The order of nature is not inherent in matter but imposed upon it by divine decree.

A fascinating aspect of this controversy is that both sides were concerned to avoid the same danger—that nature would come to be regarded as independent of God. Neo-Platonists were afraid that a mechanistic view would lead to a conception of the universe as a vast machine operating by built-in physical forces. Mechanists feared that the active principles would be conceived as independent powers inherent within matter. Both sides hoped to articulate a role for God in a world increasingly seen as a closed order of cause and effect.

NEO-PLATONIST PHYSICS

Neo-Platonists resisted the idea that creation could be reduced to a mechanism. They stressed the existence of active principles–minds or souls—in nature, which they located in phenomena they felt were not explainable in mechanistic terms. These active principles were regarded either as the immanent spirit of God at work in the world or as powers built by God into the creation. This was akin to the Augustinian notion of "seminal principles" or "seeds" implanted by God in creation.

For example, the early chemist Jean-Baptiste van Helmont (1579-1644) believed that all things have a soul or seminal principle that survives its destruction in the form of a characteristic gas. Experimenting with this idea, he burned various substances and was the first to identify carbon dioxide and several other gases. In his own eyes, however, van Helmont was not merely making a scientific discovery. He developed his chemical philosophy "as a conscious rejection of materialism," says historian Richard Westfall, "as an assertion of the primacy of spirit."[7] Van Helmont prided himself on offering a truly "Christian philosophy" that recognized spiritual powers in the world as manifestations of divine power.

In the seventeenth century, many people found van Helmont's philosophy attractive precisely because it offered an antidote to mechanistic philosophy. Yet his own views illustrate a tendency within the neo-Platonist tradition toward an equally undesirable result—namely, that the immanent spiritual powers themselves may become self-sufficient. Speaking of those powers (represented by gases), van Helmont writes:

> For that most glorious Mover hath given powers to things, whereby they of themselves and by an absolute force may move themselves or other things.[8]

Notice how van Helmont's language tilts sharply toward the concept of autonomy. The active principles are described as "an absolute force" enabling things to move and develop "of themselves." But in that case, these forces are virtually self-sufficient, and the neo-Platonist worldview has yielded a concept of nature just as autonomous as the mechanical worldview its adherents had hoped to counter.

That tendency is much more pronounced in Gottfried Wilhelm Leibniz (1646-1716), a Lutheran philosopher and mathematician. Leibniz was a close friend of van Helmont's son; like van Helmont, he was committed to the idea of active principles in matter. "The whole nature of bodies is not exhausted in their extension, that is to say their size, figure, and motion," Leibniz wrote; instead "we must recognize something that corresponds to soul." In his philosophy these souls or active principles were intimately united with matter in the basic elements of which the world is composed, which he called monads (a Greek term for unit). A monad is a kind of living particle—a point spatially related to other points but also a mind, capable of perceiving its environment. The philosophical term for this is panpsychism, the belief that matter is permeated with psychic properties such as perception and intelligence.

As we shall see later, mechanist philosophers such as Descartes sought to preserve a role for souls and spirits by treating them as completely *independent* of matter. Leibniz on the other hand, felt that the way to safeguard a place for the spiritual was to *reunite* it with matter. Hence though his monads were spiritual, they followed strict mechanistic laws. He insisted that every motion has its origin in another motion according to the laws of mechanics—laws that are never violated. He even referred to the monads as automatons and did not hesitate to designate the bodies of plants, animals, and human beings likewise as automatons.

So on one hand, Leibniz's concept of monads as souls—active principles—gives his philosophy a spiritual twist (philosopher Lewis Beck describes it as "pluralistic spiritualism"[9]). Yet the monads behave in a completely lawful manner and need no guidance or intervention from God. Again we see the active principles becoming virtually autonomous. In Leibniz's philosophy, the universe is a perpetual-motion machine that needs no input from God. As Kaiser explains, for Leibniz even miracles were not fresh interventions by God but rather instances of laws of a higher order ordained by God from the beginning.[10]

In short, Leibniz saw the world as a perfect machine and God as a perfect watchmaker who foresaw and provided for all eventualities from the outset. As he put it, after the original creation everything that followed was "purely natural, and entirely mechanical." In the words of historian Alexandre Koyré, in Leibniz's philosophy:

> God just did not do what He wanted, or would like to do. There were laws, and rules, that He could neither change nor tamper with. Things had natures that He could not modify. He had made a perfect mechanism in the working of which He could not interfere.[11]

Using Torrance's phrase "contingent order," we could say Leibniz stressed the order of creation to the point that it was no longer contingent but absolute. Though his goal was to develop a Christian philosophy of nature, his version of neo-Platonism clearly degenerated into a form of naturalism, precisely as the mechanists had feared.

Eventually neo-Platonism, with its emphasis on immanent powers, led to pantheism (where God is completely immanent in creation). And for practical purposes, pantheism became indistinguishable from atheism,[12] since both reject any signs of God's transcendent power, such as miracles. When this happened, many orthodox Christians turned against the neo-Platonic tradition in science.

MECHANISTIC PHYSICS

The mechanistic tradition explained natural phenomena as the result of the interaction of particles. For example, the chemist Nicolas Lemery (1645-1715) pictured oil as consisting of pliable branched particles that easily become entangled with each other, giving oil its characteristic viscosity. He pictured acids as tiny pointed particles that react with other substances by piercing them. Alkalis, on the other hand, consist of porous particles. The reason acids and alkalis neutralize each other when mixed, Lemery postulated, is that the acid particles stick into the alkali particles like so many pins stuck into pin cushions.[13]

On the question of God's immanence and transcendence, the mechanistic tradition came down firmly on the side of transcendence. The first to develop a full-fledged mechanistic philosophy was René Descartes (1596-1650). Descartes consciously set out to prune the world of the active principles so beloved of the neo-Platonists, who had imbued matter with psychic properties such as perception and intelligence. For Descartes, psychic properties belong to spiritual substance alone; matter is completely passive with no creative powers, no rational order of its own.

Positively, Kaiser explains, the doctrine of passivity meant that "matter was entirely receptive to the mathematical laws imposed on it by God."[14] Many of Descartes's followers were Christians—such as Marin Mersenne (1588-1648) and Pierre Gassendi (1592-1755), both members of the clergy—who saw Cartesian philosophy as an effective weapon against neo-Platonic naturalism. Since matter had no creative or active powers of its own, the only way to explain its existence and behavior was to invoke an external Creator.

Yet the mechanistic worldview soon acquired disturbing overtones of materialism. For example, Descartes reasoned that since the existence and behavior of matter depend entirely on God, the laws of physics directly reflect the attributes of God. The most important attributes of God for Descartes were His eternity and immutability; hence, he concluded the laws of physics are likewise eternal and immutable—not because matter has its own inherent laws that God cannot violate (as naturalists would say) but because the laws of physics have their source in God, and He is constrained by His own nature.[15]

As a result, the physical universe became for Descartes a machine operating by fixed, inexorable laws. He rejected the possibility of miracles because in his view God does not act otherwise than by His settled decrees. Descartes was the first to suggest the possible evolution of the universe from an original chaos of material particles, acting solely by physical processes still in action today.

Thomas Hobbes (1588-1679) gave the mechanistic philosophy a completely materialistic interpretation. A political theorist, Hobbes was the first to extend the mechanistic philosophy into the realm of human society (ethics and psychology). Whereas Descartes had insisted on two substances, matter and spirit, Hobbes reduced everything to matter. Christians who opposed the mechanistic worldview typically pointed to Hobbes's writings as evidence of its anti-Christian bias.

THE GREAT SYNTHESIS

As both the neo-Platonic and mechanistic traditions veered away from a Christian view of creation, many devout scientists sought a middle ground—in particular, Robert Boyle and Isaac Newton.

Robert Boyle

Robert Boyle (1627-1691) was a deeply religious Christian who is credited with discovering that the pressure of a gas is inversely proportional to the volume it occupies—what every chemistry student knows as Boyle's law. Boyle began as an adherent to van Helmont's active principles. Later he came under the influence of Descartes and became persuaded that van Helmont's immanent spiritism erred by confusing God with His creation, by "mixing the divine with the natural." The failure to keep these two things distinct, Boyle argued, would lead to pantheism.

Hence Boyle's judgment on neo-Platonic philosophy was that, for all its Christian terminology, it detracted from "the honour of the great author and governor of the world" by elevating the immanent powers of creation to the level of divinity. Only the mechanistic tradition, he felt, preserved the distinctive domain and dignity of the Creator. Boyle advanced an image of the world as a great clockwork "where all things are so skillfully contrived, that the engine being once set a-moving, all things proceed according to the artificer's first design."

It was Boyle who coined the label "mechanistic philosophy," and the tradition took root in England largely due to his work in chemistry. In his experiments on air pressure, for example, Boyle described air as particles behaving according to mechanical principles. His goal was to promote an atomistic view of matter—to show, as he put it, that the characteristics of bodies "may be produced mechanically," that is, "by corporeal agents" working "by virtue of the motion, size, figure, and contrivance of their own parts," which are ultimately reducible to atoms.

Despite his enthusiasm for a mechanistic view of nature, however, Boyle drew back from a full-fledged Cartesian philosophy. He criticized Descartes for treating natural laws as eternal and immutable and for refusing to countenance any evidence of God's operations in the physical world. Like other Christians of his day, he recoiled from mechanistic philosophy because it seemed to be turning creation into an autonomous machine. As Butterfield writes:

> It is curious to note that, if earlier in the century religious men had hankered after a mathematically interlocking universe to justify the rationality and self-consistency of God, before the end of the century their successors were beginning to be nervous because they saw the mechanism becoming possibly too self-complete.[16]

So in the end, Boyle took something from each tradition. From mechanistic philosophy he took the concept of matter as passive because he felt this retained a clear distinction between the realm of matter and the realm of immaterial spirits—both God and human souls. The passivity of matter made nature dependent on God to impose and maintain its lawful order. Boyle wrote frequently of God's "general concourse," by which he meant the divine supervision needed to keep a mechanistic universe operating on course.

From neo-Platonic philosophy Boyle retained the idea of active principles in matter, which he identified with certain chemical processes and especially the growth of living things. Boyle's chemical research was designed to capture and reproduce the work of those active principles (terminology we still use when we speak of the "active ingredient" in a chemical compound).[17] For Boyle active principles were "supramechanical" phenomena that could not be reduced to mechanistic forces. They represented a realm of spiritual phenomena within creation.

Isaac Newton

The great Isaac Newton likewise sought a middle ground between the two traditions. His intellectual roots were in the work of the Cambridge Platonists, a group of academicians who worked out a synthesis of the neo-Platonic and mechanistic philosophies.

A major concern of the Cambridge Platonists was to defend the realm of the spirit. On one hand, they were drawn to the mechanistic worldview because the concept of the passivity of matter seemed to require the activity of spirits, such as God and the human soul. But they

abhorred the Hobbesian form of mechanism, which reduced everything to matter and made nature self-sufficient, eliminating the need
for divine creation and providence.

On the other hand, as their name suggests, the Cambridge
Platonists accepted much of the neo-Platonic tradition. They were
attracted by its insistence that the ordering forces in the world are
active principles not susceptible to mechanistic explanation.
Mechanistic philosophy treated every phenomenon as a result of invisible particles with specialized shapes colliding with each other like so
many tiny billiard balls. But certain phenomena—light, magnetism,
electricity, heat, life processes—are not easily explained by particles in
motion. These the Cambridge Platonists explained by invoking active
principles. The active principles were regarded as evidence that the
physical world contains within itself, contrary to mechanistic philosophy, some spiritual phenomena.

This is not to say the active principles were regarded as miraculous or supernatural, for they operated according to precise mathematical law. Nevertheless, they were clearly not reducible to collisions
of material bodies and thus seemed to provide some locus in the world
for the phenomenon of spirit.[18]

Newton's thinking was similar to the Cambridge Platonists'. On
one hand, he is credited with establishing the mechanistic worldview
as the reigning philosophy in science. His remarkable accomplishments in reducing a wide variety of natural phenomena to mathematical laws—from the orbits of the planets to the tides of the
sea—persuaded many that nature is a unified, law-bound system.
Newton himself was not adverse to describing much of the world in
mechanistic terms. In the preface to the *Principia*, where he explained
the motions of the planets, the comets, the moon, and the sea according to mechanical principles, he wrote, "I wish we could derive the
rest of the phenomena of Nature by the same kind of reasoning from
mechanical principles."

Yet, like the Cambridge Platonists, Newton drew back from a
completely mechanistic worldview and looked for avenues to "fit God
in" to the world. He found four such avenues. First, from the
Cambridge Platonists he took over the idea of supramechanical or
active principles in nature, describing them as "a certain most subtle
spirit which pervades and lies hid in all gross bodies," revealed in such
phenomena as chemical reactions, light, and magnetism. For Newton
the active principles were avenues for God's ordering activity within
the world.

To the list of active principles Newton added his own discovery
of gravity. Gravity acts at a distance without any physical contact
between bodies—a concept with deep roots in the neo-Platonic tradi-

tion (see chapter 3) but anathema to mechanistic philosophy, which sought to explain all natural phenomena by the shape and size of particles impinging directly upon one another. Thus, as Newton saw it, he had discovered a major new active principle through which God acts directly in His creation.

This characterization of gravity in terms taken from neo-Platonism became a bone of contention between Newton and many of his contemporaries. The more mechanistically minded among them, such as the Cartesians, objected strongly to Newton's theory of gravity, arguing that it was an occult concept—a throwback to ideas of mystical affinities.

Newton denied the charge. He insisted that the concept of force he had introduced was not an ultimate explanation at all—either occult *or* mechanistic. It was merely a postulate used to explain observations. Ultimate explanations, Newton said, should be left out of science. This is the context in which he uttered his famous expression *hypotheses non fingo*—"I feign no hypotheses."

The reason Newton felt free to avoid ultimate causes was, of course, that for him the ultimate cause was God. He viewed gravity as an active principle through which God Himself imposes order onto passive matter—as one of the avenues through which God exercises His immediate activity in creation. As Kaiser puts it, for Newton things like gravity "depended on God's immediate presence and activity as much as the breathing of an organism depends on the life-principle within." Like breathing, these active powers were regular and natural, and yet they could not be explained in purely mechanical terms.[19]

Gravity thus served an apologetical purpose for Newton. Since it could not be derived from intrinsic properties of matter, such as mass and extension, gravity represented the imposition of a supramechanical law upon matter. Hence it served as evidence of God's active governance of the world.

A second way Newton found to "fit God in" was in his concept of absolute time and space. From the mathematician Isaac Barrow, Newton adopted the idea that time and space are expressions of God's own eternity and omnipresence. Newton took God's eternity to mean He is actually extended throughout all time—in his words, God's "duration reaches from eternity to eternity." He took God's omnipresence to mean that He is extended throughout all space—His presence reaches "from infinity to infinity." Therefore time must be eternal and space infinite.[20] Physics textbooks often describe Newton's concepts of absolute space and time as purely metaphysical without explaining that his motivation was primarily religious.

A third way Newton found a role for God in the world was as the source of its orderly structure. In the cosmic order, Newton saw evidence of intelligent design. "The main business" of science, he said, is to argue backward along the chain of mechanical causes and effects "till we come to the very first cause, which certainly is not mechanical." Newton also regarded several specific characteristics of the world as inexplicable except as the work of a Creator. "Was the eye contrived without skill in optics," he asked, "or the ear without knowledge of sounds?"

Newton's favorite argument from design, however, focused on the solar system, whose delicately balanced structure he felt clearly indicated intelligent design. If the speed of the planets were just slightly different, if the mass of the sun were just slightly more or less, the entire system would not work. Newton concluded that the solar system cannot be explained by natural causes alone—which are "blind or fortuitous"—but only by a cause "very well skilled in mechanics and geometry." In the *General Scholium* Newton writes:

> This most beautiful system of sun, planets, and comets could only proceed from the counsel and dominion of an intelligent and powerful Being.

Indeed, Newton's image of the universe as a finely tuned machine or "contrivance" in itself fostered the idea of a Creator, just as a watch implies the existence of a watchmaker. "The whole form of Newtonian science," writes historian John Herman Randall, "practically forced men, as a necessary scientific hypothesis, to believe in an external Creator."[21]

A fourth way Newton found a role for God was by assuming that the universe needs God's intervention from time to time to stabilize it. For example, the orbits of the planets exhibit irregularities when they pass close to other planets or to comets. Newton feared that over time these fluctuations would accumulate and cause chaos, and the solar system would collapse. Therefore, he argued, God must step in periodically and set things right again. If the universe is a clock, then it is a clock that on occasion needs to be repaired and rebuilt.

This argument exposed Newton to great ridicule. In his own day, Leibniz mocked him for believing that God is an incompetent workman, unable to create a perfect world and forced to tinker with it from time to time to repair its shortcomings.[22] In the early part of our own century, philosopher E. A. Burtt wrote, "Really, the notion of the divine eye as constantly roaming the universe on the search for leaks to mend, or gears to replace in the mighty machinery, would have been quite laughable" if it weren't so pitiful.[23]

The idea was laid to rest scientifically by astronomer Pierre Simon de Laplace (1749-1827), who showed that the perturbations in the orbits of the planets are not random but periodic and thus over time quite stable. The solar system does not require God's direct intervention to fix its malfunctions, for it does not malfunction in the way Newton had thought.

This is the basis for the story about Laplace frequently retold in science books. As the story has it, Napoleon Bonaparte perused Laplace's *Treatise on Celestial Mechanics* only to comment, "Newton in his book spoke often of God. But in your book I did not find the name of God even once." Whereupon Laplace answered, "Sire, I have no need of that hypothesis." The story may be apocryphal, and at any rate Laplace was a practicing Roman Catholic. But Laplace was right to reject this particular notion of divine activity that Newton had advocated. God does not act to repair leaks and cracks in His original creation but to effect His saving purpose in human history.

THE NEWTONIAN LEGACY

Today we are conditioned to think of the history of science as a warfare between science and religion. In the development of classical physics, however, what we see is not a battle between science and Christianity but a debate *among* Christians over the best way to conceptualize God's role in the world—a debate over how to construe divine action in a world increasingly understood to operate by natural law.

The neo-Platonic tradition emphasized semi-spiritual active powers immanent in matter, implanted by God at creation. The mechanistic tradition emphasized the passivity of matter and the need for God to impose order upon it. Newton effected a synthesis that brought together what he saw as the best of both traditions. His was a mechanistic world imbued with active forces.

But among his followers, only a few retained his conception of active forces as avenues for the immediate presence and activity of God. Eventually the concept of force was secularized and forces were regarded as powers inherent in matter. For example, speaking of gravity, the philosopher Immanuel Kant wrote that "an original attraction belongs to all matter as a fundamental force appertaining to its essence." Scientists sought to subject all the other so-called active principles to mechanistic explanations—light, magnetism, electricity, life.[24] Matter came to be regarded as self-sufficient, and Newton's active powers were absorbed into the materialistic philosophy he had hoped to refute.

The irony is that this materialistic, mechanistic philosophy then came to be called the "Newtonian" worldview. We won't go into detail listing its major proponents—figures such as la Mettrie, Diderot,

Holbach, d'Alembert—but will merely summarize its basic outlines. The "Newtonian" worldview held that the real world is the world of matter, and its basic components are small, hard atoms in motion. As Newton put it, "God in the beginning formed matter in solid, massy, hard, impenetrable, movable particles." All changes in nature, he said, are due to "the various separations and new associations and motions of these permanent particles"—what is sometimes called a billiard-ball view of the universe.

The "Newtonian" worldview assigned objective existence to primary qualities only—to mass, extension, weight, length. Things like colors, tastes, odors, and sounds were relegated to the human mind as secondary qualities. And the mind, in turn, was relegated to a tiny portion of the brain. As Burtt puts it, the world people *thought* they were living in—a world rich in colors and beauty, joy and love—was "crowded now into minute corners in the brains of scattered organic beings." The *real* world outside was "hard, cold, colorless, silent, and dead," a vast machine running by inexorable mechanical laws. The human mind became merely

a puny, irrelevant spectator (so far as a being wholly imprisoned in a dark room can be called such) of the vast mathematical system whose regular motions according to mechanical principles constituted the world of nature.[25]

Interestingly, the construction of the so-called "Newtonian" worldview was not primarily the work of scientists. As Butterfield points out, the translation of Newton's scientific achievements into a comprehensive materialistic worldview was wrought primarily by literary men, who wrote for a rapidly expanding educated reading public. In the aftermath of Newton's brilliant scientific work, the presses poured forth an immense stream of works by popularizers, such as the French writer Fontenelle, who produced elegant and amusing expositions to adorn ladies' dressing tables. It became fashionable to have a naturalist cabinet in the drawing room containing fossils and feathers. Science came into vogue as a pastime among the *beau monde* and then among the bourgeoisie.[26]

But it was not science per se that was absorbed so much as a new view of life and the universe. As Voltaire put it at the time, no one *read* Newton, but everyone *talked* about him. The vast majority of thinking people were only marginally interested in science for its own sake, but they were immensely interested in what it meant for a general view of the world.

The "Newtonian" worldview eventually became the paradigm for all human knowledge. Practitioners of political theory, ethics, psychology, and theology sought to restructure their disciplines in accord with mathematical physics in order to render them truly "scientific." The principle that physics bequeathed to these disciplines is that nature is thoroughly orderly and rational—that what is natural is also reasonable. Nature and Reason (often capitalized) became the dominating ideals against which all human conceptions were to be tested. Scholars in every field sought to brush aside the accretions of ancient authority and irrational tradition in order to uncover what was natural and reasonable.

Since physical science discovers laws that are general and uniform, it was assumed that the human sciences must likewise discover general laws. There was a search for universal codes of behavior, principles and customs adhered to by all cultures. Once these universal principles were uncovered, it was thought that a comprehensive system could be deduced. Just as Galileo had observed a ball rolling down an inclined plane and discovered the mathematical law of acceleration for all moving bodies—and just as Newton had observed a falling object (an apple, according to legend) and calculated the mathematical law of gravity for all matter—so scholars hoped that by observing a few simple cases they could also discover universal laws governing human behavior.

In religion for the first time since the days of St. Augustine, an influential segment of the intellectual community openly attacked the Christian tradition, putting orthodox Christians on the defensive.[27] The search was on for a natural religion, for universal beliefs underlying the accretions of particular cultures and traditions. At first the natural religion thus "discovered" bore remarkable similarities to traditional Christianity. Later, it became a substitute for it. Anything that did not commend itself to the Enlightenment definition of reason (or Reason) was eliminated, beginning with miracles. Finally only a few key principles remained, generally these three—that an omnipotent God exists, that He requires of humans a virtuous life, and that there is a future life of rewards and punishments.

Even this simple creed was eventually truncated and became a bare obligation to moral living. Voltaire wrote, "I understand by natural religion the principles of morality common to the human race."[28]

In the social sciences, theorists sought to construct a "social physics" modeled on Newtonian physics. They hoped that once they had analyzed a few principles of human nature, these could be used to construct a science of economic, moral, and political life.[29] The Cartesian dualism between mind (or spirit) and body was rejected in favor of complete materialism. The goal of the social sciences was to show that mind is merely a part of the body—to propose a purely mechanical genesis of ideas and sensations. Human thoughts and behavior would be explained as the result of atoms in the brain operating by strictly mechanical causes. Humanity would be absorbed into the giant world-machine. "Let us conclude boldly then," la Mettrie said, "that man is a machine."

We end this chapter as we began it, remarking on how odd it is that what is called the "Newtonian" worldview is so antithetical to everything Newton himself believed in. We have seen how classical physics grew out of the debate between Christians over how to understand God's role in the world—the tension between those who stressed the transcendent acts of God and those who stressed His immanent power. Both groups were seeking to understand how God relates to His creation, and both made significant scientific contributions.[30]

In the end, however, cultural dominance passed from Christianity to the Enlightenment, and Newton's physics was transmuted into the "Newtonian" worldview. But the machine image of the universe was—like all analogies—incomplete, and no sooner was it in place than it began to be challenged, primarily in the study of living things, to which we turn next.

THE BELATED REVOLUTION IN BIOLOGY:
Taking Biology from Metaphysics

*I*f any area of science seems more clearly hostile to Christian faith than others, it is biology. The evolution controversy that began in the late nineteenth century became a rallying point for anyone opposed to Christianity or the church. Reading the typical history textbook today, one gets almost no clue to the rich interaction that existed for three hundred years between Christian faith and the study of living things. That history is what we hope to capture for you in this chapter.

Historians talk about the scientific revolution as the birth of modern science. Yet it was a revolution confined primarily to astronomy and physics. Biology saw no dramatic changes to rival those instituted by Copernicus, Galileo, and Newton. Up until the seventeenth century, biology remained virtually a branch of medicine. Most of its practitioners were physicians, concerned principally with human anatomy (Vesalius, Harvey) and with botany (focusing on the medicinal properties of plants).

The scientific revolution came belatedly to biology in the eighteenth and nineteenth centuries—and then it blossomed forth suddenly in a welter of contrary philosophies and approaches. Historical treatments of biology seem to jump from mechanists to vitalists, from reductionists to holists, from essentialists to transformists, from radical materialists to natural theologians who regarded living things as evidence for belief in God. How can we make sense of this apparently chaotic ferment of ideas and ideologies?

The contrasting theories sort themselves out once we realize that biology was nourished by the same three streams of thought discussed in earlier chapters: the Aristotelian, neo-Platonic, and mechanistic worldviews. Grasp these three worldviews and you have the tools to sort through the rich diversity making up the history of biology and to understand the intellectual commitments motivating individual figures. As historian William Coleman points out, advocates of various interpretations of life "ultimately borrowed their biology from their metaphysics."[1] Each metaphysical tradition primed its adherents to look for certain kinds of facts and to apply certain interpretations.

The three worldviews we met first in chapter 3 look a bit different, however, when we meet them again a few centuries later in biology.[2] The Aristotelian worldview, though discredited in physics and astronomy, remained vigorous in natural history. Its major theme was that organic structures must be understood according to built-in purposes. The Aristotelian approach was particularly popular with anatomists, who were impressed with how perfectly the eye is constructed for seeing and the ear for hearing. Many saw in the wonderful "fit" between structure and function the hand of a wise Creator. In addition, Aristotelian logic was used in the construction of classification systems to organize the vast array of living things.

Aristotelians tended toward the descriptive side of biology. They interpreted the order in the organic world as an expression of the divine plan of creation; their reasoning was the logic of categorization; their method was observation in the wild.

By contrast, neo-Platonism stressed immanent semi-spiritual "active principles" as formative forces in nature. The nineteenth century witnessed a great revival of neo-Platonism through the romantic movement, especially in Germany where it developed into *Naturphilosophie* (nature philosophy). The romantic biologists embraced a form of pantheistic vitalism, especially popular among embryologists, who sought an inner Law of Development to explain organic forms.

By drawing an analogy between embryonic development and the development of categories of organisms, romantic biologists were the first to construct theories of evolution. Just as individuals move up through several stages of development, so all of life was presumed to move up the great chain of being from simpler forms to humanity. In most cases, this was not evolution as the term is used today but rather as its literal definition suggests—an "unfolding" of a preordained pattern, the gradual realization of an immanent or built-in pattern. Like earlier neo-Platonists (Paracelsus, van Helmont, Leibniz), the romantic biologists often spoke of "seeds" in nature—hidden, latent powers that unfold over time.[3] Each category of organism was regarded as the realization of such a seed.

The romantic biologists also searched for fundamental anatomical patterns for each class of organisms. They referred to these patterns as "archetypes"—a term reminiscent of Plato's perfect and eternal Ideas, which stand above the flux of organic nature and impart to it a logical order and coherence. Hence romantic biology is often described as an idealist philosophy of nature; the search for archetypes was labeled Transcendental Anatomy.

The romantic biologists interpreted the order in the organic world as a progression up the chain of being, a succession of archetypes; they reasoned by analogy; their method was historical.

The mechanistic worldview came to biology through Descartes, with his proposal that living things (animals and the human body) are automatons, operating solely by physical laws. Mechanistic philosophy appealed particularly to physiologists studying the way the body operates. Early physiologists focused on the mechanical operation of limbs and joints; later they experimented with chemical reactions in the body.

Mechanists interpreted the order in the organic world as a result of order in the physical world, in the atoms and chemicals that comprise living things; they reasoned by analysis; they championed the method of controlled experiment.

Now let's examine each of these movements in greater detail.

HEIRS TO ARISTOTLE

The Age of Exploration was a remarkable boon to biology. European explorers made room on the decks of their ships to carry exotic plants and animals back from all over the world. Soon naturalists signed up to join the expeditions, coming back laden with specimens to stock their vast collections. An unprecedented number of new species of plants and animals came to the attention of natural historians. (The study of living things was not yet called biology but natural history.) For although physical laws remain the same everywhere on the globe, each continent has its own fauna and flora.

With this exponential growth in sheer information, the foremost need became biological classification—the imposition of some kind of order on the stunning diversity of living creatures. Starting in 1550, "problems of nomenclature, identification, and classification rather suddenly became acute," says historian A. R. Hall, "and constituted one of the main theoretical topics in biology for nearly three hundred years."[4] Soon taxonomic systems were proliferating as fast as the discoveries that inspired them. Yet none was complex enough to cope with the needs. Elaborate diagnostic phrases were coined to name species—phrases that grew ever longer as biological knowledge expanded—until it seemed that no two persons used the same name for the same species. Clearly naturalists needed an international taxonomic system that would give them a common nomenclature. The question was: Which system would it be?

The answer was a system based on Aristotle. Aristotle had bequeathed a taxonomic system using the categories of genus and species. The term *genus* was originally used to mean any one of the higher categories. *Species* is the Latin word for "form," which we readily recognize as a key element in Aristotelian philosophy.

Aristotelian Forms not only provided a means of classification, they also expressed the idea of purpose—an idea eminently adaptable to Christian theology. Nothing, it seemed, could be more obvious than that living structures are designed for a purpose. In His providence God had given birds wings so they could fly; He had given fish gills so they could live under water; He had given tigers sharp teeth and claws to capture their prey. For many natural historians of the time, the marvelous "fit" between an organism and its environment bespoke a purposeful creation.

This synthesis of Aristotelian biology and Christian belief attracted many Christians to the study of living things. As zoologist Ernst Mayr remarks, "the study of natural history in the eighteenth and early nineteenth centuries was almost completely in the hands of amateurs, particularly country parsons."[5] So forcefully did design in the organic world seem to reveal God's handiwork that it inspired a form of apologetics known as natural theology. From the intricacy of a bird's wing to the complexity of the human eye, living structures are far beyond the power of physical processes operating by blind chance, so the argument went; they must be the "wise contrivance" of an intelligent Creator.

Note that natural theology was not a "god-of-the-gaps" argument. It did not argue from *ignorance* of natural causes but rather from an expanding *knowledge* of the complexity exhibited by living things—and from their similarity to human artifacts. Hence the strength of the argument seemed to grow stronger, not weaker, as scientific knowledge increased. Natural theology became quite popular with both orthodox Christians and deists.[6] It prospered enormously between about 1650 and 1850, inspiring most of the field work done in biology during that period.

Modern history textbooks are written from such a thoroughly secular perspective that we have lost sight of the powerful influence of Christian faith in the formative period of all the sciences, including biology. As a result, "it is difficult," as Mayr comments, "for the modern person to appreciate the unity of science and Christian religion that existed from the Renaissance and far into the eighteenth century." Indeed, "the Christian dogma of creationism and the argument from design coming from natural theology dominated biological thinking for centuries."[7]

It was Charles Darwin's theory of evolution that eventually brought about the decline of the Christian Aristotelian tradition in biology. For that tradition was implacably opposed to evolution. Aristotle had taught that Forms are eternal—that new Forms never come into existence, existing Forms never die out. Of course, individuals *within* the species are born and die; but as each individual dies, another comes to take its place. So in the endless cycle of generations, Aristotle taught, the species itself is eternal—mirroring the eternal rotations of the imperishable heavenly spheres.[8]

Christians could not accept Aristotle's definition wholesale, of course, because they believed the world had a beginning and would have an end. But they adapted the Aristotelian definition by postulating that God had created each species at the beginning of the world and that it had remained stable thereafter.[9] Note the Aristotelian tones in the words of William Harvey (1578-1657): After describing the life cycle of organisms, he concludes that "from frail and perishing individuals an immortal species is engendered."[10]

Now let's consider specific figures who worked within the Aristotelian framework.

John Ray

If the greatest challenge for natural history was biological classification, the greatest challenge for classification was to find a guiding principle for delimiting species. For example, should plants be classified according to their root system, leaf shape, blossom, fruit, or habitat? Some of the properties that make for handy classification and identification have little or nothing to do with biological function. (Flip through your child's *Golden Guide*, for example, and you'll find it groups wildflowers by blossom color.)

The early naturalists hoped to get away from such "artificial" systems of classification, useful though they may be for identification, and to uncover a "natural" system. A natural system, as they conceived it, would articulate the fundamental ordering principle God Himself had used in creating the organic world.

The botanist John Ray (1627-1705) believed he had found such a natural system—and in fact he is credited today with offering the first biological (as opposed to logical) definition of species. Based on his understanding of Genesis 1, Ray proposed that a species consists of all the descendants of a male-female pair created by God—just as the human race consists of all the descendants of the original human pair, Adam and Eve. Hence Ray's definition of species centered on reproduction. No matter how broad individual variation may be, each organism is classified in the same species as its parents.[11]

Ray's definition was adopted enthusiastically by later generations of naturalists. They used the term "common descent" to mean a literal blood relationship, not an evolutionary lineage. For Ray was no evolutionist. His definition of species assumed an unbroken chain back to the originally created species. Ray held that however vast variation might be, it would always be just that—variation, and not the creation of new species. God rested on the seventh day from His work of creating, Ray argued.[12] Afterward He allowed the free play of secondary causes *within* species, but He did not create any new basic species.

In addition to his botanical research, Ray authored several sermons and religious essays. He penned one of the most influential books on natural theology. Titled *The Wisdom of God Manifested in the Works of the Creation* (1691), it argued that living things are so complex and so marvelously designed that they must be the creation of a supremely intelligent Creator.[13]

Carl Linnaeus

Swedish botanist Carl Linnaeus (1707-1778) established the first workable and comprehensive classification system for the organic world. Like Ray, Linnaeus believed that the key to the originally created units is descent and that a natural system of classification must rest on reproduction. He took that to mean the plant's reproductive structures, and hence built his system on the shape and number of pistils and stamens.

Linnaeus's system had no place for evolution, for he held that at creation God had made each organism to reproduce only its own kind. Hence the organic world is organized into units that remain stable throughout time. The task for naturalists is to identify the created unit.

Initially Linnaeus identified the created unit with species, and he penned the line for which he was later to become famous: "We count as many species as different forms were created at the beginning." As a result, his name became closely associated with the doctrine of the complete immutability of species.

Yet Linnaeus was not committed to the species as the unit of creation. Already in his early thirties, Linnaeus was experimenting with hybridization and he decided that in many cases the stable unit in the organic world must be higher than species—perhaps the genus. So in the sixth edition of his *Genera Plantarum*, he identified the original progenitors created by God as a single pair for each genus, which contained the potential for differentiation over time into several species. Three years later Linnaeus had raised the category level of the first creations to orders. Clearly, he was still groping for some principle for identifying the created unit, which he believed lay at the foundation of order in the organic world.

For Linnaeus that unit also represented the Aristotelian Form or essence of each organism. Steeped in Aristotelian logic, he firmly believed that the natural system of classification would also be a logical system. As historian James Larson explains, Linnaeus held "a strong faith in the intelligibility of organic nature"—and for him intelligibility meant that nature followed the conceptual hierarchy of Aristotelian class logic.

It also meant nature was the handiwork of an intelligent Creator. A devout Lutheran, Linnaeus believed, as Larson puts it, that rational inquiry must inevitably lead "to the acknowledgment of and respect for an omniscient and omnipotent Creator." As a result, his "scientific work [was] something of a religious enterprise." Like Ray, Linnaeus wrote essays on natural theology in which he argued that science teaches us to see the Creator glorified in His works.[14]

Georges Cuvier

The great zoologist Georges Cuvier (1769-1832) was proclaimed by his contemporaries the Aristotle of the nineteenth century. He virtually founded the field of comparative anatomy, and he did it on the basis of Aristotelian teleology—using the concept of final cause, purpose, or function.

For Cuvier the primary feature of any organism is its functional unity, the coordination of all its parts and structures. He enunciated a principle he called "the correlation of parts," which he viewed as a natural law, as unalterable as the laws of physics. The principle states that an organism is not an arbitrary jumble of traits; rather, it is an organized whole, every part modified by the organism's overall function and way of life.

For example, the carnivore has traits eminently suited to its mode of life—keen eyesight, claws for catching prey, sharp teeth for tearing meat. By contrast, the grazing animal has flat, rough teeth for grinding and hooves instead of claws. Cuvier used to boast that from a single fossilized bone he could reconstruct an entire organism.

Like his predecessors, Cuvier adopted a definition of species based on reproduction. But he did not mean the structure of reproductive organs (as Linnaeus did). He meant the ability to interbreed. What keeps species stable and distinct is that individuals cannot interbreed with organisms outside the species. They are separated by uncrossable reproductive barriers. Though wide variation may occur *within* species, it never leads to a *new* species. Cuvier cited the familiar example of domestic dogs, which range from the tiny Chihuahua to the lumbering Great Dane without ever losing the diagnostic canine features.

Though evolution was very much "in the air" in Cuvier's day (Lamarck was one of his colleagues), he remained adamantly opposed to it. Moreover, unlike Linnaeus, he remained committed to the species as the stable unit of creation. As Cuvier put it, "We imagine that a species is the total descendence of the first couple created by God, almost as all men are represented as the children of Adam and Eve."

Yet the decisive factor precluding evolution for Cuvier was his view of the organism as an integrated whole. Any significant change in a highly integrated, interdependent functional system, he argued, would destroy the system. (Think what would happen if a child randomly moved a few wires in your computer.) Hence an organism cannot change in a piecemeal fashion. Organic change must be systemic. An organism must change all at once—with corresponding changes occurring throughout the system—or not at all.

Moreover, Cuvier argued, if species have changed gradually over history, we ought to find transitional forms throughout the fossil record. But we do not. Cuvier knew fossils better than anyone else in his day; indeed, he established the science of paleontology (the study of fossils). He argued that paleontology simply does not furnish us with the myriads of transitional forms required by evolutionary theory.[15]

Updated Aristotle

Though the biological tradition we have been describing is labeled Aristotelian, that label must be carefully qualified. It was Aristotelian in logic only (in its emphasis on function and purpose), not in ontology. For example, Cuvier's functionalism was, in Coleman's words, "a restatement of the thoroughgoing teleological interpretation of life which he had adapted from Aristotle."[16] Yet Cuvier was a Calvinist in theology, and emphatically rejected the Aristotelian tendency to see Forms or essences as independent ordering principles in the world. For Cuvier any philosophy that places the ultimate principle of order *within* creation usurps the power and prerogative of the Creator. Nature has an orderly structure not because of any inherent properties, but because it is subject to God's laws. In his rather haughty writing style, Cuvier criticized as "puerile" those philosophers who give "nature a kind of individual existence, distinct from the creator, from the laws which he has imposed."[17]

He was equally adamant in rejecting the neo-Platonism embraced by romanticism and *Naturphilosophie*, which often verged on pantheism. Cuvier criticized pantheism for failing to distinguish between

Creator and creation, for merging God and the universe. This concern to keep a clear distinction between God and His creation—and to reserve creative power to God alone—characterizes the mechanistic worldview. And indeed the Aristotelian tradition in biology borrowed its conception of the relation between God and the world from the mechanists.[18]

This explains why, for example, naturalists within the Aristotelian tradition consistently rejected spontaneous generation, a question debated repeatedly until Louis Pasteur finally laid it to rest in the mid-nineteenth century. To the Christian Aristotelians, the creation of life was a prerogative of the Creator alone, a task completed within the original creation week. Any theory granting to matter the power to create life ascribes to creation what is properly a divine prerogative.

As Pasteur put it, if we accept spontaneous generation, "God as author of life would then no longer be needed. Matter would replace Him." Clearly, this was a post-Newtonian form of Aristotelianism, as strict as any mechanist in reserving creative activity to God alone (though equally strict in opposing any purely materialistic form of mechanism).

In its conception of God, the Aristotelian tradition tended to remain orthodox (with, however, deistic tendencies). Hence theologically it served as a counterweight to both the Enlightenment materialism of the French *philosophes* and the romantic spiritualism of the German *Naturphilosophen*. To the latter we turn our attention now.

NEO NEO-PLATONISM

Most of us are acquainted with romanticism primarily as a movement in the arts—Wordsworth's nature poetry, Turner's shimmering landscape paintings, Tchaikovsky's emotive melodies. What most of us don't know is that at its heart the romantic movement was inspired by biology. It was a reaction against the reduction of living things to mere mechanisms in the Newtonian-style world machine.[19]

In 1749 the French philosopher-physician Julien Offray de la Mettrie wrote *L'homme machine*, arguing on the basis of philosophical materialism that the organism must be understood as a machine. But even as he penned those words, a reaction was setting in. Indeed, for the next hundred years, Coleman writes, the "mechanistic-materialistic conception of the organism and particularly of man attracted more abuse than adherents."[20]

However persuasive the machine analogy may have been in physics, the fact is that when machine concepts were used to construct biological theories, the results were clumsy and inaccurate. For example, Descartes had an enormous influence with his philosophical assertion that an organism operates like clockwork; its motion, Descartes wrote, follows "necessarily from the very arrangement of the parts," just as the motion of a clock follows "from the power, the situation, and the shape of its counterweights and wheels." Yet the factual content of Descartes's biological theories was exceedingly simplistic and crude—"offending," Mayr sniffs, "every biologist who had even the slightest understanding of organisms."[21]

Ultimately, the stubborn refusal of living things to fit into any simplistic mechanistic explanation prompted a rebellion among natural historians. Many turned to neo-Platonism with its concept of formative principles immanent in nature. As historian Arthur Lovejoy comments, a conspicuous aspect of romanticism was "a revival of the direct influence of neo-Platonism."[22] In an interesting twist of history, the astronomer and biologist Pierre Louis Moreau de Maupertuis (1698-1759) was the first person to bring Newtonian thought to France—and later was also the first person in France to recognize that a simplistic Newtonian paradigm of "forces and motions" is inadequate for biology. He turned to the philosophy of Leibniz, embracing his organic vision of nature.

"Leibniz's nature is a vast organism whose parts are lesser organisms, permeated by life and growth and effort," writes historian R. G. Collingwood.[23] Leibniz regarded matter itself as imbued with force, activity, and even a low-grade form of mind or sensitivity (panpsychism). Through Maupertuis, Buffon became acquainted with Leibniz's ideas, and Buffon's multivolume natural history was a key influence in the rise of romanticism and Naturphilosophie.[24]

Romanticism sought to remove physics from the heart of science and replace it with biology—to remove the machine as the dominant metaphor of science (and society) and replace it with the organism. Romantics gave the World Soul of earlier neo-Platonism a biological twist, transforming it into a universal Life Force. And since the major characteristic of life is growth and development, the Life Force became identified foremost as an agent of change and progress.

Whereas the Aristotelian tradition in biology focused on classification, the neo-Platonist tradition emphasized embryology. Study of the fertilized egg seemed to promise an understanding of the development not only of the individual organism but of life itself. The romantic biologists drew a parallel between the developmental stages of the individual and the historical progress of organic forms (the doctrine of recapitulation). In the words of zoologist and paleontologist Georg August Goldfuss (1782-1848), the fossils "prove that the animal kingdom—regarded as a single organism—actually went though a metamorphosis similar to that of the foetus."[25]

The romantic biologists tended to be vitalists. For instance, the

German anatomist Caspar Friedrich Wolff (1733-1794) argued that mechanical and chemical processes could not account for embryonic development if not guided by a "vital force"—a special developmental force that impels the unformed embryo toward its goal (i.e., the adult form). Vitalism represents a revival of the neo-Platonist "active principles," which we met in earlier chapters—here conceived as an immanent Law of Development.[26] And if there is a parallel between the individual and the human race, then there must be a single Law of Development directing the unfolding of life itself.

This was the beginning of a historical approach to biology—and not only biology but also all other areas of scholarship. Classical physics had dealt with timeless and abstract phenomena. Its theoretical models were idealized balls rolling down idealized planes; its laws hold at any time and in any place. But biology deals with phenomena that change over time—with individuals that grow and develop from embryo to adult. Hence the decision to take organic life as the defining metaphor for all reality led to a dramatic transformation in thinking. As historian John Herman Randall puts it, "the genetic and historical method supplanted the analytical and mechanical." All things—not only life but also social institutions and ideas—were conceived as processes. Everything was caught up in a great transformation from primitive beginnings to some exalted future.

Yet this was not evolution in the modern sense of the word; rather, it was an unfolding of inbuilt potential through a succession of archetypes. Here we touch on an element in neo-Platonism not discussed in earlier chapters but very important for romanticism—namely, the concept of a great chain of being (ladder of life or *scala natura*). This was a picture of the universe as hierarchically ordered from the lowliest clump of matter through simple life forms, to the higher organisms, to human beings, and then through a series of spiritual entities to God Himself.

This great orderly structure was originally conceived as static, with each individual object assigned its proper rung on the ladder. But under the influence of romanticism, the structure was historicized. The entire chain of being was toppled over on its side, as it were, and instead of being a static structure—the inventory of all the kinds of things that exist in the world—the great chain became a dynamic process, a series of stages through which the world develops as the Life Force unfolds its succession of archetypes. The great chain of being, which for 2000 years had been a static concept, was transformed into an evolutionary concept, with everything striving to move up to higher levels of perfection.[27]

This was the age of Hegel and Schelling in philosophy, of Schleiermacher in theology. The Life Force often took on the trappings of an immanent deity, a God-in-the-making, and romanticism veered off into pantheism. In contrast to the mechanists, Ian Barbour explains, for the romantics "God is not the external creator of an impersonal machine, but a spirit pervading nature."[28] As Randall puts it, "the world was no machine, it was alive, and God was not its creator so much as its soul, its life."[29] Lovejoy sums up the idea in the phrase, "theological evolutionism." As the great chain of being was temporalized, he explains, "God Himself was temporalized—was indeed identified with the process by which the whole creation slowly and painfully ascends the scale of possibility."[30]

Buffon

Georges Louis Leclerc de Buffon (1707-1788) is sometimes looked down on as a popularizer and not a real scientist. Yet his multivolume natural history was enormously influential in his day.

Buffon lived at the same time as Linnaeus, but his ideas could hardly have been more opposite. Linnaeus remained basically Aristotelian in his concern for order and design. In his view, the function of the natural historian was to name, classify, and describe every part of nature, with the ultimate goal of finding a natural system of classification (presumably one corresponding to the pattern in the mind of the Creator). But in Buffon's opinion, classification systems could never be natural. All systems were arbitrary human inventions. The real business of natural history was to uncover hidden active principles in nature that account for its structure and functioning.

Linnaeus regarded the world as created—neatly ordered and perfectly adapted by the wise design of an omnipotent Creator. Buffon saw nature as a confused welter of individuals, subject to constant change over time under the influence of climate, diet, and environment. The goal of natural history was to study the processes of generation and variation whereby organisms come into existence and develop their present form.

Clearly, Buffon was introducing a new kind of natural history— dynamic, causal, nonteleological, historical.[31] Nature is not a static being, he wrote, but a "succession of beings." For Buffon, all nature was alive; he was interested not in natural structures but in natural processes.

Buffon is often described as a materialist because he emphatically rejected any supernatural explanation of the world and its processes. But we must understand that the concept of "matter" was subject to varying interpretations. For the romantic biologists, matter was not defined as the hard, impenetrable, passive particles of Newtonian physics. Instead, they ascribed to it a number of qualities we normally associate with life—will, perception, sensitivity, the capacity to act, and other psychic qualities.

As Coleman notes, their "materialism occasionally verged on animism"[32] (all things have a rudimentary form of life), or even panpsychism (all things have a rudimentary form of mind). Here we see the influence of Leibniz's monads, elemental particles endowed with activity and sensitivity (see chapter 4). Buffon's materialism was similar: He supposed the existence of "living matter" made of "organic molecules."[33]

Neither animism nor panpsychism, as defined above, is necessarily contrary to Christian teaching. But as a historical fact, by attributing active and creative forces to nature, the romantic version of materialism tended to make nature appear self-sufficient and the Biblical Creator superfluous. Hence it was frequently associated with pantheism and even atheism. As Jacques Roger explains, "By insisting that Nature is perpetually active . . . Buffon's thought tended to eliminate God, replacing Him with nature and history."[34] The more one regards "Nature" as capable of creating things through its own power, the less necessity there is, it seemed, for a Creator.

Lamarck

Jean Baptiste Pierre Antoine de Monet, Chevalier de Lamarck (1744-1829), was a contemporary of Cuvier. Like Buffon, he reacted against what he regarded as the dry systematic approach of the Aristotelian tradition. The essence of life, he felt, is flux, motion, change. Central to his philosophy of nature is the organism as it strives to adapt and develop.

Lamarck embraced a thoroughly historical conception of the world, and proposed a theory of evolution based on the inheritance of acquired characteristics. According to the theory, as an organism strives to reach a goal, its structure changes. (E.g., as the giraffe stretches to reach the upper foliage, its neck lengthens.) These traits are passed on to the organism's offspring, eventually transforming the original species into a new one.

Like Buffon, Lamarck is often described as a materialist—and again for the label to stick we must give it a romantic definition. Lamarck did acknowledge a divine source of life, for whom he showed considerable respect. Yet he denied the Creator any real creative activity in the world. For Lamarck, says historian Erik Nordenskiöld, God's greatness "lies in the fact that He has created nature in such a way that it has developed its profuse multiplicity *without interference from without*"[35]—words that remind us forcefully of Leibniz.

Hence in Lamarck's philosophy the real creative power is nature. Listen to the way he personifies nature in this passage, cited in Nordenskiöld:

Every step which Nature takes when making her direct creations consists in organizing into cellular tissue the minute masses of viscous or mucous substances that she finds at her disposal under favorable conditions.

"A personal God," Nordenskiöld comments dryly, "could not have acted more personally." In a later work, Lamarck writes that "Nature is . . . an intermediary between God and the various parts of the physical universe for the fulfilling of the divine will."[36] Obviously, this is not materialism as you and I understand the term; it is Nature conceived as Plato's World Soul.

Hence we can call Lamarck a materialist only if we understand that his materialism, like Buffon's, verged on vitalism. Historians such as E. S. Russell have puzzled over how to classify Lamarck. A "conflict" exists, Russell wrote, between Lamarck's "thorough-going materialism," which attributed all phenomena to "mechanical causes," and his "vitalism," which explained evolution in terms of a "vital power" progressing toward an end.[37] But there is no conflict once we understand that Lamarck's definition of materialism was a romantic one, which endowed matter with psychic properties. What drives evolution forward in Lamarck's theory is the organism's internal striving, a biological form of the romanticist universal *Streben* (striving toward perfection).

Because he presented a full-blown theory of evolution, Lamarck is typically portrayed as a precursor of Charles Darwin—praised for being right about evolution in principle though mistaken about its mechanism. But the fact is that the two men lived in completely different conceptual worlds. Darwin would bring biology under the explanatory framework of the mechanistic tradition (as we shall see in the next section); Lamarck stood firmly within the neo-Platonic tradition. As historian Charles Coulston Gillispie notes:

In no serious sense, therefore, is Lamarck's theory of evolution to be taken as the scientific prelude to Darwin's. Rather . . . it was one of the most explicit examples of the counter-offensive of romantic biology against the doom [the reductionism] of physics.[38]

Gillispie goes so far as to argue that Lamarck's theory of evolution was merely a vehicle for advancing his romantic philosophy of nature.

THE PRIMACY OF PHILOSOPHY

Taking stock of where we have come so far, we can begin to sort out where individual scientists fall on any particular issue by first placing them in their proper tradition. Consider the question of spontaneous generation. A purely chronological history of biology jumps confusingly back and forth, the idea of spontaneous generation being rejected by one researcher, accepted by the next, and then rejected again. But once we understand the metaphysical traditions within which biology developed, a pattern emerges.

The Aristotelian tradition rejected the idea of spontaneous generation. Ray, Linnaeus, and Cuvier all rejected the theory—for religious, philosophical, and scientific reasons. Theologically, they believed (as John Ray argued) that God rested from His creative work on the seventh day; from then on life is transmissible only through recurring generations descending from the plants and animals originally created. Thus there was a religious objection to the idea that life could appear *de novo* from nonliving matter.

Philosophically, the Christian Aristotelians were committed to a mechanistic view of the relation between God and His creation, a view that sought to reserve creative powers to God alone. Eventually the rejection of spontaneous generation received scientific confirmation as well. Francesco Redi's experiments showed that maggots grow from eggs instead of appearing spontaneously in decaying meat. Later, Louis Pasteur's experiments demonstrated that microscopic life arises likewise only from other living organisms. In fact, at the time Pasteur's brilliant refutation of spontaneous generation was counted as scientific support for the Aristotelian tradition—and as evidence *against* evolutionary theories (including Darwin's, published just two years earlier).

Within the neo-Platonic tradition, on the other hand, many accepted the idea of spontaneous generation, including Maupertuis, Buffon, and Lamarck. A completely natural explanation of life is possible, they argued, only if nature itself possesses the characteristics of living things. So they constructed a view of nature as an unbroken continuum (great chain of being), from chunks of matter having only the most rudimentary form of life and mentality up to humans. And if matter itself is in some sense living, then it is clearly not beyond the power of nature to generate new life.[39]

Both sides of the spontaneous generation controversy counted Christians among their supporters. The neo-Platonic tradition included, for example, John Turberville Needham (1713-1781), a Welsh naturalist and Jesuit priest who claimed to have seen spontaneous generation occur numerous times under his microscope (including an experiment using gravy from roast meat). Needham sensed no contradiction between his Christian faith and belief in the active powers of nature.

In the eyes of many of his contemporaries, however, Needham's views appeared to pave the way to atheism. The greater the powers attributed to nature—so it seemed—the fewer the powers reserved exclusively for God. And indeed the neo-Platonic movement showed, as Roger puts it, "a general tendency to transfer to Nature all the powers traditionally attributed to God."[40]

REDUCTIONISM REDUX

If romanticism was a reaction against mechanistic philosophy, by the mid-nineteenth century mechanism had reappeared as a reaction against romanticism. Romantic biology with its vast vistas of the evolution of everything, with its immaterial Life Force, struck a later generation as overly speculative and metaphysical. As Mayr explains, "the evolutionism of the *Naturphilosophen* was so speculative and at the same time so sterile that it produced a violent reaction and induced the best zoologists to concentrate on straight descriptive work." They turned their attention away from historical development and concentrated on describing "functional processes," which are more accessible to the mechanistic models made popular by the physical sciences.[41]

Roger tells a similar story. In the mid-nineteenth century, he writes, a new generation of physiologists "rebelled against their teachers and insisted on reducing life to physicochemical processes." This new brand of mechanism was more sophisticated than the old Cartesian image of the universe as a clockwork, making use of new developments in chemistry, electricity, and thermodynamics. Nevertheless, it was a revival of la Mettrie's reductionistic, materialistic attitude, rejecting idealistic or spiritual categories and discarding any notion of vitalism or "soul" to explain living things.[42]

We can distinguish two groups of mechanistic biologists during this period. One group was motivated by political and religious concerns as much as by biological ones. During the 1840s, as Coleman explains, there was a surge of criticism of "political absolutism and religious conservatism." The leaders in this critical attack sought support in the philosophy of materialism. They hoped that radical materialism

> would sap the supernatural sanctions of Christianity and in so doing not only shake the dogma of the churches but also undermine the legitimacy of contemporary absolutist princes who drew strength from purportedly divine rights to power.[43]

This group included figures such as Karl Vogt (1817-1895), Jacob Moleschott (1822-1893), and Ludwig Büchner (1824-1899). They turned their hand to the popularization of science, using it to support materialism. In fact, they virtually equated the two. As a result, Roger notes, "the use of biological materialism and reduction as weapons against religion was a prominent feature of nineteenth-century intellectual life."[44]

The second group of mechanistic biologists were more moderate, focusing on physiology, not politics. They tended to treat reductionism primarily as a methodology, not an all-embracing philosophy. This group included figures such as Emil du Bois-Reymond (1818-1896), Karl Ludwig (1816-1895), and Hermann von Helmholtz (1821-1894). Their enemy was the vitalistic Life Force of *Naturphilosophie*, which they regarded as inaccessible to scientific study and hence a barrier to scientific research. By contrast, the assumption that life is reducible to the laws of physics and chemistry seemed to promise that life processes would eventually be entirely explicable.

After all, when biologists looked at the progress of the physical sciences, it seemed that successes were being chalked up daily. By borrowing the mechanistic methodology of physical science, they hoped to duplicate its successes. And with their emphasis on experimentation, the moderate reductionists did contribute greatly to understanding the processes of life—reproduction, respiration, cell metabolism, digestive chemistry, to name just a few areas.

But in the end what the reductionists borrowed from the physical sciences was much more than a method. They also adopted its doctrinaire materialism. Before long the second group became just as dogmatic as the first. "What had been manifesto in Du Bois-Reymond's introduction," says Coleman, "soon became systematic dogma." In Ludwig, physical-chemical reductionism of living things became "a declaration of faith." And Ludwig's student, Adolf Fick, gave full expression to the radical reductionist credo. All forces, he wrote, whether in organic or inorganic nature, "are in final analysis nothing other than motive forces determined by the interaction of material atoms."[45]

Yet reductionism remained a program, a goal, rather than an accomplishment. Life's complexities are too vast to be reduced to force and matter.[46] And so, ironically, the radical reductionists, while claiming to disdain metaphysics, developed a doctrine itself clearly metaphysical—in the sense that it sought to give a comprehensive explanation of life going far beyond the evidence. The reductionists merely replaced the idealist categories of romantic biology with materialist categories and became as speculative and doctrinaire as the predecessors they despised.

Charles Darwin

We hardly need to point out that Darwin was firmly rooted in the mechanistic tradition. His theory of natural selection is implacably materialistic, and the only reason to stress the point is that so many people have tried to wed his theory to design and purpose.

When one of Darwin's contemporaries, the botanist Asa Gray, tried to find a divine plan within the theory, Darwin protested that this was not what he meant at all. If each variation is predetermined to lead to some desired end, he argued, then there is no need for natural selection. The whole point of natural selection is to demonstrate how the *appearance* of design might emerge from *un*designed random changes. "If the right variations occurred, and no others," Darwin wrote, "natural selection would be superfluous."[47]

Horace Bushnell, another of Darwin's contemporaries, was perhaps more perceptive than Gray. He was acutely aware of the mechanistic nature of Darwin's theory—and as a result roundly rejected it. Under the influence of romanticism, Bushnell embraced an organic view of nature. He argued that Darwin's theory was reductionistic—that it ignored "super-mechanical forces" and reduced living organisms to parts of a great machine.[48]

Bushnell was right, of course. The central elements in Darwin's theory of natural selection—the chance origin of variations and the mechanical process of selection—were both posited expressly to get rid of any purpose or design in biology. "Adaptation to the environment" would take the place of "purposive design" in explaining the marvelous fit between the structures of organisms and their needs. "This denial of purpose," Jacques Barzun notes, "is Darwin's distinctive contention. . . . The sum total of the accidents of life acting upon the sum total of the accidents of variation thus provided a completely mechanical and material system by which to account for the changes in living forms." Barzun goes on:

> To advance natural selection as the means of evolution meant that purely physical forces, brute struggle among brutes, could account for the present forms and powers of living beings. Matter and Force . . . explained our whole past history and presumably would shape our future.[49]

Every philosophy answers certain kinds of questions, and its success in doing so becomes its credential in the marketplace of ideas. What made Darwin's theory of evolution so persuasive is that he not only answered the questions raised within his *own* tradition in biology, but he also offered alternative ways to answer questions raised within the *other* two traditions—thus, in effect, pulling the rug out from under them.

For example, the centerpiece of the Aristotelian tradition was its explanation of adaptation, the marvelous "fit" between the organism and its environment. Its explanation was couched in terms of purpose, generally conceived as divine purpose or design (natural theology). Darwin took over the idea of adaptation from the Aristotelians and offered an alternative explanation. Purpose is not real, he argued; it is mere appearance, produced by the mechanism of natural selection. As Gillispie says:

Darwin did better than solve the problem of adaptation. He abolished it. He turned it from a cause, in the sense of final cause or evidence of a designing purpose, into an effect, in the Newtonian or physical sense of effect.[50]

The romantics, on the other hand, offered a distinctively historical evolutionary outlook, which they explained by the idealistic concept of archetypes—pre-existing, immaterial ideals that guide and direct the sequence of evolution. The concept of archetypes gave primacy to the mental world—to ideas or mind. Darwin took over the concept of evolution from the romantic biologists and offered an alternative explanation. He replaced the common archetype with the common ancestor. Instead of a single archetype for all vertebrates, Darwin posited a single ancestor of all vertebrates. Henceforth, archetypes were not immaterial ideas in the world of thought; they were historical organisms in the world of nature. As Russell puts it, in the post-Darwinian world, categorical grouping of organisms

could no longer be explained as the manifestation of Divine archetypal ideas; it had a real historical basis, and was due to inheritance from a common ancestor.[51]

In short, Darwin eliminated his intellectual competitors not only by arguing negatively against their positions but also by offering a positive alternative in his own terms. He thereby made their positions seem superfluous—and not only superfluous but unscientific. Darwin's style of intellectual attack was to portray his opponents' theories not merely as competing scientific explanations but as interlopers that had no business being in the same ring at all. He criticized concepts such as divine creation and ideal archetypes not so much for being mistaken scientific ideas but for falling outside the realm of science altogether. Mechanistic, naturalistic forces were put forth not as superior scientific causes but as the *only* causes admissible in science.

As historian Neal Gillespie puts it in *Charles Darwin and the Problem of Creation*, Darwin's intention was to promote a new epistemology in science—a positivist epistemology that limited science to mechanistic explanations. In Gillespie's words:

> Darwin's rejection of special creation was part of the transformation of biology into a positive science, one committed to thoroughly naturalistic explanations based on material causes and the uniformity of nature.[52]

It was not only special creation that Darwin hoped to displace, of course; he also took deliberate aim at the idealistic progressionism of the romantic biologists. But Gillespie's point is well taken. Darwin argued that explanations of biological phenomena in terms of a "plan of creation" or "unity of design" (archetypes) provide no actual information but merely "hide our ignorance."[53]

Unyielding Despair

Though Darwin's view of nature was mechanistic, it was quite different from the mechanistic philosophy of classical physics. In earlier centuries, scientists had seen no conflict between a mechanistic picture of nature and belief in God. The world might be seen as a clock, but that only served to reinforce belief in a clockmaker who had created its gears and springs and wound it up. As historian Carl Becker writes, "Nature was regarded as a delicately adjusted machine, a stationary engine whose mechanism implied the existence of a purposeful engineer, a beneficent first cause or Author of the Universe."

But with Darwin the machine became self-generating, self-operating. Thereafter, Becker explains, "nature was conceived not as a finished machine but as an unfinished process, a mechanistic process, indeed, but one generating its own power"—eliminating the need for an external engineer or creator.[54] By the end of the nineteenth century, mechanistic philosophy had become radically materialistic and reductionistic. It pictured living things as automata in a world governed by rigidly deterministic laws—with no purpose, no God, no significance to human life.

It was a gloomy picture, but many adherents found it all the more attractive for its gloom. As Randall puts it:

> the dark picture fascinated [them]. They loved to paint the alien elements as black as possible, even as they shuddered in delicious horror before it. . . . Many believed it *because* it was so dreadful; they prided themselves on their courage in facing facts.

As an example, Randall cites the widely quoted passage from Bertrand Russell's *A Free Man's Worship*: "Man is the product of causes which had no prevision of the end they were achieving. His origin, his growth, his hopes and fears, his loves and his beliefs are but the outcome of accidental collocations of atoms." And finally, those proud, despairing words: "Only within the scaffolding of these truths, only on the firm foundation of unyielding despair, can the soul's habitation henceforth be safely built."[55]

BORROWING BIOLOGY FROM METAPHYSICS

The three traditions we have outlined did not, of course, remain surgically separated from one another. Once terms or phrases became common usage in one tradition, they tended to spill over into general discourse. Adherents of other traditions might pick them up and pay them lip service without necessarily accepting their metaphysical context. For example, Aristotelians such as Linnaeus sometimes spoke of "the chain of being," but that was largely pious phraseology.

On the other hand, there were some who consciously sought to reconcile the different traditions. Richard Owen (1804-1858), a student of Cuvier, was subsequently influenced by romantic biology and worked out a synthesis of the two. Had Owen not already become known as "the British Cuvier," comments historian Philip Rehbock, he might well have earned the title of "the British Geoffrey"—a reference to Etienne Geoffrey St. Hilaire, one of the transcendental anatomists.[56]

Louis Agassiz (1807-1873), the Swiss naturalist who headed the zoology department at Harvard University, likewise combined elements of Aristotelianism with the idealistic progressivism of *Naturphilosophie*.[57] In Germany Ernst Haeckel (1834-1919) grafted Darwin's materialistic evolution onto the roots of romantic biology and became one of Darwin's most vigorous popularizers.[58]

Clearly, science is not simply a matter of observing facts. Every scientific theory also expresses a worldview. Philosophical preconceptions determine where facts are sought, how experiments are designed, and which conclusions are drawn from them. It is only by grasping the worldview traditions that have shaped the development of biology that we really understand what motivated a Cuvier, a Buffon, or a Darwin. We end this chapter, as we began it, with the quotation by William Coleman—that the advocates of all three historical traditions "ultimately borrowed their biology from their metaphysics."

Consider a concrete illustration—the controversy that raged in the eighteenth and nineteenth centuries over embryology. The development of the microscope had shed new light on embryonic development, revealing that differentiated structures appear much earlier than the naked eye had been able to discern. A chicken egg placed under a microscope revealed within a single day the outline of the vertebrae, a beating heart, the shape of the head, the beginnings of eyes. Marcello Malpighi (1628-1694), perhaps the greatest embryologist of the century, wrote in surprise, "lo! in the egg itself we behold the animal already almost formed." How did this formation take place?

The Christian Aristotelians tended toward a view called preformationism. They assumed that God had created the basic structures of creation in the beginning and that all subsequent events merely unfold those structures according to mechanistic laws. Hence it is impossible for structures to originate *de novo*; the embryo must have a germinal structure built in from the start—a rudimentary pattern that is merely realized through embryonic development.

Conceiving exactly *how* that pattern was built in was problematic. Generally it was conceived as an Aristotelian Form, a nonmaterial "essence" embodied in the material substance. But some preformationists went so far as to imagine an entire miniature adult curled up in each sperm cell (the theory of *emboitement*), a view that laid their position open to ridicule.[59] Yet the basic insight of preformationism was sound—that the adult pattern must somehow be contained in the egg from the beginning. Today we have solved the problem by discovering the role played by the DNA molecule. As Ernst Mayr notes, the Aristotelian Form "is a teleonomic principle which performed in Aristotle's thinking precisely what the genetic program of the modern biologist performs."[60]

On the other hand, most neo-Platonists tended toward a view called epigenesis. They held that the egg is a simple, unstructured, homogeneous substance, whose structure is created *de novo* by a special developmental force, which is emphatically not mechanistic but akin to the neo-Platonist tradition's "active principles." This developmental force takes formless organic matter and molds it step by step into limbs and organs, progressing gradually toward the adult form— identified as the neo-Platonic ideal, essence, or archetype. For example, Karl Ernst von Baer (1792-1876) argued that it is the "essence" (*die Wesenheit*) of the developing animal form that guides and controls the stages of development in a fertilized egg. This view, sometimes called emergentism, was likewise based on a sound insight—that the embryo does not start out with limbs and organs; rather these emerge from undifferentiated cells through the course of development.

In the late nineteenth century, embryology was given a mechanistic interpretation. This later generation of embryologists had faith that the ultimate explanation of developmental events would be found in the laws of physics and chemistry. An embryo's overall pattern of development would be explained by the same laws that govern individual molecular and mechanical interactions. No immaterial Forms, no special developmental force, would be needed. For example, Wilhelm His (1831-1904) tried to explain the formation of certain organs in the embryo by comparing embryonic tissues to plates and tubes. He even tried to imitate the formation of these organs by folding, pinching, and cutting rubber tires.

Notice that in each case, what we have described is a research program, a set of assumptions, not a conclusion from the evidence. Science moves forward by metaphysical assumptions made in advance of actual observation and experimentation. As Coleman points out, even the research methods employed by various biologists and the instruments they design are strongly affected by prior conceptions about what life is—about what kind of facts are "out there" to be discovered. A researcher's prior interpretation of life guides him in making decisions whether or not a particular method of investigation is appropriate to the subject matter and whether or not it is likely to be fruitful.[61]

Whose Biology?

We might well wonder whether the three worldview traditions discussed here are still alive today. The answer is yes. The most visible is the mechanistic tradition. Mainstream academic biology is adamantly committed to a materialist, reductionist form of mechanism, often appealing to Darwinian evolution for support. For example, in Science on Trial Douglas Futuyma writes, "Some shrink from the conclusion that the human species was not designed, has no purpose, and is the product of mere mechanical mechanisms—but this seems to be the message of evolution." Similarly, in The Blind Watchmaker, Richard Dawkins writes that human beings are the products of natural selection, "the blind, unconscious, automatic process which Darwin discovered."[62]

Yet the older nonmaterialistic form of mechanism remains alive today as well. It is held by some theistic evolutionists, many of whom are orthodox Christians. They see evolutionary theory as merely a continuation of the mechanistic tradition begun by Galileo, Boyle, and Newton—no more inherently materialistic than Newton's theory of universal gravitation. Christian mechanists accept evolution as a limited scientific theory, but they reject any extension of evolution into a full-blown philosophy—whether materialistic reductionism or romantic progressionism. An example of a Christian mechanist approach to science can be found in Science Held Hostage, whose authors accept evolutionary forces as the source of the cosmos and humanity but believe God directs those forces.[63]

In the past few decades, the Christian Aristotelian tradition has been revived by the scientific creationist movement. Anyone who has read creationist literature will recognize there the same concepts held by Ray, Linnaeus, and Cuvier. For example, in *Variation and Fixity in Nature*, Frank L. Marsh writes, "The Genesis text apparently indicates that every basic type of organism was in existence by the close of the sixth day." In *The Natural Limits to Biological Change*, Lane P. Lester and Raymond G. Bohlin write, "By a prototype we mean 'all organisms that are descended from a single created population.'" For a revival of Aristotelianism (specifically of Cuvierian functionalism) from a non-Christian perspective, see *Evolution: A Theory in Crisis* by Michael Denton.[64]

The neo-Platonist tradition likewise continues as a minority view within biology. Its most prominent form today is a position known as organicism, which, as the name suggests, continues to view the organism as the major metaphor in science. Organicism has dispensed with vitalism, rejecting vital forces as distinct metaphysical entities. Instead it identifies the uniqueness of life with a certain level of organization. The chemicals found in living things are not different from chemicals found in nonliving things; the only difference is the far greater complexity in the way the former are organized.

Alfred North Whitehead, founder of process philosophy, was an influential organicist. A disciple of Leibniz, Whitehead borrowed his terminology of monads and his panpsychism. A contemporary proponent of Whitehead's process philosophy is Ian Barbour, whose *Issues in Science and Religion* is regarded as a classic.[65]

Whereas Christians in the mechanist and Aristotelian traditions tend to be theologically orthodox, Christians in the neo-Platonist tradition tend to be liberal, carrying on the tradition of theological liberalism that sprang from German romanticism. The Catholic priest Teilhard de Chardin, with his conception of an immanent God-evolving-in-the-world, was a romantic through and through. He continues to have an enthusiastic following in some circles today. Among biologists C. H. Waddington and Theodosius Dobzhansky were admirers of Teilhard. A contemporary follower is E. J. Ambrose, author of *The Nature and Origin of the Biological World*.[66]

This is an extremely sketchy outline; yet it suggests that the three philosophical traditions remain useful categories for analyzing contemporary approaches to issues in biology. In fact, we shall pick them up again in chapter 10 where we examine the impact of the genetic revolution on biology.

PART THREE

THE RISE AND FALL OF MATHEMATICS

MATH IN THE PAST:
Discovering the Structure of Creation

*F*ind "the ideal mate of your dreams," promised the flyer that came in the mail. Just fill in the enclosed confidential questionnaire, the ad said, and our computerized dating service will match your personal profile to someone ideally suited to you.

Amazing what mathematics can do.

The computerization of courtship is only one example of the way modern culture is dominated by mathematics. In science and industry, operations are being progressively quantified and subjected to mathematical treatment.

Yet, ironically, at the same time mathematics itself has become progressively more isolated, cut off from applications in other fields. Professional mathematicians show a marked preference for pure as opposed to applied math. They devote themselves to problems suggested by the logic of mathematics alone, without asking whether the problems (or their solutions) bear any relevance to the physical world.

This growing isolation of "real" mathematicians stems from a change in the philosophy of mathematics. For centuries, mathematics was regarded as the key to truth about the universe, an insight into the very structure of the created order. The axiomatic method of mathematics was held up as the pattern for all true inquiry, a guarantee of infallible knowledge. But today many mathematicians view mathematics as a game, pursued according to its own rules and solving its own internal problems. They no longer speak of mathematics as *true* but only as internally consistent.

In the next two chapters, we will trace this change in the philosophy of mathematics, probing the historical interaction between mathematics and the Christian faith.

IDEALS AND AXIOMS

Mathematical reasoning seems to be a created facility of the human mind. Like language, it is universal. Most ancient civilizations—the Sumerians, Egyptians, and Babylonians—developed counting systems and rules for calculation.

Yet these civilizations did not conceive of mathematics as a discipline on its own, as we do. Instead, they treated numbers and geometric figures merely as tools for practical ends, such as surveying, commerce, and calendar-making. In Egypt, for instance, the Nile river flooded once a year and created problems for landowners by blurring the borderlines of their estates. This was a great incentive for developing the art of surveying, since every year the borders had to be reestablished by geometrical measurements. Yet mathematics remained empirical, a set of rough, approximate rules and strategies for calculation based on observation.

It was the ancient Greeks, beginning with Pythagoras in the sixth century B.C., who first systematized the practical insights of mathematics and developed them into a separate abstract discipline with its own methodology. The Greeks began by asking how we acquire mathematical knowledge. Is it by experience? No, for experience cannot tell us that a principle is true for all times. Yet that is the kind of principle we deal with in mathematics.

Experience can lead to certain broad generalizations, such as "all swans are white," but it leaves open the possibility that some day we may encounter an exception, a black swan. Yet when we say $5+7=12$, we are not asserting a broad generalization of this kind, one that is true in most cases but not necessarily all. Instead, we mean it is always and necessarily the case.

In mathematics it appears that we have access to truths that go beyond experience. Upon what, then, are they based? For Pythagoras and later for Plato, the answer was that mathematics is part of an ideal world—a realm of abstract principles (Ideas or Forms) that gives rational structure to the material world.

To gain knowledge of this ideal world, Plato said, we cannot merely examine the material world. For although modeled upon the ideal Forms, material objects realize these Forms only imperfectly. Insight into the Forms themselves is gained only by the light of reason, which "sees" abstractions such as mathematical truths much as the eye sees color and shape. We have only to cast the eye of reason upon them to "see" that they are true. In the Pythagorean-Platonic tradition, the cosmos operates according to mathematical laws discoverable by reason. The underlying design of nature is mathematical.

The Greeks outlined the methodology of mathematics as well. They began by asking the basic epistemological question: How does one go about seeking the truths of mathematics—and *guaranteeing* that they really are truths? The answer was supplied by Euclid. Mathematical knowledge is absolute and infallible, Euclid said, because it begins with self-evident axioms or postulates and derives all further truths by deductive reasoning.

There are many types of reasoning, including induction and reasoning by analogy, but only one guarantees a correct conclusion—deduction. For example, in Aristotle's classic syllogism, once you grant that all men are mortal, and that Socrates is a man, then you must conclude that Socrates is mortal. The Greeks believed infallible knowledge could be attained by beginning with a few fundamental, self-evident axioms and deducing a body of truths from them. This is known as the axiomatic method.

Euclid's accomplishment was to apply the axiomatic method successfully to geometry. The geometrical principles themselves originated in the ancient world as bits and pieces of practical knowledge derived from land surveying and architecture. The word *geometry* comes from the Greek and means "to measure the earth." From hundreds of practical theorems accumulated over the centuries, Euclid culled out five postulates and five axioms from which the rest could be logically deduced. The simplicity and thoroughness of his systematization lent to geometry an aura of universal and irrefutable truth.

As a result, geometry came to be regarded as the highest form of mathematical knowledge. Euclid's elaborate network of propositions seemed, on one hand, to compose a flawlessly logical system and, on the other hand, to accurately describe physical reality. As Louis Rougier puts it, geometrical theorems

> seem to have a double truth: formal truth that originates in the coherent logic of discourse, and material truth originating in the agreement of things with their objects.[1]

For nearly 2,000 years, Euclid's approach was hailed as a model—nay, *the* model—of certainty in human knowledge. For example, when Aquinas undertook his massive systematic exposition of theology and philosophy, he was honored as the "spiritual Euclid."[2]

To summarize, the Greek heritage to Western culture had a strong Pythagorean-Platonic element, which included both a metaphysical and an epistemological principle. Metaphysics asks *what* we know, what the world is like. The answer the Greeks gave was that the nature of the world is ultimately mathematical. Epistemology asks *how* we can know. The answer was that we penetrate the world's structure through human reason, using primarily the axiomatic method. In *Mathematics: The Loss of Certainty*, mathematician Morris Kline states the two principles succinctly in these words: "There is law and order in the universe and mathematics is the key to this order."[3]

MATHEMATICAL LAWS AND THE LAWGIVER

Toward the end of the medieval period, Western culture uncovered the great well of wisdom from the classical age. Christians struggled valiantly to adapt and assimilate the new-found philosophies to a Biblical view of the world. As we have seen in earlier chapters, many believers at the time felt that they could "translate" the ideal realm taught by Plato and Aristotle into the spiritual realm taught in the Bible. The Pythagorean-Platonic concept of a mathematical order in creation was accepted enthusiastically within both the neo-Platonic and the mechanistic traditions. The origin of that order was attributed to God's own rationality. God, being a rational God, had created the world with a consistent and predictable structure.

These ideas breathed life into scientific work, especially after the Protestant Reformation. The Reformers rejected the nature/grace dualism of the medieval church and taught that one could honor the Creator by studying His creation. Scientific work acquired great dignity. Science became, as Kline explains, a "religious quest":

> The search for the mathematical laws of nature was an act of devotion which would reveal the glory and grandeur of His handiwork. . . . Each discovery of a law of nature was hailed as evidence of God's brilliance rather than the investigator's.[4]

We find these convictions expressed, for example, in the writings of Nicolaus Copernicus (1473-1543) and Johannes Kepler (1571-1630). They conceived of God as the Cosmic Lawgiver, who created the world according to mathematical laws. Listen to Kepler:

> The chief aim of all investigations of the external world should be to discover the rational order and harmony which has been imposed on it by God and which He revealed to us in the language of mathematics.[5]

This was not mere religious piety, incidental to Kepler's scientific contributions. His convictions about God and mathematics were in fact the central inspiration for his scientific work.

Indeed, acceptance of the *scientific* views of Copernicus and Kepler required at the same time the acceptance of their *mathematical* views. As we saw in chapter 3, when Copernicus first proposed the theory that the earth moves around the sun rather than vice versa, there was not enough empirical data to decide between an earth-centered and a sun-centered system. In fact, there were good, common-sense arguments *against* the idea of the earth moving—good in the sense of being consistent with the knowledge available at the time.

Copernicus's only answer to these objections was a mathematical one—that whether it seemed to make sense or not, a sun-centered system was simpler mathematically. It reduced the number of epicycles needed to explain the motions of the heavenly bodies from more than eighty to thirty-four. A hundred years later, Kepler eliminated epicycles altogether by substituting elliptical orbits for circular ones, which simplified the mathematics still further.

The heliocentrism of Copernicus and Kepler stood opposed not only to common sense but also to the weight of Aristotelian doctrine. The only thing going for the theory was mathematical simplicity. As historian A. R. Hall puts it, Copernicus's new system "rested in no way upon his discoveries in practical astronomy, which were negligible, or on the precision of his measurements, which was not remarkable." Instead it rested purely on the fact that it was mathematically simpler—and on the value judgment that this was preferable.[6]

Hence, as E. A. Burtt points out[7], the central question raised by heliocentrism was this: Is the universe fundamentally mathematical in structure? Can we devise theories about nature based on mathematical calculations? Is it proper to choose one theory over another just because it is simpler mathematically?

Answering yes to these questions would overthrow the reigning Aristotelian physics and cosmology. For the essential features of Aristotle's universe were qualities—hot and cold, wet and dry, soft and hard—not quantities subject to mathematical treatment. Mere quantity was rather low on Aristotle's list of what makes the universe what it is. By contrast, for Kepler it was a "law of creation" that "just as the eye was made to see colors, and the ear to hear sounds, so the human mind was made to understand . . . quantity." Many of the early scientists liked to cite a passage from the apocryphal Wisdom of Solomon 11:20, "Thou hast arranged all things by measure and number and weight."

In short, the eventual acceptance of the Copernican theory also marked the acceptance of a new world view—a conviction that whatever is mathematically true is true in reality as well, whether in astronomy or the terrestrial sciences. As philosopher John H. Randall puts it, the very fact that Copernicus's theory was so obviously contrary to what we see with our own eyes undercut trust in common-sense observations and "sent men to mathematics as the only unshakable knowledge." For "if men's eyes lied here, where could they be trusted?"[8]

Galileo Galilei (1564-1642) summed up the new worldview in his well-known statement that the book of nature is written by the hand of God in the language of mathematics. Today this idea has become so familiar that it strikes us as a platitude. But in Galileo's day it was, as philosopher R. G. Collingwood puts it, "a fighting speech"[9]—a declaration of war on Aristotelian philosophy and a ringing endorsement of the conviction that God had created the world on a mathematical plan.

Like Copernicus, Galileo moved science away from common-sense observations toward mathematical reasoning. Strict empiricism decrees that science shall always be based on observation. But if that were the case, we would all still be Aristotelians. For Aristotle based his theory of motion on everyday experiences—things like pushing a ball along the ground. His theories assume a real world where shapes are always approximate and motion is affected by counterforces, such as friction and air resistance.

But Galileo's great accomplishments flowed from his decision to leave observation behind and enter a world of mental abstraction. He developed his laws of local motion by imagining what would happen in abstract space. His theories are not based on real bodies known by experience but on geometrical bodies imagined in the mind, bodies with perfect shapes moving along perfect planes in a world free from friction, air resistance, and atmospheric pressure—a sort of empty Euclidean space.

As science historian Richard Westfall explains, the Galilean concept of inertia required one to imagine an ideal world of perfect spheres moving on perfectly smooth, frictionless planes. "Where is the experience of inertial motion?" asks Westfall. "It is nowhere. Inertial motion is an idealized conception incapable of being realized in fact." Indeed, many of Galileo's great insights into the nature of motion did not result from physical experiments at all but from "thought experiments," Westfall says, "carried out in his imagination where alone they are possible."[10]

Yet for Galileo that ideal world *was* the real world. Hence what he accomplished was not merely the substitution of one theory of motion for another. He also helped persuade people of a new philosophy—a philosophy that affirmed the superiority of the abstract mathematical account of nature, in opposition to the nonmathematical one of Aristotelian physics and common sense.

The new philosophy received its crowning expression in the work of Sir Isaac Newton (1642-1727). Newton's greatest work reveals the fundamental place occupied by mathematics in his physics, for it is titled *Mathematical Principles of Natural Philosophy*. In it Newton showed that the same mathematical formulas describe both heavenly and earthly motions. His theory of universal gravitation encompassed both Kepler's laws of celestial motion (the orbit of a planet) and Galileo's laws of terrestrial motion (the arc of a cannonball).

Given the scientific knowledge available when Newton began his work, it might have seemed unrealistic, even grandiose, to expect to encompass such diverse phenomena within a single set of mathematical principles. After all, Aristotelian cosmology had trained people to draw a sharp distinction between the earth, conceived as the locus of change and decay, and the heavens, conceived as changeless and perfect.

Yet in spite of Aristotle's continuing influence, says Kline, the expectation of a single explanatory system "occurred very naturally to the religious mathematicians of the seventeenth century." Why? Because of their belief in the Biblical God.

> God had designed the universe, and it was to be expected that all phenomena of nature would follow one master plan. One mind designing a universe would almost surely have employed one set of basic principles to govern related phenomena.[11]

Operating on that assumption, Newton demonstrated that the entire universe is a single uniform system, describable everywhere by the same mathematical laws. He then developed formulas for several specific phenomena—the ocean tides, the paths of comets, the precession of the equinoxes, and many other phenomena that had been observed but never reduced to mathematical formulas.

To accomplish all this, Newton used what was perhaps his greatest invention—the calculus, a method of measuring continuous movement. In this single discovery, Randall observes, Newton "had arrived at the most potent instrument yet found for bringing the world into subjection to man."

> Since any regular motion, be it of a falling body, an electric current, or the cooling of a molten mass, can be represented by a curve, he had forged a tool by which to attack, not only the figures, but the processes of nature.

With the invention of calculus Newton had forged, in Randall's words, "the last link in the mathematical interpretation of nature."[12]

God and Nature

To summarize, many of the early scientists were committed to a religiously grounded understanding of nature that had two major corollaries, one metaphysical and the other epistemological—that God made the world with a mathematical structure and that He made human beings with a mind capable of understanding that structure. These two principles are reflected in the words of Kepler, who writes that "God, who founded everything in the world according to the norm of quantity, also has endowed man with a mind which can comprehend those norms." The same two-fold conviction is expressed by the French philosopher René Descartes (1596-1650), who speaks of "certain laws which God has so established in nature and of certain notions which He has impressed in our souls."

Through the eighteenth century and into the nineteenth, mathematics and the mathematical sciences were vastly extended. Yet in terms of basic philosophical assumptions, the work done after Newton was largely an encore. Though ideas about God strayed from orthodoxy into pantheism and deism, scientists remained convinced that divine creation is the only guarantee of mathematical knowledge.

HUBRIS BEFORE A FALL

Even as mathematics and science were blossoming, however, their roots were withering. Design in nature and the human ability to know it came to be taken for granted. Design came to be regarded as an inherent structure in things, requiring no God for its existence. Likewise, the power of human reason came to be regarded as a given, needing no grounding in divine creation. Yet torn from the soil of belief in creation, mathematical knowledge lost its basis. Like a flower cut off from its roots, it bloomed brilliantly for a time and then began to wilt.

The World as Machine

The process of cutting away the roots began surprisingly early—in the works of scientists who were Christians in general outlook. It started with the adoption of a particular view of knowledge. Following in the Pythagorean-Platonic tradition, many early scientists held that mathematical order represents the most real and most certain aspect of the world.

The Greeks had defined true knowledge as certain knowledge. As a result, they denied that one could have true knowledge of the sensory world with its constantly changing events. True knowledge had as its object only things that are unchanging, immutable. For Pythagoras and Plato, that meant, foremost, mathematics.

The same definition of knowledge permeates the writings of many of the early scientists. Kepler for example, believed that what is most real are the mathematical harmonies that underlie the world known through the senses. It was a short step from there to viewing mathematical relationships as *causing* events—as though mathematics possessed the power to make things happen. In *Mystery of the Cosmos*, Kepler writes that mathematical harmonies in the mind of the Creator furnish the cause "why the number, the size, and the motion of the orbs are as they are and not otherwise."[13] As Burtt points out, this was a completely novel concept of causality. It assumed that the underlying mathematical harmonies discoverable in observed facts actually *make* them what they are.[14]

If mathematical laws cause physical phenomena, then it seems to follow that these phenomena are as certain and necessary as the mathematic laws themselves. Kepler speaks of his scientific accomplishments (the most enduring of which are his three planetary laws) as showing the necessary and rational ground of the structure of the universe. The word *necessary* implies mathematical necessity. In the sum 5+7=12, the truth of the sum follows from our understanding of the terms in the equation and does not depend on any conditions in the physical world. That is, once we understand what five and seven mean and what it means to add them together, we see that they *must* equal twelve. To speak of the laws of nature as necessary is to suggest that the same relationship exists between physical objects or events as between two sides of a mathematical equation.

In this way, physical causality gradually came to be understood as an absolute, unalterable connection, a relationship that could not be otherwise. It doesn't just happen that the sun is in the center of the planetary system; it *must* be so. It doesn't just happen that the planets move in ellipses; it *must* be so. God could not have created them otherwise—any more than He could make five plus seven equal thirteen, any more than He could make a square triangle.

We see these ideas even more clearly in the writings of Galileo. Kepler had applied mathematics to the heavens; Galileo applied mathematics to the earth—to the acceleration of falling objects and the arc of a cannonball. Like Kepler, Galileo regarded mathematical laws as absolutely true and necessary. He writes that nature is "inexorable," acting only "through immutable laws which she never transgresses."[15] Galileo believed God created the world as an immutable mathematical system, and that through mathematics human knowledge can be as objective and certain as God's own knowledge.

Emerging was a vision of nature as a vast machine, completely determined by inexorable, immutable laws. As philosopher Hans Reichenbach explains, when scientists discovered that one could express physical laws in the form of mathematical equations, it began to appear as though physical necessity were of the same character as mathematical necessity. Or, to turn it around, the certainty and universality of mathematical law was ascribed to physical phenomena.[16]

In the works of Copernicus, Kepler, Galileo, and Newton, the determinism is not complete because they believed that intelligent agents (God and human beings) transcend the machine and are able to act freely within nature. Yet intelligent agency is pushed further and further from center stage. The ultimate causality in the universe is defined not in terms of God's actions or human purposes but in terms of mathematical relationships.

In the writings of René Descartes, the tension between humanity and the world machine stretches to the breaking point. Descartes was well aware of the problem of finding a place for humanity and for God in a universe increasingly characterized as a self-contained machine running by mathematical laws. As a solution he suggested that there exist two equally ultimate substances—extended substance (material bodies) and thinking substance (intelligent agents).

These two substances are, in Descartes's dualistic philosophy, completely independent. The material world (extended substance) is a vast machine set in motion by God at the creation and ever since moving in fixed patterns in accordance with natural laws, subject to mathematical necessity. The human spirit (thinking substance) is the realm of thought, perception, emotions, will.

Descartes's goal was to defend the reality of thinking substance—to provide philosophical grounds for religious faith and human significance in a mechanistic world. Yet even his own writings clearly grant the material world greater significance. Since it can be known mathematically, the material world is treated as more certain—and hence more real—than the spiritual world. As for God, Descartes's belief in invariable laws of nature implicitly limits divine power. It creates a sphere where even God cannot act in any significant way. And as for the human mind and spirit, they are reduced to shadowy substances somehow inhabiting a physical body that itself operates strictly mechanistically—a "ghost in the machine."

The conviction that nature operates by mathematical necessity was given a tremendous boost by Isaac Newton's wide-ranging success in explaining the physical world mathematically. After Newton, belief in God remained an important background belief—but increasingly it was no more than that. The religious inspiration for scientific work grew dimmer and gradually gave way in the hearts of many scientists to a passion for purely mathematical results. Mathematical order was seen as an inherent property of the material world, needing no rational Creator for its origin.

A New Authority

If God came to seem unnecessary to explain design in the world (metaphysics), He likewise came to seem unnecessary as the ground of human knowledge (epistemology). The impressive successes of mathematical science seemed to bespeak an inherent ability of human reason to penetrate to ultimate truth. And mathematics was equated with the axiomatic method, exemplified supremely by Euclidean geometry. It became the goal of science to use the axiomatic method to find truth in all fields of knowledge.

The axiomatic method begins with basic postulates held to be infallible because they are self-evident. All other principles are derived from these starting axioms by logical deduction. The method seemed to be a means for guaranteeing absolute truth. For if the axioms are self-evident and the reasoning rigorous, the conclusions must be reliable.

For example, Descartes hoped to unify all the sciences (physics, astronomy, ethics, theology) by application of the axiomatic method— what he called "the long chains of simple and easy reasoning" used by "the geometers." As he puts it elsewhere,

> In our search for the direct road towards truth we should busy ourselves with no object about which we cannot attain a certitude equal to that of the demonstrations of Arithmetic and Geometry.[17]

The assumption here is that all knowledge is related by necessary connections, as geometric truths are. Hence we should be able to use the same deductive reasoning to move from one truth to the next.

Descartes's epistemology begins with a program of systematic doubt whereby we strip our minds of all half-baked, unfounded notions until we reach a bedrock of clear and simple ideas so fundamental they cannot be doubted. These are the self-evident truths; they serve as the axioms of any true science. By a process of deduction from these starting axioms Descartes hoped to build a solid structure of knowledge in all fields of scholarship.

Now, not all philosophers agreed with Descartes over the proper source of the starting axioms. He was a rationalist, who believed knowledge must be based on innate ideas knowable directly by the light of reason. Empiricists, on the other hand, believed knowledge must begin with ideas derived from sense perception. Yet both groups operated with the same basic epistemological method. Both began with what they viewed as indubitable premises and sought to deduce from them apodictic knowledge.

This search for certainty represented the secularization of a religious concept of truth. As Randall puts it, people were yearning for an absolute kind of knowledge attainable in reality only by divine revelation: "In a word, they were trying to arrive at that complete and perfect understanding and explanation of the universe that only a God could possess." In other words, even after Western thinkers stopped believing in the Biblical teaching of divine revelation, that teaching continued to shape their ideal of truth.[18]

Physicist and philosopher Karl Popper likewise identifies the dynamic at work here as religious. The authority of divine revelation, he notes, was simply replaced by another form of authority. Rationalists appealed to the authority of the intellect, empiricists to the authority of the senses.[19] Yet both maintained that the individual carries the source of knowledge within himself. Both denied the need for an external authority in matters of truth. Both held out the hope that once the individual has grasped knowledge in its simplest, most direct, and hence infallible form—whether innate ideas or sense data—he can then proceed to deduce a completely reliable system of knowledge.

The axiomatic method, in other words, seemed to give the individual a means of arriving at absolute, godlike knowledge on his own—a way of transcending the limitations of his particular niche in time and space. As belief in God declined, the axiomatic method modeled on geometrical reasoning replaced God as the guarantor of human knowledge.

Seeds of Doubt

To summarize, for the early scientists the reliability of mathematical knowledge rested on the belief that God had created the world with a mathematical structure and that He had created the human mind with the capacity for grasping that structure. But as belief in God declined, people had to seek a new basis for mathematical knowledge. The new basis was the belief that the universe was a massive machine operating by strictly necessary, mechanical relationships that could be known through mathematics.

Yet there was a bug in this new system—an epistemological bug. For human knowledge depends on the capacity of the human mind to penetrate the structure of things—and there was no room in this mechanistic scheme for the human mind.

The world of everyday experience is full of colors and smells, beauty and pathos. But the world discovered by the scientists was a world of mathematical entities—mass, extension, velocity—what Galileo called the primary qualities. The "real" world, as revealed by science, was composed of nothing but matter in motion.

What, then, is the status of all those vivid colors, sounds, smells, and feelings we normally experience? Well, if they are no longer properties of objects themselves, they must reside in the mind of the person perceiving the objects. Galileo called them secondary qualities and explained them as a result of the interaction between objects and the human mind.

In Descartes's philosophy the disjunction between the world of science and the world of experience became even more acute. As for the richness of human experience, Randall says:

> Descartes led the way in shoving off these qualities, so inconvenient for the mathematical physicist, into a separate and totally distinct kind of thing, the mind, . . . that served as a ready dumping-ground for everything in experience which physics did not read in mechanical nature.[20]

In short, the world science describes became totally different from the picture the mind actually sees. A great chasm opened between the world as it supposedly is in itself and the world as the mind perceives it.

This is the crisis of modern epistemology. To begin with, according to Descartes, the world and the mind are two completely opposed and independent substances. The question inevitably arises: How can such separate and disparate substances relate to each other? As Burtt puts it, "how is it possible for such a mind to know anything about such a world?"[21]

To make matters worse, many of the things the mind *seems* to know bear no relationship to the world as described by science. The mind is outfitted with all sorts of concepts (the secondary qualities) that have no basis in the real world, as envisioned by mathematical physics. If the human mind in its normal operation is so misleading, how can it be trusted at all?

Descartes resolved the dilemma through an appeal to God. He argued that since God is good, He would not deceive us by creating us in such a way that we are subject to constant illusion. Yet even within Descartes's own system, the solution seemed rather ad hoc. For his mechanical philosophy assigned no significant role to God overall. To pull Him in at this one point only, in order to solve an epistemological puzzle, seemed artificial and contrived.

Appeals to God were becoming somewhat suspect anyway in Descartes's day. As a result, the enduring legacy he left was not a ringing defense of God and the soul, as he had intended, but a corrosive method of systematic doubt. The epistemological question he sought (and failed) to answer—how the human mind can gain genuine knowledge of the physical universe—continues to haunt Western philosophy.

For the early scientists, there had been no epistemological dilemma. They believed that the Biblical God had created the world according to an intelligible pattern—*and* that He had designed the human mind to apprehend that pattern. God provided the link between the natural world and the human mind.

But when God was banished from the intellectual scene, that crucial epistemological link was shattered. In the Cartesian universe, as it came to be understood, the mind was shut up in a dark corner of the brain, an insignificant presence in an unthinking, unfeeling, mechanical world of masses spinning in space. How could one be sure that the ideas occurring in this minor and irrelevant phenomenon called "mind" had any correlation to the vast universe wandering blindly through time and space?

Thus were seeds of doubt planted that would soon flower into outright skepticism—as we shall see in the next chapter.

THE IDOL FALLS:
Non-Euclidean Geometry
and the Revolution
in Mathematics

*B*y the end of the eighteenth century, mathematics had become an idol. In the scholarly world it was a matter of faith that the universe was a perfectly running perpetual-motion machine—a view that eliminated the need for God to do anything except perhaps start it all off. In epistemology it became likewise a matter of faith that the axiomatic method led to universal and absolute truth—a view that eliminated the need for divine revelation. Under the spell of Newton's success in mathematical physics, scholars hoped to use the same method to reinterpret the social, political, moral, and even religious thinking of the age. In every field their goal was to intuit a body of starting postulates and from them deduce a universal and infallible system. (See the end of chapter 4.) As historian Rudolph Weingartner writes in the eighteenth century, "many believed that the time was near when all things would be explained by means of a universal physics."[1] Human reason would conquer the world, reducing it to scientific formulas.

Yet, like all idols, the mathematical idol was destined to fall. As Morris Kline puts it, the decline of belief in God as the mathematical designer of the universe "soon entailed the question of *why* the mathematical laws of nature were necessarily truths."[2] In this chapter we trace the decline of confidence in mathematics—what Kline in the title of his book calls *The Loss of Certainty*. We also outline the domino effect of that loss in a rising skepticism in every field of scholarship.

THE AXE OF SKEPTICISM

Skepticism appeared early on, in the work of the Scottish philosopher David Hume (1711-1776). Hume attacked mathematics at its core—the axiomatic method. That method consists of two parts: a set of self-evident axioms and a network of logical deductions from them. Mathematicians tended to honor the axiomatic method in the abstract more than in practice, as we shall see. Nevertheless, as an ideal it became immensely popular—not only in mathematics but in all fields of scholarship.

The use of the axiomatic method in the sciences rested on the assumption that relationships in nature are necessary—that is, that the necessary connections traced by deductive reasoning have analogues in inexorable and immutable laws of nature. It was at the root of this assumption that Hume laid the axe of skepticism.

How do we know that the deductive reasoning pursued by the human mind has any analogue in the outside world, Hume asked. If we restrict our attention to information actually coming in from that world, he said (good empiricist that he was), all we have are sense data. And if we examine sense data, we find nothing there of abstract, metaphysical concepts such as laws of nature or necessary causes.

No matter how thoroughly we winnow through our sense perceptions, Hume said, we never find any perception of a causal power. All we actually perceive are events following one another. In ordinary discourse we might say, for example, that fire causes heat. But all we actually perceive is the sight of fire, followed or accompanied by a feeling of heat.

To speak of fire *causing* heat, Hume concluded, is in reality merely a shorthand way of saying that we generally perceive the former accompanied by the latter. In his words, when we experience the "constant conjunction" of events A and B, we develop the mental habit of expecting B whenever we perceive A. To say A *causes* B is merely a verbal convention. It tell us nothing about the real world; it tells us only about human expectations based on previous experience. Hume's conclusion was, in the words of John Hedley Brooke, that "the idea of a causal connection had its origin in human psychology rather than in some perceived form of physical necessity."[3]

If there is no physical necessity between events, then there are no necessary laws of nature. Therefore nature cannot be known by the axiomatic method, which traces necessary relations. In fact, nature cannot be represented by *any* logically deductive system, even mathematics. In strict empiricism, Randall concludes, the fact that we can formulate a mathematical physics is nothing but a "happy accident."[4]

But if mathematics does not give us knowledge of the physical world, what status does it have? For Hume, mathematics is purely tautological. Its theorems merely spin out meanings already implicit in its starting axioms. To illustrate, when we say a bachelor is an unmarried male, we are not giving any additional information; we are merely spelling out information already contained within the term. Thus Hume pulled mathematics down from its pedestal as the supreme science, reducing it to a collection of formal definitions—which are mere tautologies.

Kant's Dogmatic Slumbers

Hume's conclusions were so repugnant to eighteenth-century intellectuals that most simply ignored them. But they troubled the great German philosopher Immanuel Kant (1724-1804). He later remarked that reading Hume awoke him from his "dogmatic slumbers." Kant was immensely impressed by Isaac Newton's discovery that diverse physical phenomena follow mathematical formulas. Yet here was David Hume arguing that mathematical knowledge of nature is impossible.

It seemed clear to Kant that Hume was wrong. Newton's work provided a stunning practical confirmation that mathematics is an effective tool for gaining knowledge of the physical world. Yet it was equally clear that Hume was right in his criticisms of the standard arguments explaining *why* mathematics works. Kant realized that if we begin by examining the contents of our own minds, there can be no guarantee that the ideas "in here" correspond in any way to the world "out there."

Indeed, there can be no guarantee that the world out there is intelligible at all. But then we come back to Newton, who showed that the world *is* intelligible, that it is mathematically ordered. How can this dilemma be resolved?

Kant's solution was to postulate that the mind itself creates order—which we then mistakenly regard as existing in the external world. The human mind itself comprises a mental grid injecting order onto a chaos of sense data—imposing organization onto the flux of perceptions. The mind contains its own furniture into which the guests must fit.

One piece of that furniture is mathematics. It provides mental forms that shape, mold, and organize our experience. Whether the world itself is mathematically ordered we can never say, Kant taught. All we know is that it appears that way to us because our minds impose mathematical order upon inherently unordered sense data. The categories of the mind impose mathematical order as a cookie cutter imposes shapes onto dough. We see an intelligible world only because we are looking through the tinted lenses of the human mind. Human perception could be described by the child's poem that begins, "Grandpa dropped his glasses in a pail of purple dye, and when he put them on again he saw a purple sky," and an entire purple world.

By locating mathematical truths within the human mind, Kant rendered them purely subjective. Yet he continued to regard them as timeless and necessary. Since the basic categories of thought are rooted in the structure of the human mind, he reasoned, all humans at all times *must* think mathematically. The reason 5+7 must be 12 is that human beings have no other way to think.

This, then, was Kant's explanation of why mathematics works—his response to Hume. An innate mental grid shapes all experience; and since that grid is mathematical, all experience is susceptible to mathematical treatment. Mathematical laws are not true in the old sense—i.e., rooted in the nature of reality—since we cannot know reality. Instead, they are rooted in the human mind. But since the human mind has an inherent structure that is everywhere and always the same, mathematical laws are universal and necessary.

It is sometimes said that Kant instituted a new Copernican revolution. Just as Copernicus placed the sun at the center of the planets, so Kant placed the human mind at the center of the universe. The human mind creates the world as we know it. It creates the laws of nature and guarantees their necessity. Newton's physics and Euclid's geometry are simply descriptions of the way the human mind necessarily organizes spatial sensations. Human experience no longer reveals the rationality of a Creator God but the innate categories of the human mind.

So Kant saved human knowledge—but only by giving up the world. In his epistemology, human knowledge is absolute and necessary, but it reveals nothing about the outside world. It was a pretty steep price to pay to solve the problem of epistemology.

Moreover, it didn't last. In the nineteenth century, new forms of geometry were developed, and mathematicians came to realize that Euclidean geometry was not an apodictic and universal science after all. Geometry—the paradigm of certain knowledge—turned out to be uncertain, as we shall see in the next section.

MOVE OVER, EUCLID

At the outset of the nineteenth century, Euclidean geometry was the most venerated among all the branches of mathematics. It was the first to be organized into a deductive system. For over two thousand years its theorems were found to be in perfect accord with the physical facts. It seemed the ideal system—both a product of reason *and* a description of the physical world.

In fact, when the early scientists asserted that the universe as constructed on mathematical principles, they meant *geometrical* principles. Galileo's famous line that the book of nature is written in the language of mathematics goes on to say, "and the characters are triangles, circles, and other mathematical figures."

Euclid's geometry is founded on ten principles he felt were so simple and obvious that everyone must see their truth, such as: the shortest distance between two points is a line; all right angles are equal to each other; two things equal to a third thing are equal to each other. But there was one axiom in Euclid's system that troubled mathematicians, for it was not as simple and direct as the others. The parallel axiom, or Euclid's fifth postulate, is stated as follows:

> If a straight line (Fig. 1) falling on two straight lines makes the interior angles on the same side less than two right angles, then the two straight lines if extended will meet on that side of the straight line on which the angles are less than two right angles.

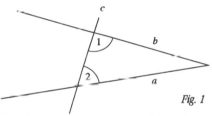

Fig. 1

Got that? No wonder mathematicians felt this axiom lacked the straightforward simplicity of Euclid's other axioms. Most of us recognize it more readily in a rewording by John Playfair (1748-1819), which goes like this: If you have a line *l* and a point *P* above the line, then there is only one line that can be drawn through *P* parallel to *l*. (Fig. 2)

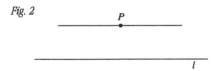

Fig. 2

Even reworded, however, the axiom was problematic, for it dealt with lines extending out into space infinitely, and experience cannot vouch for the behavior of anything infinite. Yet Euclid's axioms were supposed to be based on self-evident experience.

For two thousand years, from the Greeks onward, mathematicians puzzled over how to resolve the parallel axiom. They sought either to reword it (so that it would become self-evident) or else to derive it from one of the other axioms (in which case it would not be self-evident but a theorem to be proved). Neither strategy proved successful.

In the early eighteenth century, mathematicians hit upon a new strategy. They would assume the parallel axiom was false and then show that it led to consequences contradicting the rest of Euclid's system. This is a standard technique in logic, whereby one proves a statement is true by proving that its negation leads to results that contradict established knowledge.

There are two ways to falsify the parallel axiom. The axiom states that there is one and only one line through a given point parallel to a given line. To deny the axiom, one can either assume that there are *no* parallel lines that pass through the point or that there are *many* parallel lines. Various mathematicians experimented with each of these assumptions, using them along with Euclid's other axioms and postulates to make deductions and prove theorems—presuming that at some point they would reach a logical contradiction, thereby proving the original assumption false.

But to their great surprise, mathematicians never reached the expected contradiction. Whether they assumed that no parallel lines or that an infinite number of parallel lines pass through the point, they could make up theorems and prove them just as Euclid had done without ever running into a contradiction.

In the nineteenth century it gradually began to dawn on mathematicians that what they were discovering were new systems of geometry. The systems they were experimenting with were genuine forms of geometry in the sense that they possessed a valid logical structure. They began with a set of hypotheses and mapped out a series of deductions. Moreover, the results were perfectly consistent logically.

But would the new systems apply to the physical world? German mathematician Karl Friedrich Gauss (1777-1855) performed measurements in the hope of finding out. In the new geometries, the sum of the angles of a triangle is not precisely 180 degrees. So Gauss shouldered his backpack and hiked up a mountain to calculate the angle sum of the triangle formed by three great mountain peaks. He discovered that the sum of the three angles did slightly exceed 180 degrees but the difference was so small that it fell within the range of experimental error.

In other words, the result of Gauss' experiment was inconclusive. (As it turns out, the difference in angle sums doesn't show up until the dimensions are as large as the earth itself.) The significance of the experiment, however, was not its result but the sheer fact that it was conducted—the fact that a respected mathematician would entertain serious questions about which geometry applies to the physical world. For the first time, mathematicians were considering the possibility that Euclidean geometry was not the geometry of physical space.

Today scientists hold that any form of geometry is potentially applicable to physical space. Choosing *which* form to apply in a given context depends on empirical considerations. Euclidean geometry applies when dealing with surfaces that are ordinary planes. Hence it works well for most terrestrial applications because the surfaces are small enough that they can be treated essentially as planes. But other forms of geometry may work better for other applications.

For instance, Riemannian geometry (named after German mathematician Georg Bernhard Riemann, 1826-1866) is based on the assumption that there are *no* parallel lines passing through a given point. It applies when dealing with surfaces that have a positive curvature, like a sphere, where a "straight" line is like the arc of a great circle. Here the sum of the angles of a triangle is always greater than 180 degrees. Parallel lines do not exist because arcs of great circles always converge. (Think of the longitudinal lines on a globe.) Einstein popularized Riemannian geometry when he applied it in astronomical contexts with his concept of curved space.

Lobatchevskian geometry (named after Russian mathematician Nikolai Ivanovich Lobatchevsky, 1793-1856) is built on the assumption that there are an *infinite* number of parallel lines through a given point. It applies when dealing with surfaces that have a negative curvature, and can be pictured as two infinitely long herald's trumpets with their bells butted together. Here "straight" lines are lines that run lengthwise along the trumpet-like surface, and the sum of the angles of a triangle is always less than 180 degrees.

With the development of non-Euclidean forms of geometry, for the first time a chasm opened between what is mathematically true and what is physically true. As mathematician E. T. Bell puts it in his book *The Magic of Numbers*, with non-Euclideanism a distinction arose between mathematical geometry and physical geometry. "Mathematical geometry," Bell explains, "is a system of postulates and deductions from them, designed without reference to . . . sensory experience." Physical geometry, on the other hand, is a "practical science designed to give a coherent account of the world of sensory (and scientific) experience."[5] But is there any connection between geometry as a logical system and geometry as a practical science? That became the conundrum of modern mathematics.

BACK TO FOUNDATIONS

The intellectual fallout of the new geometries has been severe. For two thousand years, Euclidean geometry had been held up as the model of truth. But suddenly mathematicians were no longer sure which of several competing geometries was really true. It was as though truth itself had shattered. "It became clear," says Kline, "that mathematicians had adopted axioms for geometry that seemed correct on the basis of limited experience and had been deluded into thinking that these were self-evident truths."[6]

The revolution in geometry led first to a drastic decline in the status of mathematics proper. For in comparing Euclidean and non-Euclidean forms of geometry, mathematics plays a minor role. It can determine whether a system is internally consistent, but it is powerless to determine whether it is true of the physical world. Mathematicians decided that only experience can determine which forms of geometry apply to the physical world. Mathematics proper does not deal with truth after all but only with logical consistency. As physicist and philosopher Hans Reichenbach explains:

> The mathematician discovered that what he could prove was merely the system of mathematical implications, of *if-then* relations leading from the axioms of geometry to its theorems. He no longer felt entitled to assert the axioms as true.[7]

The idea that logical truth could be separated from physical truth represented a massive shift in Western intellectual history. From the time of the ancient Greeks, most Western philosophers had assumed that reality is ultimately rational—that what is logically true is also really true. The new geometries challenged that conviction. Here were several systems that were internally consistent yet incompatible with one another—which meant they could not all be true. A wedge was driven between what is rational and what is true. From now on, mathematics would concern itself only with the question of rationality—internal consistency—and not with truth.

This reduced role for mathematics created its own problems, however. Until this time, mathematicians had not worried overly much about the logical consistency of their formulas. They reasoned that if the formulas worked in the real world, that itself proved their consistency, since the world is rational. But now that mathematics had been surgically detached from the real world, mathematicians could no longer rely on workability to give them confidence. From now on, consistency would have to be proved by logic alone.

When mathematicians examined their field by the clear, cold light of logic, they were dismayed. The axiomatic method may have had its roots in mathematics, but it had been honored in the abstract more than in practice. In reality, mathematics did not live up to its reputation as a paragon of logical certainty. Instead it was riddled with logical gaps and sloppy reasoning.

Many branches of mathematics had grown up without the construction of explicit logical proofs to justify each concept or procedure. They consisted merely of collections of steps—pragmatic rules—passed on from one generation to the next. The steps were accepted because they were effective in solving practical problems in engineering, economics, navigation, and calendar-making. But often there were no reasons or proofs given for each step, no definitions of key concepts. The beautiful deductive system introduced by Euclid had been revered but not reproduced.

For example, mathematicians were divided on whether to accept negative numbers. Negatives had been introduced to meet the practical problem of representing debts. But they did not fit the technical definition of what a number is—that is, they were not quantities. For example, Blaise Pascal (1623-1662) regarded the subtraction of, say, four from zero as sheer nonsense, since you can never have a quantity less than zero.

Then there was the problem of irrational numbers, numbers that cannot be reduced to either whole numbers or their ratios. Many mathematicians wondered whether these should even be considered numbers. After all, when written as decimals, irrationals require an infinite number of digits—which means we can not pin down with precision what quantity is being expressed. To the Greeks such imprecision was anathema in mathematics.[8] According to legend, the Greek mathematician Hippasus of Metapontum first discovered irrationals while at sea. His fellow Pythagoreans were so outraged at learning about numbers that fail to represent precise quantities that they tossed him overboard.

Then there was calculus. It made use of the notion of indivisibles (infinitely small quantities) but failed to offer a logical explanation of what an indivisible is. Voltaire described calculus sarcastically as "the art of numbering and measuring exactly a Thing whose Existence cannot be conceived."[9]

Logical gaps were detected even in Euclidean geometry. In many cases Euclid worked from diagrams where certain relationships were visually obvious; as a result, he failed to articulate explicit logical proofs. He also employed some concepts, such as congruence, that were defined not logically but physically—by lifting a rigid figure and superimposing it upon another.[10]

As long as mathematicians were convinced that God had designed the world mathematically and that they were discovering that design, they remained unperturbed about logical gaps in their work.

Since mathematics gives truth about reality, they were confident that it would eventually prove to be consistent, since reality itself cannot be contradictory. In other words, religious conviction (along with practical success) moved mathematics forward even when it lacked a complete and coherent logical basis.

But when belief in God withered and mathematics was divorced from the real world, there was no longer any guarantee of its consistency. Now the only way to guarantee the logical validity of mathematical concepts was to formulate explicit logical proofs. Thus began what is called the foundations movement—the attempt to rigorously axiomatize all branches of mathematics.

Beginning in about 1820, the axiomatic method was applied with a vengeance. All branches of mathematics were, so to speak, shaken out, washed, mended, and ironed. They were reformulated to begin with sharply worded definitions and clearly stated axioms. Mathematicians aimed at constructing explicit proofs of all results, no matter how obvious these might be intuitively.

By 1900 remarkable progress had been made. Few mathematical theorems were changed as a consequence, but at least mathematicians could pride themselves on having proved that each step was logically sanctioned. It seemed that the goal of complete logical rigor was in sight.

Then the whole house of cards came tumbling down. In rigorizing their field, mathematicians had made heavy use of set theory. In fact, by the early 1900s, set theory had begun to play the role once played by Euclidean geometry, becoming the basis for all mathematics. Then mathematicians stumbled upon certain paradoxes, or antinomies, within set theory that threatened to undermine it—and the rest of mathematics along with it.

A nonmathematical illustration of a paradox would be the statement, "All rules have exceptions." This statement is itself a rule, and therefore must have exceptions. Which means there must be at least one rule with no exceptions. But the existence of such a rule would falsify the original statement. In short, if the statement is true, then it is false.

Statements that refer to themselves frequently produce such paradoxes. In mathematics, sets that include themselves likewise produce paradoxes. These antinomies were disturbing enough for set theory. But even worse, they opened mathematicians' eyes to similar contradictions in the older, more established branches of mathematics.

Was there any way to resolve these paradoxes—and to guarantee that no additional ones would crop up in the future? Finding a method capable of guaranteeing absolute logical rigor became the holy grail of mathematics. In their quest, mathematicians split into four major schools, each offering a different foundation for mathematics.

It's Pure Logic: Logicism

The first school, logicism, held that all of mathematics is reducible to logic. In the early 1900s, logic was accepted as a body of truths. Hence if mathematics could be shown to be a subspecies of logic, it would likewise be a body of truths. The problem of consistency would be solved, since truth cannot be contradictory.

The champion of logicism was British philosopher Bertrand Russell (1872-1970). He carried out his program, along with Alfred North Whitehead, in a massive work entitled *Principia Mathematica*. Their stated goal was to demonstrate that all mathematics is part of logic by showing that the denial of any of its propositions is self-contradictory.

Not all mathematicians were persuaded by their efforts, however. To reduce mathematics to symbolic logic, Russell and Whitehead were forced to assume several axioms that other mathematicians regarded as contrived or simply untrue. But even more disturbing were the philosophical implications of logicism. For if logicism is correct, then all of mathematics is purely formal. It is a purely deductive system whose theorems follow from the laws of thought alone and do not depend in any way upon conditions in the physical world.

But if that is the case, then it is difficult to explain why mathematics works so well in *describing* that physical world—why it works so well in mechanics, acoustics, electromagnetics, optics, and all the rest of science. If the contents of mathematics derive purely from the laws of thought, why do they fit the physical world so well?

In other words, if the statement 5+7=12 is a purely logical truth, then why in our experience should 5 apples plus 7 apples always come to 12 apples? As Christian philosopher Vern Poythress puts it, "Why should an admittedly contingent world offer us repeated instances of this truth, many more instances than we could expect by chance?" If someone responds that the world is not after all entirely contingent, that it has some degree of regularity, the problem still remains, Poythress says. For why should we expect "that regularity to coincide, in even the remotest way, with the *a priori* mathematical expectations of human minds?"[11]

The real blow to logicism, however, came when philosophers rejected the idea that logic expresses truths—a development that undermined the primary rationale for logicism. For if the axioms of logic are not truths but only arbitrary constructs, then they do not guarantee consistency, and there is nothing to be gained for mathematics by reducing it to logic.

A Mathematician's Intuition: Intuitionism

While logicists were developing their approach to the foundations of mathematics, a radically different approach was undertaken by a group who called themselves intuitionists. They, too, sought to guarantee the consistency of mathematics now that it no longer expressed laws inherent in the design of the universe. But the intuitionists reached back to Descartes and his concept of "clear and distinct" ideas—self-evident ideas, intuited directly, that cannot be doubted.

Why, asked the intuitionists, should we require complicated and tedious logical justifications for intuitively obvious things like the ordinary whole numbers? That's tackling the job backward. We ought to *begin* with precisely those intuitively obvious things. Members of this school of thought regarded the intuition of pure number as self-evident—as the only intuition that "could not possibly deceive us," in the words of Henri Poincaré (1854-1912). By beginning with this indubitable basis and reasoning by rigorous logic, the intuitionists hoped to build a secure foundation for mathematics.

But like all systems that claim to be built upon self-evident truths, intuitionism foundered in trying to determine *which* truths are genuinely self-evident. Adherents were soon disagreeing with one another. The difficulty is that some abstract theorems accepted by most mathematicians are not at all intuitively obvious. They may even seem to run counter to deeply ingrained ways of thinking. Even specialists in the field may have a hard time regarding them as self-evident.

As a result, some intuitionists accepted set theory; others rejected it. Some accepted classical logic; others rejected it. This disagreement over which concepts form the basis for mathematics seriously undermined the intuitionist contention that these concepts are self-evident.

Disagreements also erupted over the next step—delimiting what kinds of theorems ought to be built upon the basic mathematical intuitions. The intuitionists' objective was to accept only those mathematical propositions that could be verified (or, in mathematical language, constructed). Hence, they earned a reputation as the Vienna Circle of mathematics. Just as the strict logical positivists considered any statement meaningless that could not be empirically verified, so the intuitionists rejected anything in mathematics that could not be constructed.[12] As might be predicted, this requirement led them to toss out a large portion of modern mathematics—which in turn rendered the approach unacceptable to most mathematicians.

Finally, the intuitionists advanced no further than Kant in

explaining how mathematics applies to the physical world. Their concept of intuition was Kantian.[13] They did not mean a direct insight into reality; they meant insight into the categories and activities of the human mind. As we saw earlier, Kant taught that experience is shaped and organized by mental categories. Even such basic concepts as space and time are not derived from the outside world but are contributions of the mind. The mind does not reflect the world of experience like a mirror; instead, it actively shapes the world.

The intuitionists taught essentially a Kantian view of mathematics. They defined it not as a body of truths but as an activity of the human mind, independent of the outside world. The mind recognizes immediate certainties and then proceeds to construct its own mathematical universe. "Mathematics," said intuitionist Arend Heyting, "is a production of the human mind."[14] The relationship between mathematics and the physical world remained an unsolved puzzle.

The Form's The Thing: Formalism

A third school of thought to take up the challenge of justifying mathematics was called formalism, launched by David Hilbert (1862-1943). The formalists sought to present proofs that are valid on account of their logical form alone. They resolved to translate all mathematics into formal symbols in order to avoid the ambiguities introduced by normal language and common-sense concepts.

The idea can be illustrated by the logical syllogism. Take a familiar example: All men are mortal; Socrates is a man; therefore Socrates is mortal. If we remove the specific content and use letter symbols instead, we can recast the statement in its purely logical form: All A's are X; B is an A; therefore B is X. At this point, the argument is valid without any reference to the physical meaning of the terms. Any content whatever can be fit into the logical form—for example, all mammals are vertebrates; the fox is a mammal; therefore the fox is a vertebrate.[15]

Now consider an example from mathematics. Euclid's first postulate says that between any two points a straight line can be drawn. Restated, we could say that for any two distinct points, there is a straight line to which they both belong. We begin the process of abstraction by replacing familiar terms like "point" and "line" with letter symbols—say, P and S. We can now restate the postulate in schematic form like this: For any two distinct P's there is an S to which they both bear the relation B.

The purpose of this exercise is to bring out the postulate's underlying logical form and enable us to judge its validity. The danger in Euclidean geometry is that we may draw diagrams of points and lines and become quite convinced from visual experience that particular theorems are true. We may then make the mistake of imagining that these theorems follow logically from certain premises when in fact they do not—a misapprehension that would leave logical gaps in our proofs. The opposite danger faces us in non-Euclidean geometry. There a particular theorem may be so difficult to visualize, so far from normal experience, that it strikes us as absurd—which may blind us to the fact that it does in fact follow rigorously from its premises.

The remedy, said the formalists, is to drain all our terms of their familiar meanings, turn them into abstract symbols, and then analyze the theorems by accepted rules of deduction. In principle, someone should be able to check the validity of each proof if all he knows is logic—even if he does not understand the meanings of any of the terms of the system and has no opinion about the truth of any of the axioms or theorems.[16]

The ultimate goal of formalism was to represent theorems by symbols and then prove mathematically that they are consistent. In order to prove that a system is consistent, philosopher John Passmore explains, "it is not enough to wait and see whether contradictions eventually reveal themselves; the formalist has to show that contradictions *cannot* arise within his system."[17] Hilbert hoped that by translating an axiomatized theory T into a formal language L, he could then study the language itself as a mathematical object and prove that it is free from contradictions.

But the formalist program came crashing down with the work of a young man named Kurt Gödel (1906-1978). Gödel took Russell's own work, *Principia Mathematica*, and used it as an object for Hilbert's program. He assigned an integer to each symbol Russell used and developed a numerical coding system that allowed him to perform mathematical manipulations on the concepts presented in the book.

But, ironically, the attempt to prove Russell's system free from contradictions itself led to contradictions. In order to prove that a formal system like *Principia Mathematica* is consistent, one must first be able to say definitely of any given formula that it is or is not provable within the system. Gödel demonstrated that within any system it is possible to find the logical equivalent of a sentence that states, "This sentence is not provable"—which is self-contradictory. For if the sentence is true, then it means that the system contains at least one sentence (namely, this one) that cannot be proved within the system; but if the sentence cannot be proved, then we don't know whether it is really true. It's a vicious cycle.

Think of the well-known liar's paradox, in which someone states, "I am lying." If we assume he is telling the truth in making the statement, then he is lying. But he can't be lying because we have already stipulated that he is telling the truth.

Gödel's paradox means there is a defect endemic to all formal systems—namely, that they are not capable of proving all true statements within the system. More broadly, it implies the impossibility of proving consistency by any method that translates concepts into a numerical system—precisely what the formalists sought to do. The results of Gödel's work were shattering. Mathematicians concluded that they could not prove consistency in any mathematical system by safe logical principles. And if consistency could not be proved, then mathematicians risked talking nonsense. Any day a contradiction might arise, and the entire mathematical structure built on it would crumble.[18]

Finally, critics argued that the formalists sought to purchase consistency at too high a price—at the price of reducing mathematics to meaningless symbols. The formalists viewed mathematics as a game, like chess, operating by its own rules without any reference to the real world. Bertrand Russell complained that "the formalists are like a watchmaker who is so absorbed in making his watches look pretty that he has forgotten their purpose of telling time."[19] Formal consistency had crowded out truth as the goal of mathematics.

Sets and Numbers: Set Theory

The paradoxes that spurred the foundation movement in the first place emerged, as we noted earlier, from set theory. Some mathematicians believed that the best way to resolve them was to axiomatize set theory itself. The founder of set theory, Georg Cantor (1845-1918),[20] had used rather loose definitions of a set and other key concepts. By clarifying these definitions and selecting the right axioms, set-theorists hoped to resolve the offending paradoxes, just as the rigorous application of the axiomatic method had cleared up logical problems in other branches of mathematics.

The strategy was largely successful. Beginning with the axioms proposed by Ernst Zermelo (1871-1953) and Abraham A. Fraenkel (1891-1965), mathematicians have refined the axioms of set theory to avoid the paradoxes. Today many mathematicians regard set theory as the best foundation upon which to build all of mathematics. Admittedly, there is not yet universal agreement on which axioms to use. Neither has the consistency of set theory been demonstrated. But many of its adherents are unconcerned. Their attitude is that mathematics has faced contradictions in the past and overcome them, and it will do so again. We do not need absolute guarantees of consistency. One group of set-theorists who call themselves the Bourbakists put it this way:

For twenty-five centuries mathematicians have been correcting their errors, and seeing their science enriched and not impoverished in consequence; and this gives them the right to contemplate the future with equanimity.[21]

After Gödel's paper appeared in 1931, many other mathematicians—often out of frustration—adopted the same casual attitude toward consistency. By this time, four major separate, distinct, and more-or-less conflicting approaches to mathematics had been expounded (logicism, intuitionism, formalism, set theory), not to mention several lesser approaches. One could no longer assert merely that a mathematical theorem was proven; one had to add *by whose standards* it was proven. And yet this was the field that, for nearly two millennia had been hailed as the perfect science—the science that begins with indubitable, self-evident truths and proceeds by infallible reasoning, that represents the pinnacle of human reason, that reveals the design of the universe, that reads the very thoughts of God.

Now mathematics had lost its claim to truth. The blow to human pride was crushing. In the words of Morris Kline, mathematicians had been

worshipping a golden calf—rigorous, universally acceptable proof, true in all possible worlds—in the belief that it was God. They now realize it was a false god.[22]

One might hope that having seen their idol fall, modern thinkers would return to the true God. Alas, most did not. Instead, they used the fall of mathematics as a tool to pry loose the foundations of all other fields of knowledge.

As Kline explains, having given up God as the basis for mathematics, scientists had to accept man. They continued to develop mathematics and to search for laws of nature but with a crucial difference. They no longer believed they were discovering the design of God but only the work of man.[23] And the subjectivity and limitations that always beset the work of man now came to be seen as unavoidable in all fields of human endeavor.

THE FALL AND ITS FALLOUT

When the idol of mathematics fell, it brought down with it confidence in any universal truth. The sharp ring of truth that characterized mathematics had inspired hope that truth could be found by similar methods in other fields of scholarship. Now that hope died.

Filtered to the rest of the academic world, the crisis in mathematics was symbolized by the emergence of non-Euclidean geometries. Euclid's axioms had stood the test of time for some two thousand years. That physical space is Euclidean seemed part of common sense. But now Euclidean geometry had been relegated to one of many possible geometries. Far from being a universal truth, Euclidean geometry was a merely human invention that might apply in some contexts but not in others.

The crisis in geometry became a metaphor for the shattering of established verities, the inadequacy of deductive systems, the loss of a single, unified body of truth. As pragmatist philosopher C. S. Peirce explains, metaphysics "has always been the ape of mathematics," and "the metaphysical axioms are imitations of the geometrical axioms." Hence when Euclideanism toppled, so did many systems of metaphysics.[24]

In fact, says mathematician E. T. Bell, "all thinking was affected." Bell writes:

> The absolutism of geometric 'truth,' drilled into adolescents in their formative years, conditioned educated but uncritical minds to accept absolutism in the 'truths' of other intangibles from philosophy and religion to economics and politics.

As is obvious from his tone, Bell sees the overthrow of "absolutism" as a positive outcome. He notes cheerfully that non-Euclidean geometry encouraged "disbelief in eternal truths and absolutes" in all fields across the board. He heralds Lobatchevsky as "The Great Emancipator" who freed the human mind from the shackles of the past—freed it to make its own truths.[25]

Edward Purcell, Jr., in his book *The Crisis of Democratic Theory*, gives a more detailed account of the effects of non-Euclideanism. Euclidean geometry, Purcell says, came to represent all traditional theories, "whether classical economics or orthodox jurisprudence or customary prescriptive political theory." The fall of Euclideanism was interpreted as discrediting all these other traditional systems. In Purcell's words, "The concept of non-Euclideanism, generalized to include all types of deductive thought, robbed every rational system of any claim to be in any sense true."[26]

In logic, for example, philosophers denounced Aristotelian logic as an arbitrary system without relation either to the external universe or to any inherent requirements of reason. The so-called "laws of logic" are merely human conventions, adopted for their utility, said Harvard philosopher C. I. Lewis. He led the way in experimenting with new laws of thought and multivalued logical systems. There are "a variety of non-Aristotelian logics," declared Sterling Amprecht, philosopher at Amherst College, "akin to the variety of non-Euclidean geometries."

In ethics, philosophers such as Morris Cohen drew a parallel between Euclid's system of geometry and the Christian system of ethics. Both were ordered systems of propositions that had been considered true. Yet if deductive systems are completely formal, then deductive reasoning cannot be used to prove the legitimacy of Christian ethics—or any other system of moral propositions. Just as in geometry, one could start with a different set of postulates—and from them produce a system of ethics radically different from that of traditional Christianity. French philosopher Jacques Rueff explicitly labeled traditional Christian moral beliefs Euclidean and argued that it was possible to create non-Euclidean systems of morality.

In anthropology, non-Euclideanism came to be associated with belief in the near-infinite plasticity of human nature. Sociologists and anthropologists urged Westerners to study what they called "non-Euclidean" cultures (by which they meant non-Western cultures) to become aware of the great diversity of norms and behaviors possible within human societies. Variation among cultures, said Robert Lowie, "enlarges our notion of social potentialities as the conception of n-dimensional space enlarges the vision of the non-Euclidean geometrician."

In economics, John M. Clark urged the development of a variety of "non-Euclidean economics," which he described as "systems of economics with axioms as far removed from each other as the geometry of Euclid and the non-Euclideans."

In legal theory, Jerome Frank of the Yale Law School declared that non-Euclidean geometry "significantly affects thinking in any field." He charged that traditional legal theory was "Euclidean"—that is, it assumed that a "legal system can be worked out logically as the ancient geometers had worked out their system from self-evident geometrical axioms." Frank criticized the postulates of traditional legal theory and offered several new ones to take their place.

In political theory, non-Euclideanism became a metaphor to sweep away traditional and established theories. For example, Charles Beard questioned the effectiveness of the balance-of-powers concept, dismissing it as a "Euclidean theory."

Throughout the academic world, non-Euclidean geometry was invoked to support a positivistic, anti-metaphysical temper of thought. A culture was assumed to be analogous to a geometry. Both were built on a few postulates chosen from an indefinite number of possibilities; both consisted of internally consistent, interrelated wholes; and both were immune to judgments about their truth or falsity in any ultimate sense. Just as different geometries could all be logically valid, it was argued, so any number of different cultural and ethical systems could all be logically valid. Thus non-Euclideanism became a metaphor for the rejection of all traditional deductive systems—particularly the moral and religious tradition of Christianity. This is not to say that non-Euclideanism is intrinsically anti-Christian or anti-religious. Yet it was invoked as a symbol to deny that Christianity has any claim to a superior or exclusive truth.

WHY DOES MATH WORK?

In recent years, mathematicians have split into two sharply divided camps—pure and applied. Pure mathematicians tend to be formalists. They concentrate on problems generated from within mathematics itself and have no interest in application to the real world. They see their subject as a theoretical game, played for its own sake and according to its own rules.

That is to say, their concern is consistency, not truth. To ask whether a mathematical system is "correct" is as improper as asking whether a game—say, dominoes—is "correct." Certainly *within* a game like dominoes one can ask whether a particular operation is correct, meaning: Does it follow the rules of the game? But to ask whether the game itself is correct or true is a confusion of categories.

Applied mathematicians, on the other hand, tend to be implicit Platonists, believing in the objective truth of mathematics. They believe mathematics is genuine discovery, not construction. Yet, unlike nineteenth-century mathematicians, they show no interest in securing an infallible, indubitable logical foundation for mathematics. They treat their subject as a handy tool for solving practical problems in science and engineering. The only test of its validity that matters is the pragmatic test: Does it work? The only justification for mathematics is its value to science and engineering. Indeed, much of the best work in applied mathematics today is done not by mathematicians but by engineers, physicists, astronomers, chemists, and computer scientists.

How the mighty have fallen. Mathematicians began with the belief that they were discovering the very design of the universe. But today mathematics has been reduced to either an abstract game or a tool of science and engineering. Neither pure nor applied mathematicians worry much about truth any longer.

But if mathematics is not true, we face a puzzling question: Why does it work so well? Why does it apply so precisely to the physical world? Here is a system typically worked out independently of any empirical observations, by pure deduction from first principles—and yet it fits empirical observations. "As often as not," observes Michael Guillen, "ideas in mathematics are conceived by playful, imaginative minds whose first concern is to be rational, not realistic." Yet repeatedly over the past four centuries, these ideas were later applied to real objects and events.[27] Why does mathematics work so well in describing the world?

Imre Lakatos (1922-1974) argues that the reason mathematics fits the empirical world so closely is that it is an empirical science. Mathematics is no special form of knowledge, Lakatos insists; and it needs no ultimate guarantees. Instead, it proceeds the same way as any other science—by proposing conjectures and then testing whether they can be falsified.

The reason we misconceive of mathematics as some special form of knowledge, Lakatos says, is that our textbooks sanitize its historical development. For example, a typical textbook will state that Euler's theorem was formulated by Euler and proved by Poincaré. The process sounds so simple and clean. But in reality Euler's theorem was reformulated several times; it was also proved several times and in several different ways. Why? Because each time the proof was inadequate and was shot down by counter-examples, until Poincaré came up with a formulation and a proof that have withstood all challenges.

At least, so far. But at any moment, Lakatos says, someone may discover a counter-example that refutes even the best-confirmed, most well-established theorem. Mathematics grows by trial and error, he concludes, just as all empirical knowledge does.

The empiricist view of mathematics was proposed earlier by John Stuart Mill (1806-1873). Mill suggested that mathematics is successful in explaining the physical world because its principles were derived from observation of the physical world to begin with. Because mathematical principles are so general, Mill said, we have wrongly concluded that they are universal and certain. But in fact they are merely probable, just like the principles of physics, chemistry, and biology.

The weakness of this view, argues philosopher Carl Hempel,[28] is that mathematics cannot be falsified by empirical events. From a genuinely empirical hypothesis—such as the law of gravity—it is possible to derive predictions that are used to test the hypothesis. But consider the mathematical "hypothesis" that $5+7=12$. What events would count as falsification of this hypothesis?

Suppose we count out five objects, then seven objects, and then count all of them together. What if we come up with eleven instead of twelve? Do we conclude that the hypothesis is empirically falsified? Clearly not. We assume that we counted wrong, or that one of the objects fell to the floor, or that someone tricked us and slipped one up his sleeve. We emphatically do not consider that empirical phenomena could invalidate a mathematical proposition.

It may be true that we initially form mathematical concepts by generalizing from experience. Yet there is more to mathematics than a process of abstraction. For mathematicians, something doesn't become a theorem merely because it has no counter-examples. What they require is a rational proof that *guarantees* the nonexistence of any counter-examples.

Moreover, the idea that mathematical concepts are generalizations from experience runs up against the practical objection that many modern mathematical concepts are so abstract that they bear little relationship to any sensory experience. As Poythress comments, "To claim that transfinite numbers, topological spaces, and abstract algebras are somehow impressed on us from sense experience takes some stretch of imagination."[29] Contemporary philosophy of mathematics is still far from answering the question, why does math work?

The Unreasonable Effectiveness of Mathematics

Before tackling the question ourselves, let's summarize the progression of events covered in the last two chapters. The early mathematical scientists worked within a Christian framework. They believed that a reasonable God had created an intelligible universe and that part of that intelligibility consists in its being open to mathematical formulation. Mathematics was regarded as the scaffolding upon which God had created the world.

But the embrace of a Pythagorean-Platonic philosophy of mathematics introduced elements incompatible with a Biblical worldview. Already in the writings of Copernicus, Kepler, and Galileo, mathematical relations began to be treated as the most certain, most real dimension of the world. Natural law, working by strict mathematical necessity, came to be regarded as a semi-independent cause, which even God could not change. Eventually, the world was conceived as a huge machine, reducible to matter in motion, operating by forces expressible in mathematical terms. God's role in running the world machine was diminished until the idea of God seemed largely irrelevant and readily dispensable.

A parallel development occurred in epistemology. At the time of the scientific revolution the reliability of human knowledge was grounded in the belief that God had created humanity in His image, to reflect His rationality. But the success of the mathematical approach to science was so intoxicating that Western intellectuals no longer felt the need for any external guarantee of knowledge. They regarded mathematics itself and the axiomatic method derived from it as an independent means of gaining indubitable, infallible knowledge. They set human reason up as an autonomous power, capable of penetrating to ultimate truth. Mathematics, as the crown of human reason, was essentially worshiped as an idol.

In the words of historian Peter Bowler, "For all the concerns that Descartes and Newton might express about the link between science and religion, to later generations their achievements merely symbolized the power of reason to challenge ancient preconceptions"—and to build a new edifice of knowledge by its own power. "What had begun as a search for new insight into how God had created the world," Bowler says, "ended with the proclamation that man's ability to understand the workings of nature would make any concern for the Creator superfluous."[30]

Autonomous human reason then turned its attention upon all fields of human scholarship, determined to reject anything it deemed "unreasonable." This was the eighteenth century, often dubbed the Age of Reason. Christianity itself was eventually hauled before the tribunal of reason—and condemned. Natural law, defined as mathematical necessity, made divine miracles impossible (even God can't change a natural law) and denied human beings both freedom and moral responsibility (they are simply cogs in the mechanistic world). Moreover, the Bible, since it teaches these notions, was denounced as hopelessly unscientific and irrational.

Under this onslaught, belief in God declined. Like the ancient Israelites, Western philosophy had waxed fat and rich, forgetting that God was the source of its wealth.

But then something unexpected happened. With no grounding in divine creation, human knowledge was cut adrift. If the universe is the product of blind, mechanistic forces, how do we know it has any intelligible structure at all? If there is no Designer, how can we be confident there is a design? If human beings are not created in the image of God, how can we be sure the design we *think* we detect is really there? Where is the guarantee that the concepts in our minds bear any relation to the world outside?

As we have seen, Hume raised these questions in an especially acute form. Kant tried to answer them by defining order and design as a creation not of God but of the human mind—a product of its inherent structure. Then non-Euclidean geometry came along and showed that the human mind can conceive many *different* designs, all equally rational, all equally consistent.

At that point, mathematicians gave up the idea of truth and contented themselves with proving consistency. As Peggy Marchi puts it, mathematicians "tried to replace truth in mathematics with some other kind of certainty or guarantee of reliability."[31] But proving consistency itself turned out to be a daunting task, and mathematicians ended up splitting into four competing schools—logicism, intuitionism, formalism, and set-theory. Eventually, all four schools floundered on the rock of Gödel's paradox, which implied that no axiomatic system is ever completely provable. Lakatos advised mathematicians to give up the search for guarantees of consistency. Mathematics is merely a collection of tentative empirical hypotheses, he urged; it needs no ultimate justification.

Yet the puzzle remains that mathematics makes claims that go beyond the empirical world, while remaining uncannily accurate in its application to that world. Through mathematical formulations we grasp enough of what the world is like to fly a man to the moon, create a microchip, or remove a tumor from the brain. But there is no explanation *why* this remarkable consonance exists between the ideas in the human mind and the order of the physical world.

Physicist Eugene Wigner discusses the problem in a much-quoted article titled "The Unreasonable Effectiveness of Mathematics in the Natural Sciences." Yet Wigner does not offer any explanation of that "unreasonable effectiveness"; he merely shrugs his shoulders, figuratively speaking, and says there *is* no explanation. "The enormous usefulness of mathematics is something bordering on the mysterious," Wigner says. "There is no rational explanation for it." He describes the effectiveness of mathematics as the scientist's "article of faith"—and later as a "miracle."[32]

Similarly, Morris Kline speaks repeatedly of mathematics as having "some magical power . . . some inner mysterious strength" that is simply "inexplicable." Borrowing a phrase from philosopher George Santayana, Kline says mathematicians are reduced to acting on "animal faith."[33]

This is the dilemma of contemporary mathematical philosophy. The amazing "fit" of mathematical concepts to the physical world cries out for explanation—but without the assumption of divine creation by a reasonable God, there *is* no explanation. Mathematicians must act on sheer faith—a faith that lacks any basis.

A "Sixth Sense"

What is a Christian view of mathematics? To begin with, Christians do not try to "explain" mathematics as a branch of logic or empirical science or anything else. All such attempts are forms of reductionism. They are reminiscent of the ethicist who says goodness is "nothing but" pleasure, or the liberal theologian who says faith is "nothing but" a feeling.

More congenial to a Christian understanding is mathematician Douglas Gasking's suggestion that we consider mathematical propositions as *sui generis*, one of a kind. They cannot be analyzed into anything else; they cannot be reduced to anything else. They give information about a unique aspect of reality.[34]

How do we know this unique aspect of reality? Michael Guillen suggests that mathematical insight is a sixth sense, "an extra sense with which we perceive the natural world." "If thought of this way," he says, "the coincidence between the natural world and the mathematical world is not any more mysterious than the coincidences between the natural world and the auditory, tactile, and olfactory worlds." In other words, mathematical insight is analogous to sight, hearing, or touch. All are means for perceiving some particular aspect of a multifaceted reality.[35]

These explanations are reminiscent of the thought of Herman Dooyeweerd, a Dutchman who formulated a comprehensive Christian philosophy in the 1930s.[36] Dooyeweerd argued that the world God created is analyzable into several aspects—numerical, spatial, physical, chemical, biological, logical, economic, aesthetic, ethical, and so on. In each case, we are dealing with an irreducible aspect of God's creation; it cannot be "explained away" as anything else.

In each case, moreover, knowledge is possible because of a corresponding capacity created in us by God. We appreciate the beauty in a work of art because we are created with the capacity to experience the aesthetic aspect of creation. We recognize contradictions in an argument because of a capacity for experiencing the logical aspect of creation. We perform mathematical operations because of a capacity to perceive the numerical and spatial aspects of creation.

Of course, in mathematics we are not limited to passive perception, any more than art is limited to representation. Many branches of modern mathematics are highly creative and are as far removed from the natural world as abstract art is from photography. As in all fields of scholarship, creativity has its roots in the created world, yet reaches out to explore freely from that basis.

The primeval paradigm of human knowledge is the account of Adam naming the animals. Devising a suitable label for each animal required careful observation, analysis, and categorization, based on the way it was created. Adam couldn't very well call a fish "woolly creature with four legs" or a bird "scaled creature with fins." He had to reflect the world as God made it.

Yet Genesis tells us "God brought the animals to Adam *to see* what he would call them." God did not prescribe one right name, one correct way to describe an animal. He left room for Adam to be creative, both in the features he chose to focus on and in the terms he selected to describe the animal. In this simple paradigm Genesis gives the Biblical basis for all the arts and sciences. On one hand, we root our work in the external world God has created, and, on the other hand, we freely exercise the creativity and imagination He has given us.

Redeeming Mathematics

If the history of mathematics reveals anything, it is the crucial role that the Christian faith has played, and must play, in the world of science and scholarship. The history of mathematics was decisively shaped by its interaction with Christianity. This is not to assert that the early mathematicians were evangelicals in the modern sense of the term. Yet they did assume a broadly Christian worldview—that the world has an ordered structure because God made it; that humans made in God's image can decipher that order; that in studying the creation, we honor its Creator. The notebooks of such giants as Copernicus, Kepler, and Newton overflow with praises to God for His orderly creation.

Yet alien Pythagorean elements were also at work that eventually elevated mathematics into an idol. Inevitably the idol fell, and today mathematics is no longer regarded as a means of discovering truth about the world. Instead, it has been reduced to a product of human convenience. Pure mathematicians view it as a merely formal system analogous to a game, solving its own internal puzzles. Applied mathematicians treat it as a pragmatic tool of science and engineering

Here Christians can have a redemptive impact on mathematics. The Biblical concept of contingent order (see chapter 4) implies that the created world does have an order, a structure, that can be known mathematically. Mathematics does give truth. But it is not a closed or autonomous order independent of God. It is contingent and open. Hence Christianity can restore to mathematics its proper dignity—not as an autonomous and apodictic source of truth but as a reliable means of gaining knowledge and working creatively in the world God has made.

PART FOUR

THE SECOND SCIENTIFIC REVOLUTION

IS EVERYTHING RELATIVE?
The Revolution in Physics

The modern world began on 29 May 1919." With these words historian Paul Johnson opens his massive historical volume *Modern
Times*. On that day photographs of a solar eclipse showed that starlight
is not straight but bends when it passes close to the sun. The photographs were interpreted as confirmation of Albert Einstein's concept
of curved space, and thereby of his general theory of relativity.

Riding on widespread publicity about the eclipse, Einstein's theory hit the intellectual world like a thunderclap. It was the first time in
nearly 300 years, explains physicist and philosopher Alfred North
Whitehead, that Newtonian physics was effectively challenged.

Scientists were not alone in sensing the immense significance of
Einstein's theory. The great mass of ordinary people were also profoundly affected. Few had any clear idea of the scientific content of relativity theory, but the term itself struck a responsive chord in a society
already leaning toward relativism—already questioning traditional
certitudes. If Einstein's theory rejected Newtonian concepts of absolute
time and space, what did that imply about absolutes in morality and
metaphysics? As Johnson explains:

> Mistakenly but perhaps inevitably, relativity became confused with
> relativism. . . . It formed a knife . . . to help cut society adrift from
> its traditional moorings in the faith and morals of Judeo-Christian
> culture.[1]

No one was more distressed by this public misapprehension than
Einstein himself, Johnson remarks. Einstein did not discard absolutes

in science; as we shall see in this chapter, he merely replaced Newtonian metaphysical absolutes (time and space) with a material absolute (the velocity of light).

But what exactly does that mean? That's the question we will consider in this chapter. Our purpose is not to give a comprehensive description of relativity theory; several good popular expositions are available. We will include only enough science to clarify the theory's philosophical implications and their relevance for Christian faith.

EINSTEIN'S SPECIAL THEORY OF RELATIVITY

Many popularizations of Einstein's work highlight the bizarre consequences of his theories—clocks that slow down, measuring rods that shrink, light rays that bend. Though that approach may be dramatic, it entertains more than it instructs. Our interest here is to elucidate Einstein's reasoning and to trace the impact the theory of relativity has had on philosophy and culture.[2]

The central effect of Einstein's theory was to make time and space relative. What does that mean? Imagine yourself sitting in a subway train, looking across the tracks at another train, when yours begins to move. But wait—is it really your train moving? Or is it the other one? If the train accelerates gently enough, you may not be sure for a moment.

Nor can you answer the question simply by looking at the trains themselves. By looking across at the other train, all you can determine is that they are moving relative to each other (relative motion). To determine which train is "really" moving, you have to look at the station platform. The train that's "really" moving is the one leaving the station.

Yet, as Einstein might point out, the station itself is also moving. It's anchored to the earth, to be sure, but remember that the earth is moving relative to the sun. And the sun is moving relative to the Milky Way galaxy. And the galaxy is moving relative to the so-called fixed stars (though they are not really fixed either). In short, all motion is relative to some other reference point. Where is a frame of reference that is absolutely at rest?

There is none, Einstein said.

To make the point clearer, consider another scenario. Imagine that you are flying in a spaceship out in empty space, and you see another spaceship approaching. But wait—is it really approaching you or are *you* approaching *it?* Given that both ships are in uniform motion, you cannot answer that question. (Uniform motion is a technical term meaning motion in a straight line with constant speed.) You can observe that the distance between the two spaceships is decreasing, but you cannot tell whether only one ship is moving or if they both are. There is no celestial subway platform to use as a reference point. Is there any frame of reference that allows us to determine absolute as opposed to merely relative motion? Newton said yes. He taught that space itself is an absolute frame of reference. Space is the "subway station" within which all motion takes place—a stationary frame of reference within which all bodies are either moving or at rest.

Absolute time was also an absolute frame of reference for Newton—a smooth, never-ending flow within which all motion takes place temporally. In his own words:

> Absolute space remains, according to its nature and without relation to an external object, always constant and fixed.
>
> Absolute, true, mathematical time passes continually, and by virtue of its nature flows uniformly and without regard to any external object whatsoever.

For Newton, as we saw in chapter 4, these were quasi-religious concepts. Absolute space represented God's omnipresence, the extension of His being. Absolute time represented God's eternity, the duration of His being. Everything in creation quite literally lives and moves in Him.

But after Newton, his theological interpretations were dropped and absolute space and time became strictly metaphysical concepts. Einstein rejected them altogether. There is no cosmic "subway station" or frame of reference, Einstein said, allowing us to determine whether a body is moving or at rest in an absolute sense. Neither is there absolute time, as though somewhere out in space a cosmic clock were inexorably ticking away. For Einstein, space and time are both relative.

How did Einstein come to his ideas? As we mentioned earlier, he replaced the Newtonian absolutes of space and time with a new absolute—the velocity of light. This is crucial for understanding relativity theory. The starting point of Einstein's theory is that the velocity of light remains the same in every reference frame. Everything else flows axiomatically from this basic principle.

Michelson and Morley

The story of relativity begins with the development of electromagnetic theory by great scientists such as Michael Faraday (1791-1867), James Clerk Maxwell (1831-1879), and Heinrich Hertz (1857-1894). Maxwell discovered that light is a form of electromagnetism. But no one could figure out how electromagnetic phenomena travel from place to place. It was assumed that they need some sort of material medium.

Consider sound waves. They travel through air or water or some other medium. Where there is no medium—for example, in a vacuum—there is no sound. Before Einstein, light was likewise thought to be a wave; scientists assumed that it, too, must travel via some material medium. But what sort of medium? No one had ever detected it, so its presence remained hypothetical. Yet scientists were so confident that it must exist that they even gave it a name—"ether" because it was so ethereal—and advanced all sorts of hypothetical descriptions of it.

Ether was presumed to fill the universe, even penetrating the empty spaces within matter. It became in essence a material basis for the concept of absolute space. It was the one thing that remained fixed in the universe—a motionless background against which the stars and planets move.

Yet the ether theory suffered from severe difficulties. Besides the difficulty of detecting it, the properties assigned to it were exceedingly complex. It was said to be all-pervasive, frictionless, transparent, incompressible, and of uniform density. It was extremely difficult to explain in mechanical terms how any substance could exhibit such diverse properties. Indeed, some were contradictory. On one hand, ether had to be completely permeable to material objects. On the other hand, it had to be infinitely rigid in order to support straight light rays.

In 1887 two Americans, Albert Michelson and Edward Morley, ran what is considered by most scientists the crucial experiment on ether. They reasoned this way: If the earth is moving through the ether, that motion ought to be detectable in the form of an ether "wind," just as the air surrounding a moving car can be detected by sticking a hand out the window and feeling the wind. The "hand" in the Michelson-Morley experiment was a beam of light. Two beams of light, to be precise, beamed in directions perpendicular to one another. The beam that ran against the ether wind should slow down (show an ether "drag") compared to the other.

But when Michelson and Morley ran the experiment, they were dumbfounded by the results. The two light beams traveled at exactly the same speed. Neither showed any of the expected "drag." Regardless of the direction the beams traveled, regardless of the direction from which they were viewed, they always moved at exactly the velocity of light—neither more nor less.[3]

Scientists were puzzled; but Einstein drew a dramatic conclusion. Adopting the empiricist principle that what cannot be detected cannot be said to exist, Einstein decided there *is* no ether. Light needs no medium, he declared; space itself has the property of transmitting light. And since the ether had become closely associated with absolute space, rejecting its existence seemed to entail the rejection of absolute space as well. All space is relative, Einstein said; there is no absolute frame of reference. In fact, "space" is just a way of talking about the relative distances between bodies.

Galileo's Theory of Relativity

Einstein's special theory of relativity goes beyond the denial of absolute space, however. To understand its full meaning, we have to dip back into history and look at an earlier principle of relativity, first propounded by Galileo and Newton.

The earlier principle was devised to support the Copernican theory of the planetary system. One of the common-sense objections raised against heliocentrism was borrowed from the ancient Greeks. Aristotle had once argued that if the earth is moving, then an object thrown straight up into the air should fall back down slightly to one side (since during its time in the air, the earth would have moved slightly). Since that does not happen, Aristotle argued, the earth cannot be moving.

In Galileo's day, opponents of Copernican theory revived Aristotle's argument and restated it in a more elaborate form. If the earth is moving, they said, then we must add its movement to all calculations of motion. To be precise, if the earth is moving through space at about twenty miles per second, then to make our physics work, we should have to add twenty miles per second to our calculations every time an object moves in the same direction as the earth's orbit. By the same token, we should subtract the same amount every time an object moves in the opposite direction.

Galileo responded by developing a principle of relativity. Imagine, he said, a boat sailing on a calm sea along a straight course at a constant speed (uniform motion). Now imagine that a member of the crew facing the bow takes a ball and throws it into the air. Since the boat is moving forward, if Aristotle is right, the ball should fall slightly behind the man. But the fact is that the ball falls right back into the man's hands—just as it would if the boat were standing still.

Galileo concluded that as long as the boat is in uniform motion, the laws of physics have precisely the same effects as they have when the boat is standing still. There is no way a person can throw balls or do any other experiment on the boat to prove that it is moving, since all the results are the same as though the boat were stationary. (The only way to prove the boat is moving is by looking *outside*, at the water or the shoreline.)

In Copernican theory, the earth flying through space is analogous to the boat. The Galilean principle of relativity says the laws of physics have precisely the same effects on the earth orbiting the sun as they would if the earth were stationary. This is why we do not have to add the movement of the earth to all our calculations of motion. This is why a ball thrown into the air will land back in our hands—just as it does for the crewman on Galileo's boat. None of our physics is affected in any way by the movement of the earth. All our results are the same as though the earth were stationary.[4]

To understand why Galileo's principle of relativity works, we have to understand the concept of inertia. Inertia is defined as the way an object behaves when no external forces are acting upon it. Aristotle taught that the natural state of an object is to be at rest. After all, a ball rolling along the ground eventually stops; an arrow flying through the air eventually slows down and falls.

But Galileo realized that these everyday examples are complicated by a multitude of forces at work. The ball slows down because of friction, the arrow because of air resistance. So Galileo imagined an idealized situation where all these forces are eliminated. He discovered that there are actually two states of inertia—rest *and* uniform motion.

Imagine idealized billiard balls floating in abstract space. If a ball is at rest, and no external force acts on it, will it start moving on its own? Of course not. It will remain at rest. If a ball is in motion and there is no friction or air resistance to slow it down, will it stop? No, it will keep moving forever. Both rest and motion are inertia states.

As a consequence, the same laws of physics apply to both. When Galileo's boat is tied up at the quay, it is an inertial system. When the boat is in uniform motion, it is an inertial system. Therefore, in both cases physical laws have the same effects. If a ball tossed into the air falls back into the crew member's hands when the boat is tied up at the quay, then it will do precisely the same when the boat is moving uniformly through the water.

Point of View

But it is a different story entirely for a person standing on the shore. When the boat is tied up at the quay, a shore-bound observer sees the ball rise and fall back down in a straight line. But when the boat is moving, he sees the ball trace a parabola in the air. That's because while the ball is in the air, the boat advances a bit, which means in order to fall back into the crewman's hand, the ball has to advance a bit as well.

This appears to be a contradiction. If the crewman sees the ball travel straight up and down, but a shore-bound observer sees the ball's path curve forward in a parabola, who sees it correctly? In one inertial frame of reference (the moving boat), the ball appears to move one way; in another inertial frame of reference (the stationary spot on the shore), it appears to move another way. How does the ball "really" travel? Whose perspective is right?

Both perspectives are right, according to relativity theory. All inertial frames of reference are equivalent. If we wish to *demonstrate* their equivalence, all we have to do is transform one into the other by either adding in or subtracting out the velocity of the moving frame of reference. If the shore-bound observer wants to find out what the path of the ball looks like to the crew member, he determines the velocity of the boat and *subtracts* that figure from his calculations. If the crewman wants to know what the path of the ball looks like from the shore, he *adds* the velocity of the boat to his calculations.

Let's make this simpler. Picture yourself climbing first a stairway and then an escalator while another person clocks you from the ground. You start by walking up the stairs at a rate of, say, two miles per hour. Naturally, the observer on the ground clocks you at two miles per hour as well. But now you step onto the escalator. Again, you walk at a rate of two miles per hour. But this time the stairs themselves are moving at a rate of three miles per hour. Hence the observer clocks your advance at a rate of five miles per hour.

Other examples: If a ship sails fifty miles per hour, and you walk along the deck at five miles per hour, a person watching from the shore sees you advance at a rate of fifty-five miles per hour. If a jet flies 600 miles per hour, and you walk down the aisle at three miles per hour, then relative to a person standing still on the ground below, you are moving at a rate of 603 miles per hour.

This is called the law of addition of velocities. The velocity observed from the stationary frame of reference (V) is the sum of the velocity of the moving frame of reference (v_1) plus the movement of the object within it (v_2).

$$V = v_1 + v_2$$

The law of addition of velocities provides a means of transforming motion calculations from one reference frame to another. The Galilean principle of relativity explains how people in different frames of reference can have different observations and yet both be right. By a simple set of calculations, we can transform one set of observations into the other—thereby explaining both observations by the same physical laws.

Was Galileo Wrong?

With this background, we are ready to tackle Einstein's special theory of relativity. Einstein was interested in the velocity of electromagnetic phenomena, especially light. But he ran up against a paradox. James Maxwell's equations on wave mechanics showed that the velocity of waves depends only on the medium, not on whether the source is moving. For example, the sound waves from a train whistle take the same time to reach a listener on the ground whether the train is traveling quickly or slowly or not at all.[5]

Maxwell's equations predicted the same results for light. The velocity of light is 186,000 miles per second, or c. In a vacuum, the velocity should remain the same regardless of how the source of light is moving. (The vacuum is required because light slows down when it passes through a medium like water or air, although in air it slows down so little that we can ignore the difference in our discussion here.) If we replace the train whistle of our earlier illustration with a headlight, the light beam will take the same time to reach an observer on the ground whether the train (the light source) is moving quickly or slowly or not at all.

Given Maxwell's equations, however, we run into a serious contradiction with the law of addition of velocities. Consider what happens when the train is stopped and the engineer switches on the headlight. He should see the tip of the light beam move with velocity c. (We're imagining, of course, that someone could actually see something move that quickly.) Now consider what happens when the train is speeding along the track in uniform motion. If the engineer switches on the headlight now, he should still see the tip of the light beam move with velocity c, just as he did when the train was at rest. This is Galileo's principle of relativity: A person in a uniformly moving frame of reference will see things exactly the same as he would in a stationary frame of reference.

An outside observer, however—say, someone watching from the train station—should see something different. According to the law of addition of velocities ($V = v_1 + v_2$), when the train is speeding down the track, he sees the light move with velocity c (v_1) plus the speed of the train (v_2). If the train is going 100 miles per hour, the observer at the station should see the light from the headlight move with velocity c + 100 miles per hour.

But this contradicts Maxwell's equations, which tell us that light will reach an outside observer at the same speed whether the train (the light source) is moving quickly or slowly or not at all. In other words, the station-based observer should still see the light from the headlight move with velocity c, unaffected by the speed of the train, because a speed of c + 100 miles per hour violates Maxwell's equations.

In short, the law of addition of velocities—the transformation law that lay at the heart of Galileo's relativity theory—contradicts Maxwell's equations. This is the paradox Einstein set out to solve. Could he find a way to reconcile Maxwell's equations with Galileo's theory of relativity?

When Time Slows Down

Einstein began with the formula used in classical physics for calculating velocity—distance divided by time ($V = d/t$). We all work calculations of this sort when we take a trip. If we drive 120 miles in two hours, we know our velocity is 120/2, or sixty miles an hour.

In the case of light, however, this simple formula appears not to work. Go back to the train and this time we'll stay with our outside observer and give him a stopwatch with a specified time (t). If the train is at rest and the engineer turns on the headlight, the observer sees a light beam rushing along with velocity c. Substituting c for V in our formula, we have $c = d/t$ (light covers a given distance, d, within a certain length of time, t).

Now consider what happens when the train is moving at 100 miles per hour. This time when the engineer turns on the headlight and the station-based observer clicks his stopwatch, the light beam covers a *greater* distance within the *same* length of time, since the velocity of the train gives the light beam an additional momentum of 100 miles per hour.

Using the formula $c = d/t$, our time (t) is the same but the distance (d) is greater. Under ordinary circumstances, that would mean the velocity (V) changes. But according to Maxwell's equations, we are not allowed to change c, because the speed of light is unaffected by the speed of its source. Mathematically, there is only one possible solution: change t. Time has to run differently in the moving train relative to the observer on the ground. It has to run more slowly.

This is Einstein's concept of time dilation.

Popular books on relativity theory often illustrate time dilation with highly counter-intuitive stories, such as the Twin Paradox. One twin goes up in a spacecraft while the other stays on earth. When the earth-bound twin is an old man, the twin in the spacecraft is still a child. But these strange stories do little to clarify Einstein's reasoning. The theory of relativity results from a purely logical deduction. If the velocity of light is a universal constant, then when d changes, t has to change. It is strictly mathematical.

Time dilation is not merely a logical concept, however. Attempts have been made to confirm it experimentally as well. The change in time is extremely small, much too small to be noticed in ordinary activities. Only if our train were to approach the speed of light would any significant time dilation occur. In experimental tests involving rocket-borne clocks, they appear to run slightly more slowly than their earth-bound counterparts. And in high-speed particle accelerators, moving particles last slightly longer than their stationary counterparts before decaying. Most physicists today accept these as experimental support for Einstein's theory of time dilation.

A common-sense analogy that helps illustrate time dilation is visual perspective. If Jack stands beside me and then walks away, he appears to grow smaller. Of course, we don't believe he actually grows smaller as he walks away. We assume that immediate proximity is the "privileged perspective"—that it gives us Jack's true size—and that his apparently smaller size at fifty yards away is a function of the visual perception of distance.

But in relativity theory there is no privileged perspective. Every inertial reference frame is created equal. If we were to apply relativity theory to visual perspective, we would say that when Jack is standing fifty yards away he *really is* smaller—in that frame of reference. There is no privileged perspective that gives us his "true" size to use as a basis for comparison; every frame of reference has its own scale of size. Similarly, in Einstein's theory of time dilation, there is no framework giving us the "real" time to set our clocks by; every reference frame has its own time.

But by the same token (and here's where the theory really gets strange) *we* are really smaller from *Jack's* frame of reference as well. Each person is smaller from the other person's perspective. In my frame of reference I'm still my normal size, but when Jack is standing fifty yards away, in his frame of reference I stand about two feet tall. Like Jack, I have no "real" height. I have one height in my frame of reference and a completely different height in Jack's.

It may sound like an Alice-in-Wonderland world. But in principle it is no different from Galileo's initial insight centuries ago. A ball tossed into the air from the deck of a boat appears to the crewman to travel straight up and down, but to a shore-based observer it appears to travel in a parabola. Who is right? Both are. By the law of addition of velocities we can demonstrate that the two perspectives are equivalent.

When I walk up the escalator, am I "really" moving at two miles per hour or five miles per hour? Both, of course—depending on whether my speed is measured relative to the escalator itself or relative to the ground. When I walk down the aisle of a jet, am I "really" moving three miles per hour or 603 miles per hour? Both—depending on whether my speed is measured relative to the jet or relative to the ground. Once we take the different frames of reference into account, the two perspectives are equivalent. What Einstein did was to make time itself relative to the frame of reference.

Nothing Faster Than Light

Several other strange consequences flow from the special theory of relativity. Yet all are direct mathematical consequences of the basic assumption that the velocity of light is constant.

For example, Einstein's theory leads to the rule that nothing can move faster than the speed of light. If you are in a moving vehicle, the closer your speedometer approaches the velocity of light, the less quickly you will accelerate.

At first sight, this rule strikes us as arbitrary. Why should there be any limit on how fast a body can move? To understand Einstein's calculations, let's return again to the example of the jet. Relative to a person standing on the ground, I advance at a rate of 603 miles per hour ($V = v_1 + v_2$). But according to Einstein's relativity theory, this law, taken from classical mechanics, is not quite accurate. Remember that the frame of reference in the jet is subject to time dilation. That is, time slows down relative to an outside observer. Taking this into account, Einstein calculated a new transformation law which changed $v_1 + v_2$ into

$$\frac{v_1 + v_2}{1 + \dfrac{v_1 \times v_2}{c^2}}$$

Now, c is a large number. The velocity of light in a vacuum is 186,000 miles per second. As a result, the fraction in the denominator is ordinarily very small, which means the deviation from $v_1 + v_2$ is very slight. The deviation becomes significant only at speeds approaching the speed of light.

We are now ready to tackle the question of acceleration. Plugging in values for v_1 and v_2, we discover that as the numbers increase, the combined velocity increases by smaller and smaller amounts. Let's be really extravagant and say our jet is so speedy it has reached the velocity of light itself. And let's say I tear down the aisle likewise at the velocity of light. The total speed relative to the ground is $v_1 + v_2$, which in this case is $c + c$, or $2c$, twice the speed of light. Right?

Wrong. Plug those values into Einstein's revised formula. The numerator is $2c$, and the complete formula looks like this:

$$\frac{2c}{1 + \dfrac{c^2}{c^2}}$$

Which equals

$$\frac{2c}{2}$$

Which equals c. So when jet and passenger both move at the speed of light, the combined speed is still c. Conclusion: If Einstein's formula for time dilation is correct, nothing can travel faster than the speed of light.[6]

Mass Gets More Massive

Another unexpected consequence of relativity theory is that as things move faster, they acquire more mass. This seems an odd consequence to follow simply from moving faster. But again it follows mathematically from relativity theory. We simply plug Einstein's modifications into the formulas from classical physics.

The operational definition of inertial mass is how much force is required to get an object to accelerate—or, conversely, how much an object resists being accelerated. Newton defined the relationship between force and acceleration in the formula $F = ma$ (force equals mass times acceleration), which can be restated to find either acceleration ($a = F/m$) or mass ($m = F/a$).

Apply this formula to an electron. When the electron is at rest and then accelerates, its acceleration can be calculated using Newton's formula: $a = F/m$. But what happens when the electron is already moving and we want to accelerate it still further? Moving frames of reference require us to take relativity into account, so Einstein modified Newton's formula to get:

$$a = \frac{F}{m} \left(1 - \frac{v^2}{c^2} \right)^{\frac{3}{2}}$$

Let's be really extravagant again and say the electron is already moving with the speed of light, so that $v = c$. What happens if we attempt to accelerate it still further? If $v = c$, then the formula inside the parentheses is 1 - 1, which is 0. Anything times 0 equals 0, so $a = 0$. In other words, you cannot accelerate the electron. If it is moving with the velocity of light, you cannot accelerate it any further. Even if you keep on pushing, the electron will not pick up any more speed.

Since the definition of inertial mass is how much a body resists being accelerated, then the closer an electron approaches the velocity of light, the more its mass increases (the more it resists being further accelerated). We should not think of electrons actually growing in size, however. The principle merely means it becomes harder and harder to increase their speed. This has been tested in high-speed accelerators where physicists have found experimentally that the faster a particle is accelerated, the greater the force needed to increase its acceleration.

Mass-Energy Conversion

We now come to the most famous conclusion from Einstein's special theory of relativity. We have just said that the faster a particle moves, the more force is required to accelerate it. Why is that? The moving particle hasn't had anything added to it to make it bigger or heavier. The only thing that distinguishes a moving particle from a stationary particle is its movement. Or, we could say, its energy—since movement means the particle has kinetic energy. The more kinetic energy a particle has, the harder it is to accelerate.

We already know from experience and classical physics that the more *mass* a body has, the more force is required to accelerate it. Now we learn that the more *energy* a body has, the more force is required to accelerate it. A natural conclusion might be that mass and energy are equivalent in some way. And that's exactly what Einstein did conclude. He decided that energy has mass, just as matter does.

Moreover, he confirmed the conclusion mathematically by working from the opposite direction—by proving that mass has energy. Using relativity theory, he modified a few Newtonian formulas to get E (the energy of the moving particle) equal to W (Newton's symbol for work done) plus mc^2, or $E = W + mc^2$. If the particle is at rest—that is, if there is no work done on the particle and hence $W = 0$—then the formula becomes $E = mc^2$. Which means that even at rest a particle still has energy equal to mc^2.

This is, of course, Einstein's famous equation for the conversion of mass to energy and vice versa. He summarized it by saying, "Energy has mass and mass represents energy."[7]

Why Light Bends

This leads us to our final conclusion from relativity theory. A beam of light has energy and, as we have just discovered, energy has mass. Mass, we know, is affected by a gravitational field. Logically, then, light should likewise be affected by a gravitational field.[8]

This was the prediction so spectacularly confirmed in 1919— described at the outset of this chapter. During the eclipse (when remote stars can be seen more easily), one of the fixed stars aligned with the edge of the sun appeared to be slightly displaced. This was interpreted to mean the starlight bent slightly as it passed through the sun's gravitational field (see Fig. 1 on page 178).

Of course, if light is subject to gravity, then so is the rest of the electromagnetic spectrum. In the 1970s, the Viking landing on Mars gave further support to Einstein's theory by showing that the sun's gravitational field bent radio waves sent from Mars to the earth.

What is fascinating about relativity theory is that all these strange

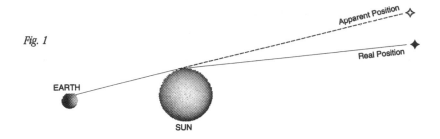

Fig. 1

and unexpected consequences flow from simple mathematical deductions. Once Einstein had derived the formulas needed to reconcile Galileo's law of addition of velocities with Maxwell's equations for wave mechanics, all he did was modify the formulas from classical physics. Despite the counter-intuitive results—time slowing down, mass increasing, and length contracting (a consequence not discussed here)—the mathematical calculations involved are simple and elegant. Once Einstein determined what it means to say that light is a universal constant, everything else in relativity theory is derived by pure mathematical deduction.

GENERAL THEORY OF RELATIVITY

Einstein's special theory of relativity showed that time and space are relative to the observer's frame of reference, which destroyed the concept of absolute time and space. Or rather, it nearly did. There was still one cogent argument against a completely relativistic account of space—an argument Einstein knew he had to answer. And in the process he developed his general theory of relativity.

Most popular books on Einstein dazzle readers with accounts of curved space and elevators flying through space but leave them wondering about the point of it all. Why did Einstein come up with such strange ideas? What questions was he trying to answer?

To understand what drove Einstein, we have to recreate the scientific context of his work. The question whether motion is absolute or only relative was not new in his day. Newton himself had debated the question with his contemporary, the philosopher and mathematician Gottfried Wilhelm Leibniz. Leibniz had argued, as Einstein did, that all motion is relative. When two bodies are in uniform motion relative to one another, he said, there is no observation capable of distinguishing which is "really" in motion. Think back to our earlier example of two spaceships in empty space. Merely by observing two bodies coming closer together or flying farther apart with no external reference point, we cannot tell which one is moving or whether both are.

Newton agreed with Leibniz to a point, but he added an important qualification. If we limit ourselves to considering motion kinematically—that is, if we regard it merely as a change of place—then motion is indeed entirely relative. But, Newton pointed out, as soon as we ask what the causes of motion are, what the active forces at work are, the picture changes completely. If we regard motion dynamically— that is, from the standpoint of the theory of forces—the relativity of motion becomes untenable.

Forces come into play when either one of our spaceships makes a *change* in speed or direction (in physics both are called acceleration). In technical language, inertia is the state of an object when no external forces act on it; acceleration is what happens when an external force *does* act on it.

And acceleration is something we can detect—through the existence of a counterforce, a force in the opposite direction. Think of a few familiar examples. If you are in a car and the driver speeds up suddenly, you are thrown backward. If the driver veers to the left, you are thrown to the right. If he turns around quickly, you are thrown toward the outside by centrifugal force. This, Newton said, gives us the tool we need to recognize absolute motion. We can detect changes in motion—acceleration—through the effects of a counterforce. And we can detect an inertial state through the absence of any counterforce.

Einstein's special theory of relativity applies only to inertial states—to uniform motion. But before he could fully establish relativity theory, he knew he had to extend it to accelerated motion as well. He had to respond to Newton's argument. Since the argument rests on the action of forces, Einstein's goal was to relativize the concept of force. He sought to show that forces are not absolute quantities but depend upon the frame of reference—in which case, they too are relative.

One of the most important forces in the universe is gravity. Newton's theory of gravity gave the Copernican system a dynamic foundation and explained the planetary orbits. So to relativize the concept of force, Einstein focused on gravity.

He began by looking for something besides gravity capable of creating the same effects. If there is some other phenomenon capable of producing the same effects, then our choice of *which* force to invoke depends upon the frame of reference we choose—which means the force has been relativized.

The alternative force Einstein identified was acceleration. Imagine you are in a spaceship accelerating at exactly one "G," the equivalent of the earth's gravity. Would you know from inside that you are in space instead of on earth? If the spaceship had windows, of course, you could look out and see, but we will stipulate that it has none. Can you tell simply from the effects within the spaceship where you are?

The answer is no. As long as the spaceship is accelerating uniformly, you can walk around just as though you were on earth—not because gravity pulls your feet down against the floor but because the floor pushes up against your feet due to acceleration. If you drop a ball, it falls to the floor—not because gravity pulls it down but because the floor accelerates up to meet it. As long as acceleration is uniform, its effects are indistinguishable from the effects of gravity.

Einstein concluded that acceleration and gravity are equivalent—that there is no possible experiment capable of distinguishing between them. In short, he had succeeded in relativizing them, making them depend upon our choice of a reference frame. We can choose to conceive of the downward force felt within the spaceship either as a result of acceleration or of gravity.[9] In his general theory of relativity, Einstein asserted the complete relativity of motion, along with space and time.

Curved Space

But Einstein didn't stop there. He went on to declare that gravity does not even exist, that it is a fictitious force. As an alternative he postulated that mass has the property of bending the space in its vicinity so that objects close by are accelerated.

As an illustration, imagine a pool table with a thin rubber sheet stretched across the top. If you place a bowling ball in the center, the sheet will sag under it. If you then try to roll a marble past the bowling ball, its path will be deflected, and it will roll toward the ball.

In an analogous way, a large object like the sun is said to warp or bend the fabric of space around it. The planets move around inside this space the way a marble can be made to roll around the inside of a large bowl. According to Einstein, there is no such thing as gravity in the sense of an invisible force emanating from masses and pulling on other masses. Instead, a mass warps the surrounding space, which deflects the paths of other masses. An object in free fall truly *is* free, in the sense that no forces are acting upon it; the direction of its fall derives from the structure of the surrounding space.

This, then, was Einstein's answer to Newton. Not only did he relativize the force of gravity, he went further and announced its complete demise. And he radically changed the concept of space. No longer is space an empty stage upon which the events of the universe take place; instead it affects those events. In the vicinity of a large mass, space has a topography, a structure, that influences celestial bodies in their choice of routes. Astronomer Eric Chaisson explains:

> Just as a pinball cannot traverse a straight path once shot along the side of a bowl, so the shape of space causes objects to follow curved paths (called geodesics).[10]

This conception of gravity is similar to a magnetic field. Just as a magnet creates certain physical conditions in the space around it, so a mass creates a physical condition called gravity in the space around it. And just as the structure of the magnetic field guides the movement of a piece of iron in the field, so the geometry of a gravitational field determines the path of any body in that field.[11]

Interestingly, Einstein's theory of relativity has very limited impact experimentally. Its empirical effects are restricted to the realms of the superfast and the superlarge. Everywhere else—which includes virtually all our normal activities—its effects dovetail with those predicted by classical physics. What attracts scientists to relativity, therefore, is not a superior fit with the facts so much as its mathematical elegance and conceptual simplicity.

IS EVERYTHING RELATIVE?

The reception of Einstein's theory of relativity has been almost universally positive. While most scientific theories have both supporters and detractors, one searches virtually in vain for critics of Einstein's theory. Only a few scientists of high academic standing have been willing to express criticism, at least publicly.[12]

Einstein's best-known critic was perhaps the late Herbert Dingle, a distinguished physicist and originally an enthusiastic proponent of relativity. Later he came to regard the theory as logically flawed on several counts. Take, for example, the idea of time dilation. The theory requires, Dingle says, that if two persons travel at different speeds, then for the faster-moving one time will slow down, and he will age more slowly. Yet since all motion is relative, either person may be held to be moving faster. "Hence, unless the theory specifies some distinguishing mark," Dingle writes, "it requires each to age more slowly than the other," a logical contradiction.[13] Yet most physicists remain unmoved by Dingle's objections.

If we are hard-pressed to find critics of relativity among scientists, it is even more difficult to find them outside science. When Einstein's theories first gained public attention immediately after World War I, enthusiasm was enormous. As physicist P. A. M. Dirac explains, "People wanted to get away from thinking about the awful war that

had just passed. They wanted something new. And that is when relativity burst upon us. . . . It aroused interest and excitement in everyone."[14]

Artists and poets eagerly picked up the theme. One artist sub-
mitted a draft to Einstein on "Cubism and the Theory of Relativity,"
claiming that cubism, like relativity, makes allowance for the "simul-
taneity of several views." Einstein wrote back that the artist had misunderstood his theory. But his words did not dampen the artist's
enthusiasm, or that of others who continued to experiment with mul-
tiple viewpoints.[15]

Poets such as William Carlos Williams, Robert Frost, Archibald
MacLeish, e. e. cummings, Ezra Pound, and T. S. Eliot all talked about
relativity in their literary works or tried to translate it into artistic
styles. Williams, for example, adopted a new variable measure for his
poems, calling it "a *relatively* stable foot, not a rigid one," which influenced other poets considerably. One novelist wrote that "the Relativity
proposition was directly responsible for abstract painting, atonal
music, and formless . . . literature."[16] An overstatement, no doubt; but
it does suggest the pervasive influence of Einstein's theory.

The general public interpreted relativity as support for the pes-
simism and relativism that permeated Western culture after the first
world war. Newspapers and magazines carried a continual stream of
popular expositions of Einstein's theories, expositions that contained
very little physics and quite a lot of philosophy—mostly a denuncia-
tion of "absolutism."[17] In 1919 the London *Times* carried an article
that concluded:

> It is confidently believed by the greatest experts that enough has
> been done to overthrow the certainty of ages, and to require a new
> philosophy, a philosophy that will sweep away nearly all that has
> been hitherto accepted as the axiomatic basis of physical thought.

A little later the same paper assured readers that the kernel of this new
philosophy was relativism: "Here and there, past and present, are relative, not absolute, and change according to the ordinates and coor-
dinates selected." The *New York Times* wondered, tongue in cheek,
whether even the multiplication tables would be safe any more.[18] As
Loren Graham explains, "the theory of relativity was seen by many
laypeople as the denial of absolute standards and values." For if time
and space themselves flex and change, how could one hold to any "reliable standards"?[19]

Since calculations in relativity take into account the observer's
frame of reference, the theory appeared to lead to subjectivism.
Ironically, it was precisely those variables that in materialistic philos-

ophy had been regarded as most real—mass and velocity—that in relativity turn out to be dependent on the observer. From the days of Galileo, mass and velocity had been reckoned as primary qualities, objective properties that characterize the object itself and do not depend on the observer (as do secondary qualities, such as taste and smell). But in relativity theory the primary qualities themselves were found to vary according to the frame of reference from which they are viewed.[20]

Einstein himself sought diligently, but alas in vain, to temper some of the radical extensions of his theory. He emphatically denied being a "philosophical relativist," that is, someone who attacks all absolute principles.[21] In fact, he was originally reluctant even to use the term "relativity theory," saying it had given rise to "philosophical misunderstandings." He preferred to call it "invariance theory" because it showed that physical laws do not vary from one reference frame to another—that every observer, no matter where he is in the universe or how fast he is moving, works with the same laws of nature.[22]

Just as Galileo had devised his theory of relativity in order to preserve the classical laws of motion across different reference frames, so Einstein devised his theory of relativity in order to preserve Maxwell's laws of electromagnetism across different reference frames. The only way he saw to keep Maxwell's equations invariant was by supposing that time and space are variant. Getting rid of absolute time and space proved highly unsettling both for science and the wider culture, but the aim was to preserve intact the laws of nature—specifically, the laws of electromagnetism, represented by the velocity of light.

The late evangelist and theologian Francis Schaeffer understood this. Despite the similarity in terms, Schaeffer argued, relativity does not support relativism, since Einstein began with Maxwell's law that "everywhere in the universe light travels at a constant speed in a vacuum."[23]

Now at first sight relativity theory may strike one as a highly uneven exchange. It seems as though we are being asked to give up fundamental metaphysical concepts such as space and time in return for a single, paltry physical fact about the behavior of light under highly specialized conditions. But as we have seen in this chapter, the velocity of light is *not* merely an isolated physical fact. It functions as the cornerstone of Einstein's entire system. Einstein replaced Newton's metaphysical absolutes, his concepts of time and space, with a material absolute, the velocity of light. The speed of light is a property of the material world–a physical quantity that you can measure in any inertial reference frame and get the same answer. Einstein hoped to rebuild physics on the basis of such invariants.

Newton had taught that space and time are absolute, but in that case the velocity of light would have to be relative. So Einstein turned it around: He said the velocity of light is absolute, and space and time intervals are relative. He then derived new transformation laws to replace Galileo's law of addition of velocities, and the rest of relativity theory is a mathematical deduction from those laws.

In fact, Einstein's theory is so strictly deductive that over time it led him away from an empiricist view of science to a highly rationalistic view. Physicist and historian Gerald Holton notes that over his lifetime Einstein moved away from an early empiricism (inspired by Ernst Mach) to a strong emphasis on the mathematical and deductive side of science. Einstein himself writes that during the course of his work he abandoned "skeptical empiricism" and became "a believing rationalist, that is, one who seeks the only trustworthy source of truth in mathematical simplicity."

This strong belief in mathematical truth explains an otherwise puzzling story. Einstein, it seems, was only mildly interested in the eclipse that dazzled the rest of the world and provided such spectacular support for his theory. A few years earlier, he had written a personal letter saying he was "fully satisfied" with his theory of relativity on purely mathematical grounds—so much so, he wrote, that "I do not doubt any more the correctness of the whole system, *may the observation of the eclipse succeed or not.*"[24]

Even when the results of the eclipse were announced, Einstein retained his serenity. A student who was with him that day records that he responded quite calmly to the news, stating he already knew the theory was correct even without this empirical confirmation. The student asked Einstein what he would have done had the results *not* confirmed his prediction. "Then I would have been sorry for the dear Lord," he replied. "The theory *is* correct."[25]

His turn toward rationalism is perhaps best expressed in his religious views. He wrote, "I believe in Spinoza's God, who reveals himself in the orderly harmony of what exists, not in a God who concerns himself with fates and actions of human beings." Baruch Spinoza was a highly rationalistic Jewish philosopher living in Holland in the 1600s, whose philosophy had the axiomatic, deductive structure of Euclidean geometry. For Spinoza, God was not a Being distinct from the universe, a personal Creator who brought the world into existence. Instead, "God" was merely a name for the principle of order within the universe.

Einstein did sometimes speak of God as a distinct Being, yet he made it clear that in his view God was completely bound by rational necessity. Einstein wrote: "God Himself *could not have* arranged those connections [expressed in scientific laws] in any other way than that which factually exists."[26] In other words, God had no choice; the laws of science reveal the only possible way He could create the world.

Few people are aware of Einstein's strong rationalistic tendencies. His rejection of absolute time and space was so revolutionary that many identify him only as the person who turned classical physics upside down. Yet Einstein's physics followed strictly deterministic laws just as Newtonian physics did. Physicist Alan Friedman says, "relativity still describes a completely knowable, causal universe."[27] Theologian E. L. Mascall writes that "the world of Einstein is every bit as deterministic as that of Laplace."[28] Priest and physicist Stanley Jaki says, "Einstein as a theoretical physicist was the most absolutist of them all."[29] Physicist Nick Herbert goes so far as to say that "Einstein's theory does not challenge classical physics but completes it."[30] And J. C. Polkinghorne, a Christian physicist, writes that Einstein's work

> is the last great flowering of the classic tradition in physics. It preserved the clarity of description and the inexorable determinism which had been the hallmarks of mechanics since Newton.[31]

In short, Einstein's theory of relativity is simple, elegant, and mathematically consistent. The real overthrow of classical physics came immediately after Einstein—with the rise of quantum mechanics. And that is the subject we turn to next.

QUANTUM MYSTERIES:
Making Sense of the New Physics

Several years ago a new magazine appeared on the shelves of health food stores, titled *Creation*. If you flipped the cover open to the statement of purpose, you learned that the magazine was designed to "bring together a rootedness in the Bible with the creation mystics of the West . . . and the wisdom of earth-centered native spiritualities, Green thinking, humanistic psychology, and the new physics."

The new physics? What's *that* doing there, along with the mysticism and the native religions?

The answer is that the new physics (relativity theory and quantum mechanics) is often interpreted as supporting various forms of mysticism. Classical physics was mechanistic—objective, deterministic, and materialistic. But the new physics appears to be subjective, indeterministic, and idealistic (in the philosophical sense of giving primacy to spiritual or mental reality over material reality).[1]

In short, the revolution in physics in the twentieth century created a revolution in worldview, undermining the Newtonian paradigm that had reigned for nearly three centuries. Gone was the image of the universe as a cold, impersonal machine. Gone the image of humans as mere cogs in the mechanism. It was a revolution welcomed by everyone who had chafed under the deterministic model inherited from Newtonian physics. They hailed the new physics as a great emancipator. It seemed to open the door once again to free will and human dignity.

But the revolution also had a disturbing side. Gone as well was the certainty of an objective order in the world. Gone was the confidence in the human ability to discover any coherent truth. British physicist John Gribbin leads off an otherwise sober book about the new physics with a sweeping assertion: "what quantum mechanics says is that nothing is real."[2]

What is it about the new physics that produces such diverse and unsettling claims? On the scientific side, the new physics has uncovered several puzzling phenomena that seem to defy explanation by the laws of classical physics. But what new explanations should be proposed— and, even more intriguing, what philosophical implications should be drawn—are still a matter of debate.

For example, quantum mechanics has revealed a realm of indeterminacy, but what exactly does that mean? Is indeterminacy a statement of human ignorance (we just don't know yet all the laws that govern quantum events)? Or is it an irreducible characteristic of matter? Does indeterminacy provide a "loophole" for human freedom? Or does it reveal mere randomness? Even today, nearly a century after quantum mechanics first appeared, scientists disagree on the answers to these questions.

The most curious feature of quantum mechanics is that it works exceedingly well as a practical and mathematical description of the atomic world, yet it has given rise to a plethora of unresolved disputes over its philosophical interpretation. Physicists harbor no doubt about the usefulness of the mathematical formulas of quantum mechanics, yet they engage in on-going debates about its ontology (what it tells us about the nature of reality).

J. C. Polkinghorne, a physicist-turned-Anglican-priest, says the situation in quantum mechanics is "rather like being shown an impressively beautiful palace and being told that no one is quite sure whether its foundations rest on bedrock or shifting sand."[3] Or as Italian physicist Enrico Fermi used to say when he applied the mathematical formulas of quantum mechanics, "It has no business to fit so well!"[4] In this chapter we describe some of the scientific puzzles raised by quantum mechanics, then trace related philosophical debates that have relevance for the Christian faith.

QUA QUANTUM

The word *quantum* has become familiar to us all. It appears in all kinds of contexts that have nothing to do with physics, from movie titles to car models. Yet the scientific concepts of quantum mechanics are still unfamiliar to most people.

The word *quantum* simply means a discrete unit of something. It entered the vocabulary of physics when German physicist Max Planck (1858-1947) discovered that hot material radiates energy in discrete lumps or packets—which he called quanta. The change in energy is not continuous but discontinuous.

In the world of everyday objects, we see both kinds of change. Continuous changes occur in color, size, weight, temperature, and motion. Discontinuous change includes the increases in height as you go up a flight of stairs, the alterations in pitch as you play a scale on the piano, or the increases in value as you add up money. The unit of change in each of the cases could be called a quantum—a single step up, a single note on the piano, a single cent.

Classical physics assumed that energy varies in a continuous fashion. But Planck made the startling discovery that on the atomic level energy increases or decreases in discrete units—in quanta (measured by Planck's constant or h). Yet classical physics offered no explanation why this should be so. A quantum constitutes a lower limit on how much energy can be exchanged, just as a cent constitutes a lower limit on how much money you can add or subtract. (You cannot calculate with half pennies or quarter pennies). But why would a lower limit exist on quantities of energy?

Consider what happens when you bounce a ball. Depending on how hard you throw it, a ball can bounce up one foot, two feet, three feet, and so on. Now imagine a ball that could bounce up to only certain prescribed heights—one foot or two feet but nothing in between. What force would prevent a ball from bouncing up one and a half feet? No mechanical model can account for it. Yet that is exactly analogous to what happens on the atomic level. Atomic particles have only certain levels of energy and nothing in between.

The existence of quanta gave scientists their first hint that the atomic world is unlike the macroscopic world familiar to us in everyday experience. Newtonian physicists had assumed that atomic particles would follow the same laws as the world of normal experience— that they would behave like microscopic billiard balls. But they do not. As Planck wrote, the quantum

> must play a fundamental role in physics, and proclaim itself as something quite new and hitherto unheard of, forcing us to recast our physical ideas, which, since the foundation of the infinitesimal calculus by Leibnitz and Newton, were built on the assumption of continuity of all causal relations.[5]

The Danish physicist Niels Bohr (1886-1961) made an even sharper break with classical physics when he applied the quantum concept to the structure of the atom. The model of the atom at the time resembled a miniature solar system with electrons circling the nucleus the way the planets circle the sun. But there was a problem with this model. According to Maxwell's equations, the circling electrons should use up energy, their orbits should shrink, and eventually they should fall in on the nucleus. Clearly atoms are much more stable than this model allowed. Otherwise the world would soon cease to exist.

Now, in the presence of a contradiction, scientists may conclude either that the scientific model is wrong or that the relevant scientific laws are wrongly formulated. In normal scientific practice, researchers tend to assume that the laws are pretty well confirmed and that the place to tinker is the model. But Bohr took the other alternative. He entertained the possibility that the laws of classical mechanics are wrong—or at least invalid on the atomic level. He then proposed a model of the atom that defied the requirements of classical physics—one in which electrons move around the nucleus in quantum paths without any loss of energy, gaining or losing energy only when they jump from one path to another (the energy always being in the form of a single quantum).

There was no classical explanation why only certain quantum paths were available and not others in between. Nor was there any cause to account for why or when the electron would jump. Nevertheless, the results of Bohr's model matched experimental results well, and it gained favor rapidly among working physicists. It proved to be the first of several quantum puzzles that seemed to fly in the face of classical physics.

A PARTICLE IS A PARTICLE IS A . . . WAVE?

The second quantum puzzle was defining exactly what an atomic particle is. The question first arose in connection with light: Is light a wave or a stream of particles? The argument has careened back and forth through history.

Isaac Newton treated light as a stream of particles because that model explained certain experimental results. On the other hand, the Dutchman Christian Huygens (1629-1695) and later Thomas Young (1773-1829) treated light as a wave—because that model explained *other* experimental results such as diffraction (the ability of light to bend around corners). When Maxwell derived equations for the transmission of electromagnetic waves (including light), that seemed to clinch the argument in favor of the wave model.

But Einstein revived the particle theory of light to explain the photoelectric effect, in which light behaves as a stream of tiny bullets knocking electrons out of a sheet of metal. Einstein called the particles photons and equated them with Planck's quanta (a photon being a quantum of light). It began to appear that light was somehow *both* a wave *and* a particle—a wave/particle duality.

The French physicist Louis de Broglie (1892-1987) extended the concept of a wave/particle duality from light to all atomic entities. De Broglie reasoned that if light, which appears to be a wave, can act like a stream of particles, then perhaps the reverse is true as well. Perhaps things such as electrons, which appear to be particles, can act like waves. De Broglie's theoretical deduction was later confirmed experimentally. The classic demonstration is an experiment in which a stream of electrons pass through a metal plate containing two thin parallel slits and then smash into a photographic screen on the other side. The resulting zebra-stripe pattern on the screen matches precisely the interference pattern produced by the superposition of two waves.[6] (Figs. 1 and 2)

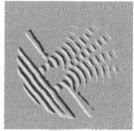

Fig. 1 The left hand illustration shows a water wave spreading out from a single slit while the illustration on the right shows the interference pattern obtained with two slits.

Fig. 2 An experimental observation of the two-slit interference pattern obtained with electrons.

Fig. 3 Details of a double-slit experiment performed with electrons. Interference patterns were once thought of as evidence for wave motion. However, close observation of detail shows that the electrons arrive in individual lumps. In the left illustration so few electrons have arrived that we see an almost random pattern of bits. The illustrations to the right show what happens as the exposure becomes longer: more and more electrons arrive until eventually the familiar interference pattern becomes visible.

The two-slit experiment demonstrates graphically the dual nature of electrons. The electrons hit the photographic screen as individual particles, producing tiny dark spots on the plate like bullet holes in a garage door. Yet the structure they form—the zebra-stripe interference pattern—is characteristic of waves. Why should individual particles travel together as a wave?

What's truly amazing is that the electrons form an interference pattern *even if they are emitted one at a time.* If we narrow the aperture on our experimental apparatus to allow only one electron to emerge at a time and fly toward the photographic screen, they still construct the same pattern—one by one. Inexplicably, the solitary electron flying through the air seems somehow to "know" that it is part of a larger wave pattern.[7] (Fig. 3)

What happens if we use only one slit instead of two? If we block one of the slits in the metal plate, the electrons hit the photographic screen in a single cluster, like a barrage of bullets hitting a target. Again, there is that uncanny sense that the individual electron "knows" something. It "knows" whether a second slit is open (in which case it acts as a wave) or whether only one slit is open (in which case it acts as a particle).[8]

These puzzling characteristics apply not only to electrons but to all atomic entities. All exhibit a dual nature. Under certain experimental conditions they act like particles; under other conditions they act like waves. In 1906 the great physicist J. J. Thomson received the Nobel Prize for establishing experimentally that the electron is an elementary particle; ironically, thirty years later, he saw his son awarded the Nobel Prize for establishing that the electron is a wave.

The wave/particle duality would not be such a problem if it were simply a matter of seeing different parts of a whole—like the blind men and the elephant, where each man touched a different part of the elephant. But the problem is more vexing than that because waves and particles exhibit characteristics that are flat-out contradictory. A wave is continuous and can spread out over an enormous area; a particle is discontinuous and localized, confined to a tiny region. A wave is easily split in an infinite variety of ways, some parts going in one direction, some in another; a particle's travel is confined to a single direction. Two waves can interpenetrate and emerge unchanged; two particles crash together. How can a single entity exhibit all these contradictory attributes?[9]

The answer is, it can't. As physicist Alan Friedman writes, the definitions of wave and particle "are mutually exclusive and do not permit conceiving of a single entity that can have features of both."[10] As a result, when physicists first encountered the paradox, Sir George

Thomson says, "It seemed that Nature was irrational, a curious feeling that those who experienced it will not forget."[11]

Today physicists resolve the paradox by decreeing that an electron (or any other quantum entity) is neither a particle nor a wave but something else entirely—something unknown in itself (like Kant's *Ding an sich*). It exhibits either "particlelike" or "wavelike" features, depending on the conditions. This is the Complementarity Principle proposed by Niels Bohr. It declares that we can say nothing about what the quantum world is like in reality; instead we recognize the validity of alternate and mutually exclusive approaches to it.

It is important to keep in mind—especially as we proceed to some of the strange interpretations of quantum mechanics—that even though we cannot describe the electron in everyday categories without paradoxes, yet mathematically there are no contradictions whatsoever. All physicists agree on the mathematical formalism of quantum mechanics. It provides a unified correlation of a wide range of observations, as well as a method for calculating predictions. What we lack is a unified mental picture of events on the atomic level to explain *why* the mathematical formalism works. Whereas Aristotelian science had its dominant metaphor (the world as an organism), and classical physics its metaphor (the world as a machine), quantum mechanics offers no metaphor, no picturable representation of the atomic world.[12]

This lack of a unifying metaphor has introduced a new vein of subjectivity into physics. Classical physics assumed that there is an objective world which we can observe and measure without essentially changing it. But on the quantum level, it seems impossible to observe reality without changing it. Depending on which experiment the researcher selects, he can make atomic entities exhibit either wavelike or particlelike characteristics. As Friedman puts it, "Entities cannot be said to have particle or wave properties independently of the observations made to measure these properties. Subject and observer are inseparably linked in quantum theory."[13] The classical distinction between subject and object has collapsed. The classical ideal of objectivity is impossible.

Some physicists go even further. If the experiment determines which properties an atomic entity has, they say, then the act of observation has become an act of creation. The observer creates what he observes. In the words of physicist Fritjof Capra: "The electron does not *have* objective properties independent of my mind."[14]

It is easy to see why many interpret quantum mechanics as support for philosophical idealism (which holds that the realm of ideas or mind is the primary reality). Capra goes so far as to claim that modern physics supports the mystical worldview of Eastern religion, which treats the material world as a creation of consciousness. But before we delve further into such philosophical conundrums, let's look at a few more quantum puzzles.

PROBABLY SO

The realization that atomic particles are not strictly particles–but are in some sense also waves–led to a breakthrough in atomic theory. Bohr's quantum model of the atom, you may remember, gave no explanation why electrons move only in certain prescribed orbits. De Broglie's proposal that electrons behave as waves supplied the missing explanation.

De Broglie assigned to every moving electron a definite wave length. The circumference of the quantum orbits could now be explained by postulating that each must contain an integral number of wave lengths. In other words, as the orbits increase in circumference, they do so by full wave lengths (one crest and one trough), never by half or quarter wave lengths. The Austrian theoretical physicist Erwin Schrödinger (1887-1961) topped off de Broglie's wave theory by deriving a strikingly simple mathematical formula for wave mechanics.

This was a remarkable theoretical achievement. Yet despite the mathematical refinements, physicists were still no closer to a physical explanation of the troublesome wave/particle duality. What is the physical nature of this wave? How does it relate to the particle with which it is associated? These questions remained a puzzle. Finally physicists gave up trying to find a physical explanation and contented themselves with simply describing the results of experiments, using the terminology of probability theory.

Consider the interference pattern produced by the two-slit experiment (Figs. 2 and 3). Physicists describe the pattern as a range of probabilities. Where a larger number of black spots appear on the photographic screen, there an individual electron is more likely to hit. Where fewer spots appear, there an electron is less likely to hit. In other words, most physicists don't even try to explain the quantum wave as a physical entity existing somewhere in space; they treat it merely as a mathematical construct that allows us to make statistical predictions about experimental results—about where electrons will end up.

Probability is not a new concept in physics, of course. But this is a radically new understanding of it. In classical physics, things like gases were treated statistically simply because there are too many molecules for anyone to track them all. Yet it was assumed that each molecule follows a completely determined path that could be predicted in principle, if only we could trace all the forces acting on it. In short, the universe was still regarded as a smoothly running clockwork, even if some of the gears were so tiny that we had to treat them in aggregates, applying statistical laws.

But in quantum physics, particles move in mysterious ways, spread out along wavelike paths. A single electron could be anywhere within the wave pattern. We can never say exactly where it is; we can only say that it is more likely to be in some places than in others. The only reason things in everyday experience seem to follow predictable patterns is that they are composed of so many atoms that the statistical probabilities average out. John Wheeler of the University of Texas at Austin states the idea colorfully:

> I cannot believe that nature has 'built in', as if by a corps of Swiss watchmakers, any machinery, equation, or mathematical formalism which rigidly relates physical events separated in time. Rather I believe these events go together in a higgledy-piggledy fashion and that what seem to be precise equations emerge in every case in a statistical way from the physics of large numbers.[15]

This is a completely novel concept of probability. The old view of probability rested on the assumption of an underlying lawfulness, even determinism. But the new view suggests an underlying randomness. Statistical laws are not merely a convenient device; they are ultimate. Newtonian physics still holds for macroscopic objects, but only because they are constituted of huge numbers of atoms where the statistical variations average out.

Hence, whereas physicists used to call the waves associated with atomic particles "matter waves," they now refer to them as "probability waves." Making an observation that reduces the probability to a specific outcome is described as the "collapse of the wave function." In other words, when we direct a stream of electrons toward a photographic screen, we cannot determine the path taken by an individual electron; it could be anywhere within the quantum wave. But once the electron strikes the photographic screen and makes a black mark there, the wave function has been collapsed on that single black spot.

At that point, the electron passes from a probabilistic to a deterministic state—from an indefinite position to a definite position. The range of possible positions collapses into the position corresponding to the result actually obtained in the experiment.

What a remarkable power this appears to give the observer and his measuring device—the power, some would say, to create a definite state out of what was formerly a fuzzy, probabilistic state. In fact, the collapse of the wave function has given rise to all sorts of interesting philosophical interpretations, as we shall see. But first, one final quantum puzzle.

A CERTAIN UNCERTAINTY

The centerpiece of classical physics was mechanics–theories of motion. Galileo made his greatest contributions in the understanding of local motion (the acceleration of falling bodies, the arc of a cannonball's flight). Newton's greatest contributions connected local motion to celestial motion (planets and comets). The laws of motion, it seemed, would unveil the secrets of the whole universe. One law would describe the leaf falling from a tree and the planet whirling in its orbit.

In the study of motion the most important properties to ascertain are position and velocity. If we know where an object is to begin with, and if we know its velocity (in physics, velocity includes both speed and direction), then we can plot its course. We can set up a co-ordinate system giving numerical values to the position of the object at each instant of time. All of Newtonian physics is built on the trajectories of particles, from the flight of an arrow to the orbit of the moon.

If it is true that the laws of mechanics lay open the inner workings of the universe, then it follows that the universe is a vast machine. Thus Newtonian physics led to a philosophy of determinism. Pierre Simon de Laplace (1749-1827), the quintessential Newtonian, argued that if a superhuman intelligence could but grasp the position of every particle in the universe, along with the forces acting on it, the entire future could be predicted. For such an intelligence, Laplace wrote, "nothing would be uncertain and the future, as the past, would be present to its eyes."

Imagine, then, the blow to physics when it turned out that in quantum mechanics precisely this knowledge is impossible. We cannot plot the trajectory of an atomic particle because we cannot know the initial conditions. We cannot determine both its position and its velocity. This is the so-called Heisenberg Uncertainty Principle, named after its discoverer, the German theoretical physicist Werner Heisenberg (1901-1976).

To understand the Uncertainty Principle, we must analyze what it means to see something. You see this book because light strikes the page, bounces off, and travels to your eyes. The book is not noticeably affected by the light because it is so much larger than the photons hitting it. By the same token, when we shine a flashlight on something, it is not knocked down. When we take a photograph of someone, he is not pushed over by the light of the flash.

But consider what happens if we flash a beam of light onto subatomic particles—say, electrons. Electrons are so minute that the photons *do* knock them off course. They alter the electron's velocity (more precisely, their momentum—which is velocity multiplied by the particle's mass). In other words, when dealing with subatomic particles, the very act of measuring a quantity such as momentum *alters* the quantity.

Hence we must make a choice. We can use a high-frequency beam of light (with high-energy photons), which makes it easier to make out where the electron is, but then we throw it off course, and its momentum becomes unpredictable. Or we can use a low-frequency beam of light (with low-energy photons), which doesn't knock the electron off course as much, but then the picture becomes fuzzy, and it is difficult to make out where the electron is.

The upshot is that we cannot determine both a particle's position and its velocity at the same time. In seeking to know one quantity, we cannot avoid altering the other. There is an inherent limit on the precision we can attain in investigating atomic events. Hence every experimental situation is plagued by an unavoidable uncertainty. We can measure either the position or the momentum of an electron, but the more accurately we measure one, the less accurate the other becomes.[16]

The illustration here is actually somewhat misleading since it uses classical terminology implying that the electron *has* an exact position and momentum, which we simply cannot read accurately. What quantum physicists actually say is that the electron *does not have* a definite position or momentum at any instant.

Uncertainty is not a new problem in science. Physicists have always had to deal with extraneous effects in experiments. Consider, for example, measuring the temperature of water in a glass by inserting a thermometer. The thermometer has its own temperature, which affects the temperature of the water.[17] Of course, when dealing with ordinary objects like glasses of water, the difference is minuscule and can either be disregarded or compensated for. But on the atomic level, the extraneous effects distort the results to such a degree that we cannot sort them out from the phenomenon itself.

The Uncertainty Principle means we cannot trace the trajectory of an individual atomic particle the way we can trace the trajectory of a planet or a Patriot missile. To do so would require that the position and momentum of the particle could be numerically given at each instant of time. Since it is impossible to pin down both of those attributes at the same time, we cannot say where an individual particle is at any given moment and we cannot trace its path.

The Uncertainty Principle represents a striking departure from classical physics, which assumed that there is in principle no limit to the accuracy of measurement. Limits were imposed merely by our technological inability to produce sufficiently sensitive measuring devices. By contrast, in quantum mechanics complete accuracy is impossible in principle.

Historically, scientists have disagreed in their interpretation of the Uncertainty Principle. Optimists—including Einstein, Planck, de Broglie, and David Bohm—maintain that the uncertainty in quantum physics is merely a statement of current human ignorance. They continue to insist that events in the quantum world, like those in the classical world, are rigidly causal and deterministic. To be sure, our current methods of investigation are inadequate, and our current measuring devices unavoidably disturb the system. But these are limits on our knowledge only, optimists insist, in principle no different from the way putting a thermometer in water limits the accuracy of our measurement of the temperature. Someday we may refine our methods or discover new laws that eliminate the troubling element of uncertainty. This is the context in which Einstein made his famous statement, "God does not play dice with the universe."

A Christian proponent of the optimist view is astronomer Hugh Ross. Writing in *The Fingerprint of God*, Ross says, "It is not that the Heisenberg Uncertainty Principle disproves the principle of causality, but simply that the causality is hidden from human investigation."[18]

Other physicists, such as Niels Bohr, view uncertainty not as a result of temporary ignorance, solvable by further research, but as a fundamental and unavoidable limitation on human knowledge. The atomic world simply does not fit human conceptual categories. Our categories are shaped by the ordinary world describable in Newtonian terms, says philosopher of science Philipp Frank, so that we inevitably think of an atomic particle in those terms—as a tiny billiard ball possessing both position and momentum.

But atomic particles simply do not possess these properties, Frank argues, at least not in the ordinary sense of the terms. In fact, we have no idea what atomic particles are in reality. We must remain agnostic about the ontology of the atomic world and talk only about the results obtained under certain experimental conditions. We choose which results we are interested in and then run the appropriate experiment.[19]

A third interpretation, proposed by Heisenberg, ascribes the uncertainty to nature. Nature is not deterministic, as classical physics assumed; it is indeterminate. Heisenberg revived the Aristotelian terminology of potentiality and actuality. The atomic realm is a realm of potentiality, he said; future events are not predetermined since any one of a range of possibilities may occur. When the scientist intrudes his measuring device into an atomic system, he forces a particular outcome to be actualized from what was before a fuzzy realm of potentialities. As Heisenberg writes, "the transition from the 'possible' to the 'actual' takes place during the act of observation."[20]

A fourth interpretation is the idealist one. If we *choose* which property will be exhibited, this "comes very close to saying that we *create* certain properties," writes Gary Zukav.[21] Zukav takes this as evidence of the compatibility of modern physics with the mysticism of Eastern religion, in which the material world is a creation of the mind. Likewise Michael Talbot, in his book *Mysticism and the New Physics*, says, "It is the consciousness of the observer that intervenes and triggers which of the possible outcomes is observed."[22] Zukav and Talbot, along with Fritjof Capra, have brought the New Age interpretation of quantum mechanics to a large popular reading audience.

A PALACE BUILT ON SAND?

Quantum theory has been spectacularly successful. It has helped scientists explain atomic structure, radioactivity, chemical bonding, and many effects of electric and magnetic fields. It has made possible major developments in practical hardware, including the electron microscope, the laser, and the transistor. It has been confirmed to an extremely high degree of accuracy. Most scientists use the theory with complete confidence. Physicists Davies and Brown conclude: "No known experiment has contradicted the predictions of quantum mechanics in the last fifty years." It is often cited as the most successful scientific theory ever produced.[23]

And yet this remarkable edifice stands on a quagmire of questions regarding its philosophical meaning. What is the nature of the reality described by quantum theory? What ontology does it imply? These questions remain unanswered. As Nick Herbert says, "Like a magician who has inherited a wonderful magic wand that works every time without his knowing why, the physicist is at a loss to explain quantum theory's marvelous success."[24] And recall the words of J. C. Polkinghorne, quoted earlier, who said that working in quantum mechanics is like being shown a beautiful palace and then learning that "no one is quite sure whether its foundations rest on bedrock or shifting sand."

The varying interpretations of quantum physics can be categorized according to which parts of quantum theory are taken to be fundamental and which parts are disregarded as mere mathematical formalism, having no counterpart in the real world. We have already hinted at some of the interpretations; now we will develop them more fully.

The Copenhagen Interpretation

The Copenhagen interpretation proposed by Niels Bohr takes as its starting point the Uncertainty Principle. On the atomic level, we encounter paired attributes (e.g., position and momentum) where measuring one attribute more accurately leads to a corresponding *in*accuracy in the measurement of the other. When we first learn of this dilemma, our common-sense understanding of it tends to be realist. We assume that things like electrons really *have* a definite position and momentum, but because the particles are so small we unavoidably disturb them in our experiments.

But that was not what Bohr said. According to the Copenhagen interpretation, an electron does not really *possess* these attributes until they are measured. Based on the empiricist dictum that what we cannot measure does not exist for physical science, Bohr denied any reality to the notions of electron position and momentum. It is the act of measuring that imparts reality to what was until then a fuzzy ghost world. (Hence one book about quantum mechanics is titled *The Ghost in the Atom*). Position and velocity are not inherent in the electron; they are a product of its interaction with the measuring device. If we try to speak of the quantum world in the terminology of classical physics, Bohr stated bluntly, "There *is* no quantum world."

The Copenhagen interpretation is currently dominant in quantum physics. Yet it is easily misunderstood, and it is helpful to clarify what it does *not* mean. To begin with, the Copenhagenist does not say *all* attributes of atomic entities result from interaction with a measuring device. Static attributes—charge, mass, and spin—are stable. Their value remains the same under all measurement conditions. With respect to these things, atomic entities behave like ordinary objects. It is only the dynamic attributes that are problematic— position, velocity, and spin orientation (the direction its spin is pointing). The Copenhagenist maintains that dynamic attributes do not exist in themselves but are a result of interaction with an experimental set-up.

An analogy might be color, which is not an innate attribute of objects but depends on the kind of illumination, the material's absorption spectrum, and the perceptual apparatus (the sensitivity of the human eye). Color is the result of an interaction of all these factors. In the same way, Bohr taught that the dynamic attributes of atomic particles do not exist in themselves but are a result of interaction with the measuring device.[25] In philosophical terminology, dynamic properties are not primary qualities but secondary qualities.

Yet even when carefully qualified to include only dynamic properties, the Copenhagen interpretation still represents a significant conceptual change in physics. All of classical mechanics was based on particles in motion. Hence position and velocity were the most important attributes. If you knew a particle's initial position and velocity, you could in theory predict all its future motion. But in quantum mechanics, it is exactly these fundamental attributes that cannot be precisely known—at least not at the same time.

Another common misunderstanding is that the Copenhagen interpretation leads to subjectivism. But Bohr did not hold that quantum entities are a creation of our minds: They exist objectively. Yet in regard to things like position and momentum they exist in an indefinite state (until we run an experiment and make one or the other definite). As a result, we cannot know what the quantum world is in itself. We can only know the various ways it responds to our probings. As Heisenberg wrote, "Natural science does not simply describe and explain nature; . . . it describes nature as exposed to our method of questioning."[26]

To say the quantum world is indefinite is to say it exists as an entire range of probabilities. This is perhaps the oddest part of the Copenhagen interpretation. It says that somehow all possibilities exist in a potential state until the wave function collapses and one particular state is actualized. For example, until it is observed, an electron is said to be neither a particle nor a wave; it exists as possibilities of both. When a measurement takes place, the wave function collapses and one of the possibilities becomes an actuality.

SCHRÖDINGER'S CAT

Critics of the Copenhagen interpretation say it grants altogether too privileged a status to the act of measurement. Bohr seems to claim that interaction with a measuring device calls forth dynamic attributes from a shadowy ghost world of possibilities. Erwin Schrödinger, who disagreed with Bohr's interpretation of quantum mechanics, sought to show its absurdity in what has come to be called the Schrödinger cat paradox.

The story begins by supposing that we seal a cat into a box containing a tiny chunk of radioactive rock, whose rate of decay is known. (Radioactivity, like all atomic events, is purely probabilistic. We do not know when or why an atom will fire off an alpha particle; we only know the probability that after a given interval a certain number of atoms will have done so.) We set up the experiment so that within an hour there is a precise fifty-fifty chance that a single atom will fire. If it does, it will trigger a relay mechanism that smashes a flask of poisonous gas and immediately kills the cat.

We set up the experiment, wait an hour . . . and then what? Has an atom fired? Is the cat dead or alive?

According to the Copenhagen interpretation, until a quantum system is observed, it exists as an indefinite state of all possibilities. In this experiment, that means that until we actually open the box and look inside, the atomic decay has neither happened nor *not* happened: It exists in an indeterminate state that includes both possibilities.

Yet in this hypothetical experiment we have connected the quantum system to a macroscopic system—namely, the cat—which allows us to observe its effects. To be a strict Copenhagenist, therefore, we would have to say that after an hour the poor feline is neither dead nor alive but exists as possibilities of both. But what in the world does *that* mean? What is a live/dead cat? When we translate quantum concepts into the world of ordinary objects, they fail to make sense.

Of course, if we open the box and look, the cat will clearly be either dead or alive. The wave function will collapse into one of the two possibilities. To be a strict Copenhagenist we would have to say the act of observation has forced the cat to appear either alive or dead. But how can that be? Isn't the cat already either dead or alive before we look at it? Does the act of observation have some magical power to create reality?

As Nick Herbert argues, the Copenhagen interpretation seems to endow the measuring instrument with magical properties—the power to make the cat either dead or alive. He goes on:

> It's hard to believe that nature endows the act in which humans make contact with quantum entities with a special status not granted to all the other interactions in the universe. Any interpretation of measurement which attributes supernatural powers to the act itself must be regarded with suspicion. There's something philosophically fishy about a measurement-centered cosmos.[27]

Though the Copenhagen interpretation remains the reigning orthodoxy, several physicists have smelled this fishiness and have offered alternative interpretations.

Observer-Created Reality

The Copenhagen school has spawned a more radical interpretation that focuses not on the measuring device but on the measurer—the human observer. As we noted earlier, each interpretation takes a different part of quantum theory as fundamental. This one centers on the scientist's decision regarding which experiment to run. That decision determines which attributes a quantum system will possess.

If we want the quantum entity to appear as a particle, we choose a particle experiment. If we want it to appear as a wave, we choose a wave experiment. Likewise if we want to know its position or velocity. In each case, the act of observation seems to impart reality to the attribute in question. As physicist John Wheeler puts it, "No elementary phenomenon is a real phenomenon until it is an observed phenomenon."

Proponents of observer-created reality disagree, however, over what counts as an observation. Some say the essence of an observation is making a record. For that purpose, a dark spot on a photographic screen, the click of a Geiger counter, or an image on film does just as well as a human being.

Others insist that only a conscious observer will do. After all, the argument goes, everything is made of atoms—even the recording device. It is therefore subject to the same uncertainty as the atomic particles being measured. Hence we need a second recording device to observe the first device making its observation. But the second device is likewise composed of atoms, so we need a third device—and so on, in an infinite regress.[28]

Logically, the only step in the process of observation that does not consist of atoms in motion is the moment when a physical signal in the brain becomes an experience in the human mind. So argues the eminent mathematician John von Neumann. Hence this is the point at which the infinite regress can be broken. Things come into full existence—their dynamic attributes are actualized—when they are perceived by human consciousness.

Von Neumann's theory avoids the criticism that it imparts magical powers to the measuring instrument but only by transferring those magical powers to the human mind—more specifically, to the point where the brain connects to the mind, a highly problematic point that no one fully understands. In short, von Neumann replaces the mystery of quantum indeterminacy with the mystery of the mind-brain connection.

A few of von Neumann's followers go even further. They propose that *all* properties—not just dynamic ones—are created by the mind and that the universe itself exists in a half-real state of limbo until human observers make it fully real. Wheeler, who adopts this view, calls it the Participatory Universe theory.[29]

Most of us would agree that such a view is, as Polkinghorne puts it, "astonishingly anthropocentric." When we run an experiment with electrons hitting a photographic screen, are we really to imagine that the image on the screen is indeterminate until someone takes it out and looks at it? Are we really to imagine that any place in the universe that human beings have not yet investigated, there no electron has ever had either position or momentum?[30] Are we really to believe that the entire universe, with its myriads of stars and galaxies, existed in some sort of fuzzy indeterminate state until human beings came on the scene?

If Bohr attributed supernatural powers to measuring devices, surely this interpretation attributes supernatural powers to the human mind—and is equally fishy philosophically.

Quantum Holism

The intricate involvement of the observer in quantum physics may be difficult to puzzle out, but the fact remains that it is real. The classic distinction between observer and observed seems to have collapsed. You can not ask what happens in the atomic world *in itself*; you can only ask what happens when the experimenter manipulates it in certain ways. You must consider the entire experimental arrangement. This has led some physicists to declare that quantum physics leads us away from individual things to a philosophy of things-in-relationship—to the entire world as a seamless, indivisible whole.

This holistic interpretation often cites as support the famous EPR experiment. Named after the three men who proposed it—Einstein, Podolsky, and Rosen—the experiment seems to show that paired electrons influence each other even when separated by vast distances. The influence happens much too quickly to be an ordinary signal (which is limited by the speed of light, according to relativity theory). In fact, it appears to happen instantaneously. The two electrons seem to be bound together by some mysterious unity. Some physicists conclude that beneath phenomena, the underlying world is a seamless whole.

As British physicist David Bohm puts it, the separate parts of the universe are not really separate parts: "One is led to a new notion of *unbroken wholeness* which denies the classical analyzability of the world into separately and independently existing parts." In his words, quantum mechanics affirms the "interconnectedness of the whole universe."[31]

Not surprisingly, this conclusion has been enthusiastically picked up by New Age physicists such as Fritjof Capra (*The Tao of Physics*) and Gary Zukav (*The Dancing Wu Li Masters*). They present it as evidence of a new confluence of modern science and ancient philosophy, as embodied in oriental religions such as Hinduism, Buddhism, and Taoism. The New Age physicists claim that atomic physics confirms the mystical experience of "oneness." As Capra puts it:

> Quantum theory forces us to see the universe not as a collection of physical objects, but rather as a complicated web of relations between the various parts of a unified whole. This, however, is the way in which Eastern mystics have experienced the world.[32]

And Nick Herbert says the result of the EPR experiment is:

> a simple consequence of the oneness of apparently separate objects . . . a quantum loophole through which physics admits not merely the possibility but the *necessity* of the mystic's unitary vision: 'We are all one.'[33]

Yet critics say the connection between modern physics and Eastern mysticism is merely a surface similarity. As Ian Barbour argues, "Asian traditions speak of undifferentiated unity. But the wholeness and unity that physics expresses is highly differentiated and structured, subject to strict constraints, symmetry principles, and conservation laws."

The rise of New Age physics can be understood as an overreaction to the reductionism of classical physics. Classical physics was analytical and atomistic. It defined everything in terms of the behavior of its smallest components and failed to take account of integrated systems. But New Age physicists fall off the horse on the opposite side. Whereas classical physics exaggerates the role of parts, Barbour argues, people like Capra exaggerate wholes.[34]

A full critique of quantum holism would include arguments against the philosophical monism implicit in New Age physics, which goes beyond our purposes here. Suffice it to say that a Biblical view of reality is not monistic but dualistic, because God is ontologically distinct from His creation. We are not God, despite what Shirley Maclaine may tell us; we are created beings. And our problem is not that we are individuals who need to experience our oneness with the Whole; our problem is that we are sinners who need to understand our brokenness before a holy Creator.

Many Worlds

Of all the interpretations of quantum mechanics, perhaps the most outrageous is the many-worlds view. It was devised by Hugh Everett, a Princeton graduate student, in looking for a way to take the magic out of the act of measurement. Why should our experiments enjoy the privileged status of being capable of creating reality? Why should our acts of observation have the power to collapse the wave function and from many possible outcomes to create just one?

Everett denied that the act of observation has any such power. But the only way he saw to deny it was to deny that the wave function really collapses. Instead, all possible outcomes actually happen—in different universes.

Suppose that an attribute has five possible values. In that case, the universe splits into five universes, each with a measuring device that registers one of those values. In the standard interpretation, the wave function collapses from five possibilities to just one—namely, to the outcome obtained in our experiment. But in Everett's interpretation, the quantum system realizes all five outcomes in five experiments in five universes.

Thus the universe is forever splitting into parallel worlds, though we have no way of experiencing any of them except the one we see at the moment. Even you and I are forever splitting into near-mirror images of ourselves, each inhabiting a different world.

The idea of innumerable, unobservable universes co-existing alongside the one we see at any instant is too extravagant to be widely accepted, though its supporters include several prominent theoretical physicists. As physicists Davies and Brown put it, the many-worlds interpretation "introduces a preposterous amount of 'excess meta-physical baggage' into our description of the physical world."[35] In general, scientists prefer the simpler scientific theory, and this endless multiplication of universes hardly qualifies as simple. Rudolf Peierls, formerly at Oxford, dismisses the theory with a simple question: "Since we have no means of seeing or ever communicating with the other universes," he asks, "why invent them?"[36]

Why indeed? It is possible that the motivation for accepting the many-worlds interpretation has less to do with science than with theology. Quantum mechanics has found its way out of the laboratory and into the astronomy department, where it has been incorporated into speculations on the origin of the universe. In the fraction of a microsecond after the Big Bang, so the theory goes, when the constituents of matter were first forming, events took place on the quantum level.

But as we have already said, quantum phenomena are intricately bound up with an observer. We have no idea what happens in itself, only what happens in a particular experimental arrangement. This poses a problem: How can we apply quantum mechanics in the infant stages of the universe when there was as yet no human observer? When we are dealing with the entire universe, says David Deutsch, astrophysicist at the University of Texas at Austin, "it's logically inconsistent to imagine an observer sitting outside it."[37] In the absence of an observer to collapse the wave function, Deutsch and Everett suggest instead an infinite multiplication of universes.

But even if we grant that the only alternative to this troubling multiplication of universes is to posit an observer—are we limited to human observers? Centuries ago, the Irish bishop George Berkeley (1685-1753) suggested that the universe remains in existence because it is observed by God. While we do not endorse Berkeley's philosophical idealism, it does offer an alternative for those who believe the universe must be observed to be fully real. Apparently, supporters of the many-worlds interpretation would rather multiply an infinite number of unseen universes than acknowledge an infinite, unseen God.

Neo-Realism

Until the rise of the new physics, most scientists were realists. They believed that the world exists objectively, independently of our perception of it.[38] Even today, the majority of practicing physicists are unreflective realists—unreflective in the sense that they believe they are investigating the way things really are, and they don't stop to think how they would support that assumption philosophically. Yet quantum mechanics has seriously shaken that implicit belief. In response, several physicists have sought to develop updated versions of realism.

Bohr counseled agnosticism about the ontological status of the quantum world but realists disagree. They believe the quantum world really exists—and, most of them would add, it is populated by ordinary objects. After all, what do we actually see in quantum experiments? Patterns of tiny black marks on photographic screens. Curly tracks in cloud chambers. Pointer readings. These are clearly real, ordinary objects. Must we account for them by resorting to bizarre, unordinary interpretations? Isn't it more natural to think the electrons that made the marks are likewise ordinary objects—with normal position and momentum attributes?

Historically, most of the founders of quantum mechanics were realists—Einstein, Max Planck, Louis de Broglie, Erwin Schrödinger. (When Schrödinger saw the anti-realist direction in which quantum mechanics was heading, he said "I don't like it, and I'm sorry I ever had anything to do with it.") Most realists believe the quantum world is built in the old-fashioned classical manner, out of particles and fields—with quantum waves as a type of force field, like magnetic waves.

Yet in order to account for the puzzling features of the quantum world, realist interpretations have taken some strange turns—so that we might more accurately call them neo-realist. David Bohm, for example, has developed a neo-realist theory in which particles have a definite position and momentum, and waves are separate and real entities, not merely mathematical constructs. In Bohm's theory, each particle travels along its own wave (he calls it a pilot wave) like a cork bobbing on the sea.

However, to make this ordinary-object model of quantum reality work, the pilot wave has to behave in unusual ways. It spreads out as an invisible field, probing the environment and changing whenever the environment changes, simultaneously causing the particle to alter its behavior accordingly. This explains why an electron seems to "know" whether there are two slits (in which case it creates an interference pattern) or a single slit (in which case it acts as a barrage of particles). The particle's corresponding wave precedes it like a field and sends the information back.

Obviously, this theory involves some pretty strange concepts. To begin with, in order to take into account all possible influences, the pilot wave has to connect in principle with every other particle in the universe, somewhat as gravity does (except that, unlike gravity, the wave does not weaken with distance). Second, it has to communicate information about the world instantaneously to the particle, enabling it to switch its attributes accordingly. This violates Einstein's dictum that nothing can travel faster than the speed of light. As a result, Bohm regards his theory as merely a starting point in constructing an ordinary-reality model of quantum reality.

Irish physicist John Bell has pursued Bohm's theory further, arguing that the EPR experiment supports the pilot wave concept. The experiment gives evidence that quantum objects can indeed influence one another in mysterious ways not restricted by distance across space—in short, not affected by locality. Bell calls his interpretation nonlocal realism.

Well, realism it may be, but it differs sharply from common-sense realism. Polkinghorne muses that neo-realists have jumped out of the frying pan of indeterminacy and into the fire of nonlocality.

Yet human nature being what it is, most practicing physicists continue to be realists of one sort or another, tending to visualize electrons *as if* they were ordinary objects flying along a path (even though our knowledge of the path is only statistical). And their calculations and experiments come out just fine. What else can scientists do, since quantum mechanics has yet to construct an alternative metaphor for the world?

As we saw in earlier chapters, various metaphors have contended for dominance in science—the world as mystical puzzle, as organism, as machine. Following Newton, the image of the world as a giant clockwork was accepted nearly universally by physicists. Today quantum mechanics has shattered that image yet offers nothing to replace it. Indeed, an undeterminate universe may even be inherently impossible to picture. As a result, most physicists continue to work within a basically Newtonian worldview in practice, even if they reject it in theory. They rely on common-sense realism, speaking of electrons in the same way they speak of billiard balls and inclined planes.

Perhaps that is as good a reason as any to prefer a realist philosophy. As Polkinghorne says, "Your average quantum mechanic is about as philosophically minded as your average garage mechanic." Yet, he goes on, just as the latter might have an intuitive grasp of how a car works that ought to be taken into account by anyone prone to theorizing about motors, so practicing physicists might have an intuitive grasp of their subject that ought to be taken into account in any philosophical interpretation. We may not believe that any particular realist interpretation has it quite right yet. But, Polkinghorne concludes, "I submit it might be wise to look for an interpretation of quantum mechanics which comes as near as possible to being in accord with the attitude so widespread among its users."[39]

PHYSICS AND PHILOSOPHY

The rise of the new physics has profoundly affected all three traditional branches of philosophy—epistemology, metaphysics, and ethics. In epistemology it has inspired new philosophies of scientific knowledge. In metaphysics it has reopened the debate between materialism and idealism. And in ethics it has revived the debate between free will and determinism. Let's examine each of these briefly.

Epistemology—What Do You Know?

POSITIVISM

The Copenhagen interpretation is often associated with a philosophy of science known as positivism.[40] The positivist maintains that the electron does not really "exist" in the full, common-sense notion of the word. But no matter, since science is not about constructing an ontology (a theory of reality) anyway; it is merely about consistently correlating observations.

And for this consistency to be achieved, say Davies and Brown, "it is unnecessary for the atom 'to exist really' as an independent thing." The word *atom*, they insist, is "simply a convenient way of talking about what is nothing but a set of mathematical relations connecting different observations." In practice, as long as the physicist applies the rules of quantum mechanics, he or she can correctly predict the results of actual measurements while ignoring questions of ontology.[41] Bohr likewise spoke of quantum mechanics as merely a calculational procedure, "a tool for deriving predictions." The task of quantum physics, he wrote, is not to find out what nature *is* but only what we can *say* about it.[42]

The typical working scientist finds this epistemology unsatisfying. It is doubtful that scientists expend great time and effort in their work because of a driving desire to harmonize laboratory observations. As Bohm argues, "If the only purpose of physics is to explain experiments, then I think physics would have been a great deal less interesting than it has been. I mean, why do you want to explain experiments? Do you enjoy doing it or what?"[43]

For most scientists, the real motivation for their work is the urge to make sense of the world, to discover what makes it tick. As Polkinghorne comments, "I have never known anyone working in fundamental science who was not motivated by the desire to understand the way the world is."[44] Similarly, Del Ratzsch, professor of philosophy at Calvin College, writes: "Modern scientists have generally (not unanimously) been *realists*; that is, they have seen themselves as . . . trying to find out what the *sub*structure and *hidden* mechanisms of the world really are. Thus, positivist anti-realism is simply not true to scientific practice." It is unfaithful "to the realist tradition within the scientific community."[45]

INSTRUMENTALISM

Today logical positivism has largely been succeeded by instrumentalism,[46] a form of pragmatism. It regards theories as tools to be judged by how well they work, how useful they are in accomplishing scientific purposes.

Like positivism, instrumentalism dismisses questions about the actual existence of electrons and other particles as irrelevant. The aim of science is not to discover nature "as it is" but to develop concepts useful for making predictions and achieving technical control. To borrow an analogy from Nick Herbert, whereas the realist sees scientific theory as a guidebook describing a real landscape, the pragmatist sees theory as a cookbook full of recipes useful for ordering and manipulating the facts.[47]

Instrumentalism is open to the same criticism as logical positivism. Working scientists do not devote their lives to developing useful tools for laboratory work. They hope to discover and explain how the world behaves. They treat theories not only as useful guides but as premises that could be shown to be false. As philosopher of science Frederick Suppe argues, everyone speaks of laws in science as true or false, which means instrumentalism "is *prima facie* objectionable."[48]

REALISM

Whatever philosophers of science may say, most working scientists remain realists—not only in regard to the ontological status of the quantum world (as we discussed earlier) but also in regard to scientific knowledge.[49] The realist believes that theories aim to describe the world and therefore can be true or false, not just useful, and that science consists largely of discovery, not just construction.

These concepts are the stock-in-trade of every scientist. As Barbour notes, "*scientists usually assume realism* in their work."[50] Even in particle physics, scientists speak of the discovery, not the invention, of a new particle. And they engage in extensive and costly research to discover whether the entities referred to in their theories really exist.

As an example, Roy Clouser, professor of philosophy and religion, tells the story of the neutrino (the word means "little neutral particle"). The existence of the neutrino was first hypothesized by Wolfgang Pauli because it made sense of a number of observations. Later the hypothesis solved other explanatory gaps in atomic theory as well. But no neutrinos had ever been detected, which bothered physicists. Neutrinos are so minute that physicists had to invest a tremendous amount of ingenuity, equipment, time, and money before they finally acquired good evidence that the tiny particles actually exist. The first thing to note in this story is that it *bothered* physicists that a neutrino might be merely a useful concept (instrumentalism), or a linguistic convention that made sense of experiments (positivism), rather than a real entity. The second thing to note is that scientists were willing to expend a great deal of time and effort to confirm that neutrinos were in fact real. "Clearly, their motive was the belief that theories are attempts to know reality," Clouser writes, "that is, to discover what exists and to know its nature."[51]

The fact that scientists instinctively operate on realist assumptions is perhaps a good reason to start with a realist stance whenever possible. There is, in fact, a growing trend in the philosophy of science today to define science according to actual scientific practice—what scientists actually do and think—rather than to prescribe what they *ought* to think. For this and other reasons, Ratzsch says, over the past fifteen years or so philosophy of science has turned in a realist direction.[52]

Nevertheless, it must be acknowledged that quantum mechanics does modify many older forms of realism. First, realism has traditionally been associated with the ability to picture the world in some concrete model or analogy—such as the Newtonian image of the machine. But the quantum world cannot be pictured. We cannot picture something, for example, that is both a wave and a particle.

But a realist epistemology should not have been tied to pictorial representation in the first place, argues theologian E. L. Mascall. Rather it should have been tied to intelligibility. "The paradigm of a real world," Mascall writes, "is not its sensible imaginability but its intellectual apprehensibility."

In other words, Mascall goes on, "The world does not lose its claim to reality by ceasing to be imaginable as an infinite Euclidean receptacle populated by tiny, passive lumps drifting uniformly down the stream of time." For "the essential character of the objective world is not sensibility but intelligibility." Though the quantum world is difficult to picture, it is highly intelligible mathematically. It can be grasped simply and elegantly in mathematical formulas. This is all that a realist epistemology requires.[53]

Second, quantum physics provides an antidote to an extreme form of realism—what Del Ratzsch calls "hard" realism—which takes theories to be precise, literal descriptions of the world and denies the impact of a scientist's personal beliefs and commitments upon his work. In its place Ratzsch proposes "soft" realism, which recognizes that the data are often ambiguous and that competing theories may fit the same observations. "Soft" realism acknowledges that theories are not simply copies of nature; they are approximations, metaphors, and

models. Nor are they derived mechanically simply by tabulating observations. Prior beliefs about what is real and what is scientifically plausible greatly influence what we choose to study, what results we look
for in our experiments, and how we interpret those results.[54] The
unavoidable impact of the observer in quantum mechanics has driven
these truths home in a new way.

Metaphysics—Mind over Matter?

In the early days of quantum mechanics, many took it to be a repudiation of materialism and an open door to philosophical idealism. In
fact, from the 1930s to the 1950s the idealist interpretation of quantum physics was quite widespread, thanks to popular works by James
Jeans and Arthur Eddington.

Arthur Eddington enlisted the new physics for the cause of idealism with the argument that it made matter insubstantial. Newton
described atoms as solid, hard, and impenetrable, like tiny billiard
balls. But modern physics reveals that atoms are mostly empty
space, consisting of a tiny nucleus surrounded by oscillating electrons. And even these are not material in the old sense; they are
something like wads of condensed energy. Compared to the solid,
substantial world of everyday perception, physics presents us with
a "world of shadows."[55]

Critics argue that Eddington confused energy with spirit or idea.
A world of energy is just as physical as a world of matter. What quantum mechanics has done is merely replace old concepts of materialism
with new concepts of materialism. It has *not* led to mentalism.

James Jeans adopted a different argument for idealism, a mathematical one. In quantum theory we cannot picture the universe in any
coherent image; we can only describe it mathematically. But mathematics is a form of mental activity; hence, Jeans argued, the world is
primarily mental. This is what he meant by his much-quoted line, "The
universe begins to look more like a great thought than like a great
machine."

Critics argue that Jeans misrepresented the nature of quantum
physics. From his argument you might think it had become a branch
of pure mathematics, a free creation of mathematical thought. But even
in quantum physics, scientists still test their theories against experience.
The tests may be very indirect, yet scientists still refer their theories to
a physical world and not merely to a mental or mathematical world.

Today the idealist interpretation of quantum physics has declined
in popularity,[56] living on primarily in works by New Age physicists. In
these books, a major argument centers on the active role of the
observer in quantum mechanics, interpreted to mean that the mind

actually creates properties of the world. As Gary Zukav writes, "Because . . . we can know either the momentum of a particle or its position, but not both, *we must choose* which of these two properties we want to determine." Thus, he concludes, "Not only do we influence our reality, but in some degree we actually *create* it."[57]

But Zukav overstates the case. In quantum physics the observer does influence the outcome of experiments, but it is not directly through his mind or consciousness. Rather it is through the tools he uses. A conscious observer doesn't need to be present for black marks to appear on a photographic screen, for a Geiger counter to click, or for tracks to appear in a cloud chamber. Indeed, for millennia radioactive rocks have been decaying under the surface of the earth with no one observing them.

New Age idealism may claim support from quantum physics but ironically it strikes a deathblow to physics—and all other branches of science. For science must begin with the assumption that there is an objective reality "out there" to be investigated. Even if we cannot know it perfectly, even if our act of observation affects it, even if it changes over time, still there must be something there, independent of our consciousness, in order for scientific investigation to proceed. There must be a world with its own inherent structure to which we can submit our theories to test them.[58]

But if the world is a creation of our own consciousness, as New Agers would have it, then it *has* no inherent structure. It can be altered to suit our beliefs. Hence there is nothing objective to test ideas against, and science is rendered impossible. It is curious that New Agers are so eager to claim scientific support for a philosophy that destroys the validity of science.

Christian faith, by contrast, teaches that the world was created by God and that it exists independently of our perception. It is the handiwork of God, not the product of our minds. As we saw in chapter 1, this conviction is one reason the scientific revolution took place in Christian Europe and not in the Hindu East.

Morals—A Matter of Choice

The Enlightenment pictured the world as a vast machine. In the mid-eighteenth century la Mettrie wrote *L'homme machine*—man is a machine, his behavior completely constrained by physical or biological forces. Human will, choice, and moral responsibility were discarded as mere illusions.

Challenges to the machine image came from time to time from Christians, idealists, and romantics. But most of the protesters were scientific outsiders, and it was all too easy to accuse them of merely being "against science." Freedom and moral responsibility were dismissed as irrational wishes, held only in the face of scientific facts. In the late nineteenth century, Darwin's theory of evolution seemed to confirm that humans are nothing more than a part of nature, completely subject to immutable natural laws. Darwin's associate Thomas Huxley argued that human beings are "conscious automata," that all our thoughts and feelings are "the expression of molecular changes" in our protoplasm.[59]

Then quantum physics announced a realm of indeterminacy at the very heart of matter—and "for the first time," says social theorist Floyd Matson, "the image of the great machine came under direct attack by science itself."[60] All the arguments against free will based upon classical physics crumbled. Physicist Pascual Jordan writes: "We may say then that the attempt to prove man a machine, to deny him free will, has been refuted by the sheer facts of science."[61]

This explains why the claim is frequently made that physics is now more compatible with Christianity than it was in the previous three centuries. At the very least, argues James Jeans, the new physics has reopened questions about human freedom and dignity. Writing in his colorful style, Jeans says:

> The classical physics seemed to bolt and bar the door leading to any sort of freedom of the will; the new physics hardly does this. . . . The old physics showed us a universe which looked more like a prison than a dwelling place. The new physics shows us a universe which looks as though it might conceivably form a suitable dwelling-place for free men.[62]

This should not be taken to mean that the new physics actually provides a positive basis for moral freedom. All it does is remove a barrier to affirming human freedom that had been erected by classical physics. In itself, however, quantum theory speaks merely of occurrences that have no causes—or whose causes are hidden. And an uncaused act is not the same thing as free, responsible behavior, any more than a determined act is. In the words of physicist and philosopher Michael Polanyi, quantum mechanics allows for a range of random variables that is strictly unaccountable; yet "human judgment is anything but a strictly unaccountable, random choice."[63] In a similar vein, Barbour writes:

> The electron's behavior shows randomness, not freedom. To be sure, both freedom and chance result in unpredictability, but they have little else in common. We would hardly attribute freedom to

a roulette wheel simply because its stopping point is not predictable.[64]

The underlying issue here is not determinism versus indetermin-
ism so much as reductionism: Do we reduce human beings to the characteristics of the atoms that compose their bodies? As Barbour shows,
both sides in the debate over free will often fall prey to reductionism.
They assume that human behavior can be explained in physical-chemical terms. One side argues: If atoms are determined, then so are people. The other side argues: If atoms are indeterminate, then so are
people.[65] The debate will never be resolved until we develop a more
Biblical view that takes our physical constitution into account but
refuses to reduce human beings to the level of atoms.[66]

GOD VERSUS THE MACHINE

Many Christians have eagerly embraced quantum physics, finding it
more congenial not only to human freedom but also to theology. And
little wonder. Classical physics was often seen as hostile to any notion
of miracles or providence. "In the days of classical determinism, the
Christian concept of providence became untenable," explains Richard
Bube, former president of the American Scientific Affiliation. "A world
responding throughout time to the inexorable laws of nature replaced
the concept of a world upheld by the sovereign power of God."[67]

Liberal theology, arising in the nineteenth century, was essentially
an adaptation to the dictum laid down by classical determinism that
nothing can intervene in nature's fixed order. It was an attempt, that
is, to devise a nonsupernatural Christianity. As recently as 1958,
Rudolf Bultmann wrote:

Modern man acknowledges as reality only such phenomena or
events as are comprehensible within the framework of the rational
order of the universe. He does not acknowledge miracles because
they do not fit into this lawful order.[68]

For Bultmann, presumably, what "modern man" does not acknowledge, Christians must get rid of.

Yet if, as quantum physics tells us, events in nature are not fixed
and inexorable after all, then a powerful barrier to supernaturalism has
crumbled. No longer can science be used to rule out Biblical teachings
about God's mighty acts in history.

But quantum mechanics does not give a positive basis for divine
activity any more than it gives a positive basis for moral freedom. It
does not provide a physical "gap" where we can "fit God in," as

though God acts in the world by choosing which quantum possibility to actualize (as some Christians have argued). Quantum mechanics merely recognizes a realm of indeterminacy, which is not at all what we mean by miracles or providence.

The real issue for Christian faith is not whether the order of nature is fixed but rather whether it is closed. As Colin Brown argues in *Miracles and the Critical Mind*,[69] both human freedom and divine action raise in principle the same question: Does the regular pattern of natural law rule out free action by a personal agent? The answer is no. When human beings make choices, we do not destroy or transgress the laws of nature; rather we feed new events into the chain of cause and effect. We induce nature to do things it would never accomplish under its own power—but after that, the normal laws of nature take over.

For example, when a builder constructs a house, he interferes with nature in the sense that he does something that natural substances—wood and stone—would never accomplish if left to themselves. Yet once the house is built, it is immediately subject to all the laws of nature, the effects of wind and weather and sun. Even the scientist in his laboratory demonstrates this dual aspect. Human initiative sets up conditions in the petri dish or test tube, after which natural processes take over.

Miracles are in principle similar. As C. S. Lewis argues, miraculously created bread nourishes the same way ordinary bread does (the feeding of the five thousand). Men miraculously raised from the dead proceed to age the same way other men do (Lazarus). Even the miraculous conception of Jesus was followed by normal pregnancy, and nine months later a child was born. Lewis concludes: "The divine art of miracle is not an art of suspending the pattern to which events conform but of feeding new events into that pattern."[70] The attempt to base human freedom or miracles on quantum randomness is not only misguided but unnecessary.

Crisis of Causality

The underlying issue here is again reductionism. Do we define the structure of nature by the structure of the atom? Historically, the answer has been yes. In analytical thought, the essence of anything is to be discovered in its smallest component. As Western thinkers turned away from God as the final cause of the universe, they turned to matter—dissecting it down to its smallest building blocks in a search for the key to its structure and origin. "Since the Renaissance," writes Arthur Koestler, "the Ultimate Cause had gradually shifted from the heavens to the atomic nucleus."[71]

With the rise of quantum physics, that "Ultimate Cause" seemed to dissolve into chance. Though everyday objects still behave according to the laws of classical physics, that is merely due to the statistical averaging of large numbers of atoms. The atoms themselves do not follow any discernable laws of cause and effect. In the words of Percy Bridgman:

> Whenever the physicist penetrates to the atomic or electric level in his analysis, he finds things acting in a way for which he can assign no cause, for which he never can assign a cause, and for which the concept of cause has no meaning, if Heisenberg's principle is right. This means nothing more or less than that the law of cause and effect must be given up.[72]

In short, the philosophical basis traditionally offered for a deterministic universe has crumbled. Classical physics assumed that order in the macroscopic world results from order in the microscopic world (much as the structure of a crystal derives from the structure of its atoms). But if atoms are not strictly determined, what is the basis for determinism? Bertrand Russell states the problem forcefully:

> But if the single atom is lawless, why should there be this regularity as regards large numbers? . . . The theory of probability is in a very unsatisfactory state, both logically and mathematically; and I do not believe that there is any alchemy by which it can produce regularity in large numbers out of pure caprice in each single case.[73]

This has been described as "the crisis of causality." Although the laws of classical physics remain pragmatically valid for large objects, as Matson argues, "the *principles* which formerly supported them are in shambles."[74] Engineers still use classical physics to construct bridges and buildings, but they can no longer appeal to an atomistic, deterministic philosophy to explain *why* physics works.

"My Dogma of Infallibility"

Comparing our discussion here to the chapters on mathematics in Part Three, we notice a similar sequence of events. The early scientists were Christians, working on the assumption that the world is ordered and that we can discover that order. But Newtonian physics achieved such spectacular successes that many Western intellectuals began to believe science could be divorced from the Christian faith which gave it birth. Science would start from infallible premises—whether the self-evident truths of the rationalist or the sense data of the empiricist—and on that basis alone construct an edifice of trustworthy knowledge. Physics reached for the Laplacean ideal of completely objective, godlike knowledge, capable of tracing every path of every particle in the universe.

George Bernard Shaw describes the Newtonian faith in vivid terms: "Newton's universe was the stronghold of rational determinism. Everything was calculable; everything happened because it must." This creed became a substitute for traditional religion for those who prided themselves on being modern—including Shaw himself: "Here was my faith. Here I found my dogma of infallibility. I, who scorned alike the Catholic with his vain dream of responsible free will and the Protestant with his pretense of private judgment."

But the Newtonian faith splintered upon the rocky shores of the new physics. "And now—now," Shaw laments, "what is left of it? The orbit of the electron obeys no law, it chooses one path and rejects another. . . . All is caprice, the calculable world has become incalculable."[75]

For Shaw and others of his generation, it seemed that the bottom had fallen out of physics—and out of *any* attempt to construct an intelligible model of the world. The most fundamental assumptions of classical physics—objectivity, determinism, atomism—were rejected. How was the human mind to be trusted when the greatest achievement of science, Newtonian physics, could crumble so suddenly? How could we have confidence that our scientific theories give us a handle on reality? No wonder the twentieth century has seen the rise of various antirealist philosophies denying that science is about truth and reducing it to a tool for manipulating nature.

For Christians, these developments can be a welcome antidote to scientific dogmatism–what Shaw called "my dogma of infallibility." Koestler, for example, celebrates the collapse of the "arrogant self-confidence of the nineteenth-century scientist."[76] Christian philosopher Gordon Clark rejoices that scientists today are "more willing to admit that science does not discover absolute truth," more willing to recognize that science does not utter pronouncements about ultimate reality.[77] Perhaps the lesson is best expressed by British philosopher of science Mary Hesse: "God is in heaven and men are upon the earth," she writes, "and men must not presume to the transcendence and objectivity of God."[78]

Yet Christians also need to be cautious about accepting wholesale the more radical interpretations of the quantum revolution—the irrational, subjectivist, even mystical versions popularized by the New Age physicists. Historically, Christians have held that the world does have an order, a lawfulness, not imposed by the human mind but built into creation by a rational, faithful God. That order is not absolute but contingent (see chapter 4); nonetheless, it is real. It was precisely this conviction that inspired the early scientists.

Perhaps the most beneficial result of the new physics is simply that it has revived the dialogue between science and philosophy, between physics and metaphysics—a relationship often fraught with tension. At its most blustery, science has denounced all philosophy, metaphysics, and religion as mere fairy tales. But today microphysics has become intricately intertwined with speculations about the ultimate nature of things and can no longer relegate such questions to the back of the academic bus. As historian Carl Becker puts it, "Physics, which, it was thought, had dispensed with the need of metaphysics, has been transformed by its own proper researches into the most metaphysical of disciplines."[79]

It is perhaps more accurate to say that physics has merely recaptured its true nature. After all, through most of its history physics has been deeply intertwined with questions of metaphysics. Historical figures such as Galileo, Descartes, Newton, and Leibniz offered their scientific theories within a context of philosophical and theological discussions. The new physics has merely brought us out of the temporary aberration of positivism and has reunited science with the broader fabric of human knowledge.

A CHEMICAL CODE:
Resolving Historical Controversies

It is a truism that modern science has given us modern technology. But the reverse is also true: Technology provides concepts that drive science forward. As we design more complex machines, we discover principles that help us better understand plants and animals. In fact, scientist often fail even to recognize certain functions in the living world until they develop machines that perform the same functions.

For instance, we did not appreciate the engineering miracle in the arch of the foot until engineers had constructed bridges along the same principle. We did not grasp the ingenuity of the lubrication system in our joints until chemists tried to find the perfect lubrication for machines and vehicles. We had no conception of the complexity of the eye until optics experts had developed cameras with focusing devices and, more recently, computer systems for transmitting images.

But the analogy between the biological world and human technology is most striking on the molecular level. Enlarged to a size where we could walk around in it, the cell would resemble a fully automated modern factory. We would see a vast range of products and raw materials continually passing through conduits in an orderly fashion to various assembly plants. We would see robotlike machines—tens of thousands of different kinds—in charge of production. These are the proteins. Some of them (enzymes) act as catalysts, regulating the cell's processes like little robots with stopwatches. In fact, we would see analogues to nearly every feature of our own advanced machines. Much of the terminology needed to describe this fascinating molecular reality we would have to borrow from late twentieth-century technology.[1]

Nowhere is this more true than in the case of deoxyribonucleic acid, or DNA. The DNA molecule functions as a code, and it is best explained using concepts borrowed from modern communications theory. In human societies, the problem of information storage and retrieval has been solved by various means throughout history, from clay tablets to papyrus to paper scrolls to books. Today the printed page is being superseded by computer disks, videotapes, and CD-ROMs. Scientists are even speculating on the possibility of developing chemical coding devices.

This is old hat, of course, for the biological world. It has operated with a chemical coding system all along. The cell exploits the properties of the long, chainlike DNA molecule to store information. It is a superbly economical solution; compared to its size, the capacity of DNA to store information vastly exceeds that of any other known system. It is so efficient that all the information needed to specify an organism as complex as a human being weighs less than a few thousand millionths of a gram and fits into less space than the period at the end of this sentence.

Today most of us are so familiar with DNA that we may forget that the code was discovered as recently as the 1960s—a discovery that is revolutionizing biology not only practically but also theoretically. It suggests new answers to such philosophical questions as: What is life? What makes it different from nonlife? How did life originate?

Our aim in this chapter is to relate briefly the story of the DNA revolution[2] and then describe some of the philosophical interpretations arising from it. In the field of biology, the three historical streams of thought traced in chapters 3 through 5 remained alive and active right up to the present (see the end of chapter 5). Representatives of all three traditions have sought to absorb the new findings of molecular biology into their own conceptual framework—to make sense of the new data in their own terms. The discovery of DNA has even stimulated a contemporary restatement of the classic argument from design.

CHEMICAL CODE

The story of DNA begins with protein. Before biologists discovered the role played by DNA, they were convinced that the hereditary material of the cell must be composed of proteins. After all, up to 90 percent of the dry mass of the cell consists of proteins. Most fascinating among the proteins are enzymes, which act as tiny automated machines, cutting and splicing together the various products the cell needs for its operation, functioning much like an assembly line in a factory.

The secret to an enzyme's remarkable abilities lies in its shape. An enzyme consists of a long chain of amino acids curled up into a complex three-dimensional structure like a tangled ball of yarn. Each type of enzyme has its own distinctive structure dictated by the sequence of its amino acids. This three-dimensional structure is what enables enzymes to recognize, by touch as it were, the particular atoms and molecules they are designed to work with. They grab onto the molecules and either slice them up into parts or else push them together until they react to form larger molecules.

The functioning of a living cell depends crucially on the functioning of its proteins—which in turn depends on their amino acid sequences. And what determines the amino acid sequences? In "a very real sense," says Nobel-prize winning biologist Jacques Monod, "it is at this level of chemical organization that the secret of life lies." Biologists were convinced that if they were able "not only to describe these sequences but to pronounce the law by which they assemble, one could declare the secret penetrated," the riddle of life solved.[3]

But in 1952 scientists' hopes were dashed. In that year the first description of a complete protein sequence was published. To their shock, biologists discovered that the amino acid sequence followed no apparent law at all. There was virtually no regularity, no pattern. In other words, if a protein were composed of 200 amino acids and scientists knew the exact order of 199 of them, there was no rule to predict what the last one would be.[4]

Despite their disappointment, biologists realized that the discovery implied something extremely important. The *lack* of overall pattern told them that the sequence of amino acids could not be described by a general law of assembly. Instead, somewhere there had to be a set of instructions that specified each amino acid in the chain—one by one. As Monod put it, a protein consists of "a sequence with no rule by which it determined itself." Hence biologists realized "it had to have a code—that is, complete instructions expressed in some manner to tell it how to exist."[5]

Back in the 1940s, experiments by Oswald Avery had indicated that the chemical basis of heredity was not protein after all but nucleic acid—specifically, the deoxyribose type, now known as DNA. Bacteria injected with DNA showed permanent hereditary changes. Yet scientists remained skeptical. At the time, says Nobel Prize-winning physiologist George Beadle, DNA "was believed by many to be a rather monotonous polymer built of four kinds of nucleotide units arranged in segments of four that were repeated manyfold."[6] Another Nobel Prize-winner, Max Delbrück, stated the same idea more colorfully: "At that time it was believed that DNA was a *stupid* substance," far too stupid to carry instructions for specifying the complex proteins in a living cell.[7]

Yet DNA did *not* turn out to be stupid, and the reason is that the nucleotides in DNA are not "repeated manyfold." They do not form a simple repeating pattern. Instead, like proteins, they are composed of apparently random sequences. Like letters in a word, and words in a sentence, the nucleotides in DNA can be arranged and rearranged in any number of linear sequences to spell out a complex message. In fact, the similarity between DNA and human language is so close that to describe its processes biologists have been obliged to borrow the language of editors and linguists. They speak of DNA as a code or symbol system; they speak of molecules that copy and translate the message; they speak of proofreading functions and error correction.

This was a revolutionary discovery, and many have compared its significance to the revolution in physics prompted by relativity and quantum mechanics. Indeed, the two revolutions are in a way connected, since it was physicist Erwin Schrödinger, of Schrödinger cat fame (see chapter 9), who is credited with the earliest mention of the idea of a code. In 1944, in a booklet called *What Is Life?*, Schrödinger wrote that a fertilized egg must contain "an elaborate code-script involving all the future development of the organism," a "miniature code."[8] And it was physicist George Gamow, celebrated proponent of the Big Bang theory, who apparently first suggested the way the code must work—that a sequence of nucleotides in DNA must correlate in some way with the sequence of amino acids in proteins.[9]

The difficulty was in figuring out exactly *how* the two sequences correlate. Solving that problem is what biologists mean when they talk about cracking the genetic code.

Cracking the Code

Most people today are familiar with the double helix structure of the DNA molecule. It may be pictured as a long ladder twisted into a spiral. The sides of the ladder are composed of sugar and phosphate molecules. Its "rungs" are composed of four bases—adenine (A), thymine (T), guanine (G), and cytosine (C). A nucleotide consists of a base linked with sugar and phosphate molecules. During replication, the two sides of the "ladder" split, and each half attracts a new set of nucleotides from the surrounding cytoplasm (the part of the cell outside the nucleus) in order to replace the missing half.

As long as the hereditary material in the cell was thought to be protein, the problem of inheritance was regarded essentially as a problem of self-replication—proteins making other proteins. But the discovery that the hereditary substance is DNA posed a completely new problem for biologists—the problem of coding. As philosopher Michael Simon puts it, there had to be some way in which the structure of molecules that are *not* proteins could determine the structure of other molecules that *are*.[10]

The solution to the problem was the hypothesis of the genetic code—the idea that the DNA molecule transmits information in a manner analogous to a written language. The alphabet of DNA is its four bases: A, T, G, and C. The sequence in which the bases are arranged along the DNA molecule spells out a set of instructions for building proteins.

But that's only the first step. Next we need to ask how the instructions in the DNA code are communicated to the rest of the cell. In a sense, the cell contains not one language but two—the DNA code written in an alphabet of four bases, and proteins written in an alphabet of twenty amino acids. When DNA constructs proteins, a translation takes place from one language to the other. When biologists talk about "cracking the genetic code," they mean finding the rules of translation between the two chemical languages—determining which particular base sequence in DNA codes for a particular amino acid sequence in a protein.

Geneticists now know that the four bases of DNA combine into groups of three—called codons—which function as three-letter words. Each word codes for a particular amino acid. For example, the codon GUA codes for the amino acid valine; the codon GCA codes for alanine. A few codons function as punctuation marks, indicating the place to begin and end the amino acid chain. Some codons even act as synonyms. Just as English contains different words that have the same meaning (*happy* and *glad*), so different codons can specify the same amino acid. While GUA codes for valine, so does GUC, GUG, and GUU.

In protein construction, the DNA stays in the cell nucleus while another form of nucleic acid—RNA—does the work of communication and translation throughout the rest of the cell. Messenger-RNA (mRNA) peels off a sequence of bases from a section of the DNA molecule, as though making photocopies from a text (Fig. 1). Then it acts as an express mail service to carry the message throughout the cell where its sequence acts as a template for protein construction. Transfer-RNA (tRNA) rounds up the amino acids. Each tRNA molecule grabs hold of an amino acid with one hand, so to speak, and seeks out a strand of mRNA, where it grabs hold of the appropriate codon with the other hand. It keeps holding on until the necessary chemical reactions take place to link that amino acid onto the end of a growing chain. In this way amino acids are linked together one by one in the correct sequence to form a functioning protein. The assembly line structure that holds all the pieces together is called a ribosome (Fig. 2).

It turns out that the "stupidity" or simplicity of the DNA molecule is deceptive. When you think that sophisticated modern computers operate on a two-symbol code (a binary code), it is obvious that the four-symbol code in DNA is quite adequate to carry any amount of

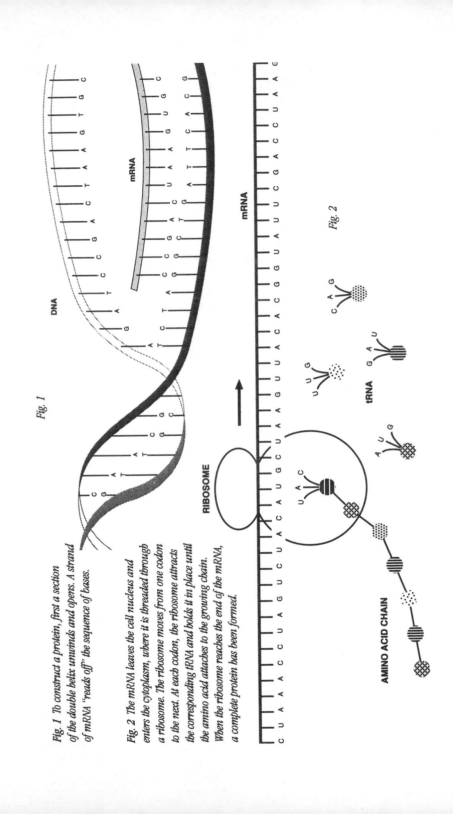

Fig. 1 To construct a protein, first a section of the double helix unwinds and opens. A strand of mRNA "reads off" the sequence of bases.

Fig. 2 The mRNA leaves the cell nucleus and enters the cytoplasm, where it is threaded through a ribosome. The ribosome moves from one codon to the next. At each codon, the ribosome attracts the corresponding tRNA and holds it in place until the amino acid attaches to the growing chain. When the ribosome reaches the end of the mRNA, a complete protein has been formed.

Fig. 1

DNA

mRNA

Fig. 2

RIBOSOME

mRNA

tRNA

AMINO ACID CHAIN

complex information. In fact, the amount of information contained in a single human cell equals the entire thirty volumes of the *Encyclopedia Britannica* several times over.

Codes and Complexity

The discovery of DNA has opened a whole new level of organic marvels—a world of codes much more complex than any human coding system. For example, in one tiny virus the DNA actually layers message upon message. Molecular biologist Frederick Sanger discovered that in this particular virus (virus øX174), the mRNA starts at one place on the DNA molecule and "reads off" one message. Then it starts a single letter down to read off a *second* message. It's as though you picked up a Shakespeare play and started at the beginning to read *Romeo and Juliet*—and then started a single letter down to read *A Midsummer Night's Dream*. This is astonishing complexity, meaning packed upon meaning.[11]

Another fascinating discovery is that in higher organisms the DNA message is stored in short segments connected by "junk DNA"–sequences that do not code for anything, as far as scientist can tell. For example, imagine a gene in a bacterium that reads, "Here are the plans for the construction of a protein to digest lactose." The equivalent gene in a higher organism might read this way: "Here are the plans gibble gabble for the construction of hubba hubba a protein to digest lactose." After mRNA copies this message, the "gibble gabble" and "hubba hubba" are edited out; otherwise a faulty protein would be produced.[12] No one knows the function of "junk DNA," but one of the practical results is that once the meaningful segments of DNA have been spliced out, they can be shuffled and reattached in new patterns. This has given rise to the entire field of recombinant DNA.

Moreover, genes can be switched on and off by small proteins that bind to specific DNA sequences. This discovery has opened up fields such as embryonic development, studying how genes are switched on and off during the developmental process.

The discovery of the DNA code has transformed our scientific understanding of the nature of the living cell. We now know that at the heart of life is a language, a code, a set of instructions. As Lila Gatlin puts it, "life may be defined operationally as an information processing system."[13] And Jeremy Campbell writes:

> Evidently nature can no longer be seen as matter and energy alone. Nor can all her secrets be unlocked with the keys of chemistry and physics. . . . A third component is needed for any explanation of the world that claims to be complete. To the powerful theories of

chemistry and physics must be added a late arrival: a theory of information. Nature must be interpreted as matter, energy, and information.[14]

The question of life's origin must likewise be recast to take account of these findings. The origin of life is now in large measure the origin of information. As Bernd-Olaf Kuppers writes, "The origin of life is clearly basically equivalent to the problem of the origin of biological information."[15]

The development of genetic theory also sheds new light on age-old controversies in biology between mechanists and vitalists, reductionists and holists, evolutionists and creationists. We shift our focus now to philosophical interpretations of DNA, organizing our discussion around the three historical streams of scientific thought outlined in chapter 5—the mechanist, neo-Platonic, and Aristotelian worldviews.

WRITTEN IN THE ATOMS

At the time of the scientific revolution, the mechanistic tradition was often propounded by Christians. But today it tends to be materialist and reductionist. Biologists within the mechanistic tradition are committed to reducing life to a product of physical-chemical forces. They have been quick to seize upon the DNA revolution as confirmation of a materialist worldview.

The reasoning is simple. If we grant that DNA is the molecule of heredity, and if we also grant that it specifies the structure of proteins—thereby specifying virtually all the chemical reactions in the cell—then we must conclude that DNA is capable of both transmitting and maintaining life. And since nucleic acid is indisputably a chemical substance, then we must agree, so the argument goes, that life is essentially reducible to chemistry.

This argument has perhaps greatest impact in debates over the origin of life. In the materialist view, the DNA code is reduced to the sequence of its bases, and its origin is attributed to physical-chemical forces acting among its constituent elements. We find this conviction expressed in the writings of Francis Crick and James Watson, co-discoverers of the double-helix structure of the DNA molecule. "So far, everything we have found," Crick says, "can be explained without effort in terms of the standard bonds of chemistry."[16] Likewise, Watson insists that the characteristics of living organisms "will all be completely understood in terms of the coordinative interactions of small and large molecules."[17] In short, according to the mechanistic view, life is mere chemistry, and the origin of life can be explained by the ordinary operation of chemical and physical processes. To quote Crick again, "The ultimate aim of the modern movement in biology is in fact to explain *all* biology in terms of physics and chemistry."[18]

The earliest attempts to formulate a mechanistic theory of life's origin leaned heavily on chance—on random interactions of chemicals in a warm pond on the early earth. Given the complexity of life, its chance origin was a highly unlikely event, of course. But biologists hoped to vault that barrier by injecting immense quantities of time. Given enough time, they said, the most improbable event becomes not only possible, not merely probable, but inevitable.

However, at a symposium held in 1966 at the Wistar Institute in Philadelphia, the computer revolution caught up with the biologists. Using high-speed computers, mathematicians simulated the trial-and-error methods of chance. The outcome was devastating. Computers showed that the probability that life arose by chance processes is essentially zero, no matter how much time is allotted.[19]

Since that time, there has been a gradual shift away from chance models of life's origin to models that rely on some force inherent in matter. Chance has proved to be the materialist's God-of-the-gaps, continually pushed back by advances in scientific knowledge.

Predestined for Life?

As chance theories lost credibility, they were replaced by theories that rely on some inherent self-ordering force within matter. Cyril Ponnamperuma of the University of Maryland sums up the guiding assumption in the field today in these words: "There are inherent properties in the atoms and molecules which seem to direct the synthesis in the direction most favorable" for producing the molecules of life.[20]

By "inherent properties" biologists mean such things as chemical bonding forces. In 1969 a book appeared titled *Biochemical Predestination*, which argued that the specific sequences characterizing long chain molecules—protein and DNA—are due to differences in chemical bonding forces. The study of chemistry is based on the fact that chemical compounds do not react completely randomly. Instead, each compound reacts more readily with certain substances than with others, due to differences in size, shape, and chemical activity. Biologists began to wonder whether in the prebiotic soup these differences in chemical bonding forces might dictate the formation of an ordered sequence.[21]

But this particular form of predestinist theory has lost its initial plausibility. To begin with, it has not been confirmed experimentally. Experiments designed to simulate conditions on the early earth have not revealed any significant ordering effects due to differences in chemical bonding forces.[22] Dean Kenyon, one of the authors of *Biochemical Predestination*, has since rejected the theory on experimental grounds. "If you survey the experiments performed to date designed to simulate conditions on the early earth," he said in an interview,

> one thing that stands out is that you do not get ordered sequences of amino acids. Nor do you get ordered sequences of nucleotides, the building blocks of DNA. These simply do not appear among the products of any experiments. If we thought we were going to see a lot of spontaneous ordering, something must have been wrong with our theory.

What the experiments do yield is primarily a sludge of gummy brown tar. Or as Kenyon expresses it more elegantly: "The dominant trend in simulation experiments is the formation of non-biological materials."[23]

This may come as a surprise to many readers. Frequently, it seems, we read headlines announcing that biologists are right on the brink of creating life in a test tube. Just before this book went to press, *Time* magazine ran an upbeat cover story titled "How Did Life Begin?" (October 11, 1993), subtitled "Scientists find some surprising answers to the greatest mystery on earth."

But the truth is that the "answers" discovered so far by science are painfully sparse. Experiments simulating conditions on the early earth have produced small amounts of organic material—notably amino acids. But the initial excitement created by these experiments has largely died down among scientists in the field. The organic materials that form are quite meager (about 2 percent of the total yield). They are generally swamped by large quantities of tarry sludge. More highly refined experimental techniques have not changed that pattern; it is now a well-established trend. As chemist Robert Shapiro comments:

> A mixture of simple chemicals, even one enriched in a few amino acids, no more resembles a bacterium than a small pile of real and nonsense words, each written on an individual scrap of paper, resembles the complete works of Shakespeare.[24]

No Chemical Rules

This is not the place for a comprehensive critique of origin-of-life experiments.[25] But Shapiro's illustration of words on scraps of paper suggests a second problem with any materialist theory of life's origin—the role of information. Inherent forces within matter would not produce a molecule capable of conveying information.

The DNA molecule stores and transmits vast quantities of information, more than any computer invented by human technology. And the reason is that each of its bases—each of its chemical letters—is almost equally likely to be followed by any other. If you start with one base, you cannot predict which will follow next. Each is equally probable. This flexibility for arranging and rearranging its symbols in a wide variety of sequences is precisely what gives DNA its enormous capacity for information storage.

Consider an analogy to the English language. If you read a book that begins, "Once upon a time," you have no idea how the story will continue. Whatever follows must follow the formal rules of grammar and sentence construction, of course; but there are no rules or laws constraining the actual content of the story. This flexibility in a human language is what allows words to be combined and recombined in an almost infinite variety of sequences to form sentences and paragraphs, conveying potentially unlimited amounts of information.

The DNA molecule exhibits a similar flexibility—a feature that cannot be explained if its sequence is the result of material forces or laws. A law produces regular, predictable patterns. Recall our earlier discussion of proteins. Biologists originally hoped to find a general law of assembly for proteins. And how did they expect to discern the effects of a law? They looked for regularities, patterns. It was when geneticists *failed* to find an overall pattern that they realized they were dealing with something not produced by natural law.[26]

The same reasoning applies to DNA. If we were to find regular, repeating patterns, that would constitute evidence of an underlying law. But a repeating pattern encodes little information. Computer buffs sometimes like to create wrapping paper by commanding the computer to print "Happy Birthday!" again and again until the page is filled. The result is a repeating pattern that conveys very little information; the entire page conveys no more information than the first two words.

If the origin of the DNA sequence were a material force, such as chemical bonding forces, then we would get something analogous to computer-generated wrapping paper. The entire DNA molecule would consist of repeating patterns, which would encode very little information.

Two for One

So severe are the problems of explaining DNA by its intrinsic chemistry that many scientists have reverted to chance theories, many of which focus on RNA.

Explaining the genetic code is a much broader problem than

merely accounting for the base sequence in DNA. What must be accounted for is the entire coding system—the translation process between DNA and protein. If it is difficult to explain how *one* of these complex molecules came into existence by natural causes, think how much more difficult it is to explain how the entire coordinated system came into existence.

This problem has inspired many scientists over the past several years to take a new look at RNA. Some forms of RNA contain elements of both DNA and protein (both code and enzyme). Originating one complex informational molecule by random interactions seems a lot easier than originating two different kinds of complex molecule.

Yet as Shapiro argues, RNA is complex enough that its origin by chance is still in the realm of vanishingly small probability, given a plausible scenario of the early earth. The odds "are still so unfavorable that the formation of the replicator [RNA] by chance would seem miraculous."[27]

Nevertheless, biologists in the mechanistic tradition have not given up the quest: They still hope to formulate some explanation that invokes physical forces alone. Biologists in other traditions, however, are not so sanguine. They argue that the DNA code requires us to use conceptual categories beyond those supplied by physics and chemistry. This argument has become popular in the neo-Platonist tradition, to which we turn now.

LIFE'S IRREDUCIBLE STRUCTURE

Although mechanistic philosophy dominates biology today, neo-Platonism remains a strong minority viewpoint. Its adherents are convinced that life cannot be reduced to physics and chemistry—that life is "something more." Exactly *what* that "something more" is has been a matter of dispute, however.

In the nineteenth century, the neo-Platonist tradition was represented by the romantic biologists, many of whom accepted vitalism or animism (see chapter 5). Vitalism assumes the existence of some sort of agent—a life force—that actively selects and arranges matter in living things. Animism dispenses with a purposeful agent, but nevertheless proposes the existence of special vital forces in inert matter.

Vitalism and animism are no longer viable theories in scientific circles today. But their place has been taken by an approach known as organicism. Organicists defend the idea that life is "something more" than physics and chemistry, while rejecting older ideas of a special metaphysical substance or force permeating living matter. Instead, they attribute the uniqueness of life to its complex organization.[28]

Organicists acknowledge that living things are constituted of ordinary physical elements—mainly very common elements such as carbon, nitrogen, oxygen, and hydrogen. They also acknowledge that the atoms and molecules which comprise living cells act individually according to the laws of physics and chemistry. What is distinctive about life, they say, is the unlikely *organization* of these components into a systematic whole that is different from anything in the inanimate world.

A striking analogy is the computer. In a computer, each component behaves according to the laws of electronics and mechanics. Yet the machine itself cannot be reduced to a collection of wires and silicon chips. What makes a computer perform its remarkable feats is the highly unlikely organization of those parts—an overall plan that "harnesses" the electronic and mechanical processes and makes them serve the functions of the apparatus as a whole.

By the same token, organicists argue, a living organism cannot be reduced to the atoms and molecules that compose it. What makes it function differently from an inanimate object is a system of organization, an overall plan, that "harnesses" chemical reactions to serve organic processes.

What Makes a Watch Tick?

One of the most influential organicists in recent years was the chemist-philosopher Michael Polanyi, who breathed life into the movement with a novel attack on reductionism.[29] Historically, most reductionists found their home in the mechanistic tradition; hence for centuries vitalists contested *reductionism* by arguing against *mechanism*—by arguing that the functions and structures of living things cannot be accounted for by any machinelike mechanism.

But Polanyi realized that mechanistic philosophy does not entail reductionism. In fact, in a remarkable tour de force he turned the table on the reductionists. You say life is a machine? he asked. Fine. We accept the analogy. But that does not force us to accept physical-chemical reductionism. Just the opposite. The machine analogy actually supports the organicist view that life is more than physics and chemistry.

Consider, after all, what a machine is, Polanyi argued. To be sure, it is constituted of physical atoms and molecules—iron, steel, plastic, whatever. But what defines an object as a machine is not the physical matter that constitutes it but rather its function.

Analyzed in terms of atoms, there is no difference between a lump of iron and an iron padlock. The difference between them is not on the level of matter; it is on the level of human purpose, which shapes the padlock to serve a particular function. The same applies to any tool or machine. The principle determining its structure is the purpose or goal for which it is designed.

Think of a watch. If a child asks you what a watch is, you probably would not answer by describing what the gears and housing are made of. Watches can be made of a variety of substances and utilize a variety of mechanisms, from antique grandfather clocks to modern atomic clocks. What defines a watch is that it tells the time. A machine is defined by its function, its purpose.

Imagine a group of extraterrestrial scientists who land on earth and have never seen a watch before. They are puzzled by the novel contraption and analyze it exhaustively in terms of the materials that make it up: the weight, size, shape, and motions of its gears and other parts. When they finish, have they figured out what the unfamiliar object is? No. A comprehensive analysis on the physical-chemical level cannot reveal that it is an object designed for telling time. The defining feature is the operational principle by which the physical components are organized—something that cannot be discovered on the physical level.

Now, let's apply this reasoning to an organic structure, such as the eye. If we analyze all its physical components—lens, iris, rods and cones—that still does not tell us what an eye is. The defining feature of an eye is that it is an organ for seeing. All its physical components are structured and organized for that purpose. In order to understand organic structures, we have to consider not just the physical-chemical components but, more importantly, the operational principle or purpose by which the components are organized.

Hence we may freely consider the organism a machine, as mechanists are so fond of doing, says Polanyi. But that does not lead us inexorably to physical-chemical reductionism. The principle that organizes the physical elements in a machine is itself beyond physics.

This distinction is common in everyday experience. A novel by Charles Dickens consists of words on paper, but no one would say it was "nothing but" a collection of words. What makes a novel different from random babbling are the artistic principles that structure those words. A Mozart symphony consists of musical notes, but no one would say it was "nothing but" a collection of sound waves. What distinguishes it from mere noise are the musical principles that order the notes. A house consists of bricks and boards, but it is not a random pile of building materials. What makes the difference are the architectural principles by which the materials are put together. In same way, organicists argue, life consists of chemical elements, but we cannot maintain that it is "nothing but" chemicals. What makes life distinctive are the organic principles by which those chemicals are put together in living organisms.

The Language of Life

If Polanyi's argument is sound, we need at least two levels of explanation to account for living structures—a physical and an organizational explanation. This is best illustrated in the DNA molecule. The bases, sugars, and phosphates that comprise the nucleotides in DNA are ordinary chemicals and react according to ordinary chemical laws. Yet those same laws cannot explain the sequence of bases that spells out the message in DNA.

In Polanyi's words, the sequence of bases is "extraneous to" or "independent of" the chemical and physical forces in the DNA molecule. That is, the sequence is not determined by inherent physical forces. It is precisely this "physical indeterminacy" that gives the DNA molecule the flexibility to appear in a variety of sequences, like words on a page.[30] And if physical forces do not determine the structure of the DNA molecule, then we need to search *outside* physics for its organizing principle. We need a second level of explanation.

This becomes clearer if we draw an analogy to human language. The words you are reading right now are written in ink. Yet their sequence did not arise from the chemicals in the ink, nor from any chemical interaction between the ink and the paper, nor even from the electronic impulses in the computer when it was originally keyed in. The information is completely independent of the material medium used to store and transmit it.

Exactly the same reasoning applies to the information in DNA. It is independent of the material medium—the strand of chemicals— used to store and transmit it. If we knew how to translate the message encoded in a DNA molecule, we could write it out using other material. We could write it in Magic Marker, in crayon, in finger paint. We could even write with a stick in the sand. And it would still be the same message. Changing the material medium does not change the message. Information is independent of the material substance that stores and conveys it.

And because a message is independent of the material medium, it does not originate from the medium. The DNA message does not originate in the chemistry of a DNA molecule—any more than the text on this page arose from the paper and ink used to print it. Yet that is precisely what the reductionist maintains. He proposes that the forces in the chemicals themselves originated the information in DNA. This is tantamount to saying that the ink wrote the words on this page, that the ink molecules spontaneously organized themselves into a complex arrangement of words and paragraphs.

In reality, of course, the words on this page were constrained by the principles of the English language—rules of grammar, interpretation, and sentence construction—along with the rules of logic and reasoning. By the same token, Polanyi argues, the information in the DNA molecule is constrained by special organic rules and principles—principles not reducible to the laws of physics and chemistry.

Polanyi's arguments have been embraced not only within the neo-Platonist tradition but also within the Aristotelian tradition, whose modern representatives in biology are most visible in the creationist movement. But creationists propose to take Polanyi's logic a step further. They use it to construct a new version of the argument from design.

WHO WROTE THE GENETIC CODE?

Aristotle is enjoying a surprising resurgence of popularity among modern biologists. In the 1970s, Max Delbrück delivered an address titled "How Aristotle Discovered DNA," in which he half playfully suggested that, if Nobel Prizes were ever awarded posthumously, Aristotle ought to receive one. The Aristotelian concept of Form, Delbrück argues, is remarkably similar to the modern concept of a genetic program—a "preimposed plan" according to which the embryo develops into an adult.[31]

Aristotle comes in for praise from B. C. Goodwin of the University of Sussex as well. Aristotle understood that a living thing cannot be grasped from an analysis of its physical substance alone, Goodwin writes. Instead, it must be understood in terms of a "principle of organization," a Form that governs the development from embryo to adult.[32]

On a similar note, zoologist Ernst Mayr remarks on a "renewed appreciation" for Aristotle in recent years. In earlier centuries, Mayr notes, philosophers and physicists were "completely deaf to the assertion of naturalists such as Aristotle that something more than the laws of physics was needed to produce a frog from a frog egg or a chicken from a chicken egg." But today Aristotle has been vindicated. "He clearly saw that raw material lacks the capacity to develop the complex form of an organism. Something additional had to be present"— a teleonomic principle, which Aristotle called *eidos* or Form. "Only when the dual nature of living organisms was fully understood in our time," Mayr says,

> was it realized that the blueprint of development and activity—the genetic program—represents the formative principle which Aristotle had postulated.[33]

Finally, Jeremy Campbell gives Aristotle credit for anticipating information theory. "Plan, purpose, and information were among the *active* forces Aristotle saw at work in nature"—precisely the ideas at the frontier of biological research today. DNA represents "a coded model of a biological goal," Campbell writes. "It is the form of the matter."[34]

This compatibility between Aristotle and modern genetics has not gone unnoticed by modern descendants of the Christian Aristotelians discussed in chapter 5—namely, the creationists. Campbell's concept of "plan, purpose, and information" fits neatly into a creationist understanding of organic structure. Hence modern creationists have enthusiastically embraced Polanyi's argument that the DNA code cannot be explained by the current working of physical-chemical causes. But they also take the argument a step further, asserting that the best explanation is an intelligent agent.

Natural Order

The mechanistic view of life gains its initial plausibility from the fact that some kinds of natural order do result from purely physical-chemical forces. Take, for example, a snowflake. Its intricate pattern is an impressive display of order in nature. Yet there is nothing mysterious or supranatural about its structure. It is explained by the laws describing dendritic growth during the phase change of H_2O from liquid (water) to solid (ice).

The growth of ice and other crystals is often cited by materialists as evidence that order is self-originating. A crystal is simply a large orderly array of atoms or molecules in their solid state. In a solution, the atoms (or ions; the difference needn't concern us here) float around freely. But if they bump against each other, they have a natural tendency to slot into a particular position and layer themselves in a fixed, orderly pattern.

For example, when sodium and chloride ions are dissolved in a solution and the water evaporates, the product is crystals of sodium chloride—table salt. Regarded separately, there is nothing in sodium or chloride ions to create an expectation of crystals. Yet because of properties we can think of as their "shape," the ions tend to layer themselves in a fixed pattern, which gives salt its crystalline structure. "If we could shrink ourselves to the atomic scale," says zoologist Richard Dawkins, "we would see almost endless rows of atoms stretching to the horizon in straight lines—galleries of geometric repetition."[35]

That geometric pattern is what makes each crystal unique. Graphite and diamonds both consist of pure carbon atoms; the only difference between them is the geometrical pattern in which the atoms are packed. In diamonds the carbon atoms form a tetrahedral pattern.

In graphite the atoms form flat hexagonal sheets layered on top of each other. If the growth of crystals illustrates the spontaneous origin of order, materialists argue, then similar processes might explain the origin of life. Pick up any book on the origin of life—especially one written for a popular audience—and you are likely to find an analogy drawn between the formation of crystals and the formation of the first living structures.

In fact, one theory receiving a good deal of attention today is that life actually started out as a crystal. Chemist A. G. Cairns-Smith at the University of Glasgow has suggested that life began on the surface of the crystals that make up certain clays. The crystalline structure acted as a template, a molecular mold, that incorporated life's building blocks and organized them in precise arrays. Cairns-Smith goes so far as to suggest that in its earliest stages life was not an organic structure at all but a crystalline mineral—that prior to DNA there were what he calls "crystal genes," with flaws in the crystal analogous to mutations.[36]

But these proposals all contain a glaring contradiction. The structure of a crystal is strictly repetitive—"galleries of geometric repetition." By contrast, the sequence of bases in a DNA molecule has no regular pattern at all. As we noted earlier, it is precisely the flexibility among nucleotides to spell out any base sequence whatsoever that allows DNA to function as a language. If the forces that shape DNA were the same as the forces that shape a crystal, then DNA would consist of a single or at most a few patterns repeating over and over—just like the geometric patterns in a crystal—and it would be incapable of storing and transmitting information.

The truth is that the process of crystal formation throws no light at all on the origin of life. Consequently, some scientists have turned to a new analogy, developed by physicist Ilya Prigogine. When you pull the plug on a bathtub, the water running down the drain often forms a whirlpool. When scientists heat oil, at a certain temperature hexagonal patterns form on the surface. These are called nonequilibrium systems, and Prigogine developed a set of mathematical formulas for describing them. His work is often touted as new evidence for the power of self-organization in nature. Mechanistic accounts of life's origin today are likely to appeal to Prigogine's work for analogies of spontaneous ordering.

But Prigogine's new examples are not essentially different from the old example of crystals. The order represented by a bathtub whirlpool and hexagonal patterns in oil are similar to the order in a crystal. What we see in DNA is an entirely different kind of order, but only in recent years have scientists begun to recognize the difference.

It is information theory that gives us the conceptual and mathematical tools we need to get a handle on the difference.

Measuring Information

"One if by land, two if by sea." Paul Revere was not familiar with information theory, but he was intuitively using its principles. Information theory treats the ways intelligence can be represented. In Paul Revere's case, intelligence about the enemy's route of approach was translated into a simple but effective code.

Information theory rests on the idea that intelligence can be quantified and measured. In fact, any kind of order or organization can be quantified. As chemist Leslie Orgel explains, "the information content of a structure is the minimum number of instructions needed to specify the structure," to tell someone how to build it. The more complex a structure is, the more instructions are needed to specify it.[37]

A structure with no order at all—for instance, a random set of letters—requires few instructions. If you want to write out a series of nonsense syllables, you need only two instructions: 1) "Select at random a letter of the English alphabet (or a space) and write it down," and 2) "Do it again." In the natural world a pile of leaves is random. It can be specified by saying: 1) "Select at random some type of leaf—oak, maple, birch—and drop it on the pile," and 2) "Do it again." A random structure can be specified using few instructions. Hence it has a low information content.

A highly ordered structure likewise has a low information content—if the order is repetitive. Recall our earlier example of a computer buff creating wrapping paper by printing "Happy Birthday!" again and again. This is a highly ordered pattern, and yet it can be specified by just a few instructions: 1) "Print 'H-a-p-p-y B-i-r-t-h-d-a-y-!'" and 2) "Do it again," until the paper is filled.

In the natural world, we see this kind of order in crystals—a single structure repeated over and over. A crystal is highly ordered, yet it is low in information content. If we were to tell a chemist how to make a crystal, we would need only two instructions. After saying what kind of atom or molecule we want the crystal to be made of, we would describe what geometrical pattern we wish the first few atoms to form. Then we would say, "Do it again." As Orgel explains, the "structural information has to be given only once because the crystal is regular."[38]

But a second kind of order exists that is completely different. It is high in information content and requires a large number of instructions. For example, if you want your computer to type out Longfellow's entire poem starting with, "Listen, my children, and you shall hear / of the midnight ride of Paul Revere," you must specify every letter—one by one. There are no shortcuts.

This is the kind of order we see in a written message. It is also the kind we find in DNA—though we might prefer to call it complexity, rather than order, to keep the distinction before our minds. It would be impossible to produce a simple set of instructions telling a chemist how to synthesize the DNA of even the simplest bacterium. You would have to specify every chemical letter—one by one. Hence DNA has a high information content.

Information theory gives us a mathematical and conceptual tool for distinguishing between these two kinds of order—the kind we see in inorganic matter and the kind we see in organisms and human artifacts (such as written messages). Nonliving structures may be random, like a pile of leaves, or they may be ordered, like a crystal, but in both cases the information content is low. Living structures, by contrast, are high in information content. Their assembly must be specified step by step.[39]

This is why crystal growth and the emergence of patterns in oil have nothing to do with the origin of life. They are examples of order, not complexity. As information specialist Hubert Yockey argues, Cairns-Smith does not solve the problem of information with his crystal genes because he "does not make a clear distinction between 'order' and 'complexity.'"[40] Complexity, in this specialized sense of the word, means a structure with high information content.

How Does a Molecule Become a Message?

How can we account for this second kind of order—or complexity—with its high information content? The physical-chemical forces at work in the inanimate world can explain order but not complexity. They can create a crystal but not a code. What force or agency is capable of creating complexity—of specifying each base in the DNA molecule?

Let's return once again to the analogy between DNA and a written message. The letters in the words you are reading are not ordered. They do not fall into repetitive patterns like computer-generated wrapping paper. In a certain sense, the letters in a written language are randomly distributed.

Think of it this way. If you see a paragraph written in Greek and you cannot read that language, then you have no way of knowing—just by examining the letter sequence—whether the paragraph is a random collection of letters and spaces or whether it consists of real words. To turn it around, someone who did not know English could not tell, just by examining the letters, that "The boy runs" is a meaningful sentence but that "Het yob surn" is not.

Every language consists of essentially arbitrary letter combinations. There is nothing inherent in the letters themselves that gives the sequence *b-o-y* meaning. Nor is there anything intrinsic to the sequence *J-u-n-g-e* that gives it meaning in German, though not in English. In fact, the same sequence of letters can have different meanings in different languages. In English *g-i-f-t* means a present, but in German it means a poison.

What confers meaning on an essentially arbitrary sequence of letters is a linguistic convention, formalized in dictionaries. From a potential infinitude of different letter combinations (corresponding to sound combinations), English selects comparatively few and confers meaning on them.

The situation is precisely analogous in the cell. The sequence of bases that spell out a message in the DNA molecule is chemically arbitrary. There is nothing intrinsic in the chemistry of any base sequence that makes it carry a particular meaning. In fact, there are many base sequences possible *besides* the ones actually used in the cell—all of them equally probable in terms of chemical forces. By merely examining the physical structure, you could not detect any difference between these useless base sequences and those necessary for life. There is nothing in their physical make-up that distinguishes the two sets of molecules. Out of a vast number of possible base sequences, somehow only a few carry meaning.[41]

What was it that conferred meaning on an arbitrary sequence of bases in the DNA molecule? What turned a chain of molecules into a message? As physicist H. H. Pattee asks, what are the "constraints that endow what otherwise would indeed be ordinary molecules with their symbolic properties"?[42] Information storage depends on an arbitrary sequence of bases that is somehow endowed with symbolic properties. Henry Quastler calls it an "accidental choice remembered."[43]

If the physical components of the DNA molecule are not distinguished in any way, then it seems clear that no analysis of the physical components can explain what makes it unique—what makes it function as a symbol system. Instead, the answer is found in the analogy between DNA and a written message. What confers meaning on particular sequences of letters in a message are linguistic conventions—rules of usage, grammar, and sentence structure. By the same token, says Pattee, "it is only the integrated set of rules of grammar and interpretation that gives these particular physical structures their symbolic attributes."[44]

But where do rules of grammar come from in nature? Linguistic conventions do not arise out of chemical reactions. As Monod acknowledges, the genetic code is "chemically arbitrary, inasmuch as the transfer of information could just as well take place according to some other convention."[45] In fact, linguistic conventions do not arise from any known natural laws. As biologist Peter Calow says, the design of living things is written out in a "system of symbols whose use and effect is established by convention, not by the laws of nature."[46] If the linguistic convention in the DNA code is not established by the laws of nature, then where does it come from? In the broader arena of human experience the answer is simple: Linguistic conventions come from the mental realm of information and intelligence.

The role of intelligence becomes even clearer if we turn from the code to the encoded message. Discussions about DNA are often muddied by confusion among three things: 1) the molecule itself, which is the material medium for the message; 2) the code, which consists of the rules of grammar and translation; and 3) the message, the actual content that is translated into protein structure. Mechanistic biologists concentrate on the material medium. They assume that once we explain the origin of the molecule itself by physical-chemical forces, the origin of everything else is thereby also explained. Once the nucleotides can be induced to come together and form a chain, the base sequence somehow "acquires meaning." It's as though we took Scrabble letters, randomly arranged the letters and spaces in a long line, and then hoped that a linguistic convention would arise from it, with rules to give the letter-groups meaning.

The neo-Platonist biologist realizes that the reductionist approach is inadequate, that we need to posit the existence of rules of grammar, "principles of organization," distinct from physical-chemical forces. The trouble is, the neo-Platonist leaves it at that, as though invoking "principles" were enough to explain the origin of the genetic message. But organizational principles, like laws of nature, have no power to make events happen. They only describe what pattern those events assume once they are initiated.[47]

Recall the examples used earlier. A novel by Charles Dickens consists of words organized according to artistic principles, but artistic principles themselves do not create novels. They are merely the rules by which the author works. A house consists of bricks and boards organized according to architectural principles, but architectural principles themselves do not create houses. They are merely the rules by which the builder works. By the same token, it is a confusion of categories to speak as though principles of organization account for the message in DNA. What is lacking is an agent—an author who creates the DNA message, composing it according to the principles of grammar and recording it on a material medium. Creationists argue that the unique informational properties of DNA are best explained by an author, a creator of life.

Design in DNA

A 1991 Gallup poll found that some 90 percent of Americans believe God created the world, either by fiat or by directing natural processes. If you were to ask these 90 percent to give a reason for their belief, many might simply wave an arm to indicate the entire natural world. From time immemorial, the order in nature has led people to conclude that there is some kind of intelligent agent behind it all.

Put in logical format, this is the argument from design, and it became immensely popular during the scientific revolution. Probing the deeper structures of nature, scientists uncovered a far more complex order than prescientific ages had imagined. As a result, the argument from design·has always been particularly popular among scientists. "It is the most empirical of the arguments for God," notes Frederick Ferré, based on "observational premises about the kind of order we discover in nature."[48]

The design argument rests on an analogy between the order found in nature and the order exhibited by objects of human manufacture. The best-known formulation is by William Paley in 1802. Piling detail upon detail, Paley described the intricate adaptations found in living things. Ascribing these marvels to physical causes, he argued, would be like finding a watch on the heath and ascribing it to natural forces such as wind and erosion. The kind of order we see in watches indicates clearly that they are the products of human intelligence; and since we see an analogous order in living things, Paley argued, they are products of *divine* intelligence. If we are to believe the recent Gallup Poll, a great many Americans still agree with Paley.

The crux of Paley's argument was the analogy between living things and watches. But today molecular biology has given us a much more striking analogy—between the base sequence in DNA and a written message. Updating Paley, we could say that ascribing DNA to phys-ical-chemical causes would be like finding a book or computer disk on the heath and ascribing its contents to the effects of wind and erosion. If books and computer programs require an intelligent origin, so too does the message in the DNA molecule. Though no one has actually witnessed the creation of life, creationists argue, still we recognize the distinctive complexity that in our experience results only from intelligent activity.

In the scientific establishment today, few are willing to follow this argument. Confronted with the implausibilities of any material-ist origin of life, mechanists nevertheless adopt an attitude of wait and see. Yet several decades of origin-of-life experiments have already revealed consistent trends, and these well-established trends are not likely to be reversed. In fact, with each passing year, they become more pronounced. Today we can say quite definitely what atoms and molecules will do when left to themselves under natural conditions—and what they will *not* do. And what they will not do is spontaneously organize themselves into the complex structures of life—into protein and DNA.

Even if they did, creationists argue, these molecules would not function as a coded message system. To construct a code, you need more than a material medium, more than chemical "paper and ink." You also need a linguistic convention—a dictionary to link meaning to symbols, and rules of grammar to link symbols into meaningful sequences. Where in the inanimate world do we find analogues to dictionaries and grammatical rules? Nowhere. The only analogues are in the world of human language. Hence it is reasonable to conclude, creationists argue, that the DNA code originated from a cause similar in relevant aspects to human intelligence.

SCIENCE AND DESIGN

What, then, does the DNA revolution mean for biology? We suggest that it confirms the central insights of each of the three worldview traditions. It confirms the mechanistic conviction that all the cell's functions are rooted firmly in a material substance—the sugars and bases of the DNA molecule. To explain living structures we do not need to appeal to any metaphysical entities, mysterious substances, or psychic sensitivities within living matter. Vitalism and animism are utterly dead.

On the other hand, the DNA revolution also confirms the neo-Platonist conviction that life is not finally reducible to physics and chemistry alone. The difference between inorganic matter and living organisms does not consist in the substance of which they are composed but in their organization. Information-bearing molecules exhibit an organizational structure that is not accounted for by purely material forces.

The central issue in biology today is not vitalism versus mechanism but the origin of complex organization. Individually, all the atoms and molecules in a living cell act according to the laws of physics and chemistry: The mechanists are right about that. But together these molecules are organized into structures that transcend the laws of physics and chemistry—the supreme example being the coded message in the DNA molecule. The neo-Platonists are right about *that*. Informational molecules exhibit a kind of complexity that is quite different from anything we see in inanimate matter, and to be complete a science of life must include some account of that complexity.

Finally, the DNA revolution confirms the Aristotelian conviction that organic structure and development are attributable to an inner intelligible pattern or plan—now identified with the message encoded in the DNA molecule. Creationists take that insight a step further, arguing that an intelligible pattern is evidence of an intelligent source. The existence of informational molecules has become the basis for a new version of the age-old design argument.

Critics often dismiss appeals to design as merely a temporary measure to bridge current ignorance, to fill gaps in scientific knowledge. In earlier centuries, that may well have been the case at times—for example, when lightning or disease was attributed to direct divine action. Later, when natural causes were discovered for these phenomena, it may have seemed that material causes would eventually be found for *every* phenomenon, filling in any remaining gaps in knowledge.

The contemporary design argument does not rest, however, on gaps in our knowledge but rather on the *growth* in our knowledge due to the revolution in molecular biology. Information theory has taught us that nature exhibits two types of order. The first type is produced by natural causes—shiny crystals, hexagonal patterns in oil, whirlpools in the bathtub. But the second type—the complex structure of the DNA molecule—is not produced by any natural processes known to experience.

Yet experience does offer another example of the second type of order, namely, the letter arrangements in a written message. In our experience, a written message is always the product of an intelligent agent; hence we can construct a positive argument that informational structures such as DNA are likewise the result of an intelligent agent.

This is an updated version of the design argument, and we get a hint of its power when we read Francis Crick's autobiography, *What Mad Pursuit*. After surveying his role in the DNA revolution, Crick remarks, "Biologists must constantly keep in mind that what they see was not designed, but rather evolved."[49] The words sound almost as though Crick has to persuade himself—*against* the most natural reading of the evidence—that life really is a result of natural causes alone. It's as though a geologist were to gaze on the four presidential faces carved into Mt. Rushmore and then to insist, despite the obvious marks of human workmanship, that the faces are the product of natural forces alone—of wind and water erosion. In DNA the marks of intelligent workmanship are equally evident.

But Is It Science?

The most common objection to any notion of design is that it falls out-side the range of science—that any theory involving reference to an intelligent agent is unscientific. But this objection assumes a particular definition of science. It assumes that there exists what some philoso-phers of science call a "magic fence" that enables us to divide real sci-ence on one side—astronomy, physics, chemistry, biology, geology—from pseudoscience like acupuncture, astrology, parapsy-chology, and the writings of Velikovsky.[50] In this scheme, any concept of a designer, an intelligent cause, falls on the side of pseudoscience.

But philosophers of science have been notoriously incapable of specifying acceptable criteria for delimiting these two realms—for mapping the dividing line where the magic fence should be erected. Observability, testability, repeatability, falsifiability, and a host of other criteria have been offered, but none has been universally accepted.

In fact, many philosophers of science now recognize that pro-posed principles of demarcation are themselves philosophically charged—that they reflect the metaphysical presuppositions of the per-son proposing them. Larry Laudan writes that the principles offered for defining science really function as weapons in philosophical battles. "No one can look at the history of debates between scientists and 'pseudo-scientists' without realizing that demarcation criteria are typ-ically used as *machines de guerre* in a polemical battle between rival camps," Laudan writes. He goes on:

> It is well known, for instance, that Aristotle was concerned to embarrass the practitioners of Hippocratic medicine; and it is notorious that the logical positivists wanted to repudiate meta-physics and that Popper was out to get Marx and Freud. In every case, they used a demarcation criterion of their own devising as the discrediting device.[51]

Similarly, philosopher of biology David Hull writes that he is "highly sceptical" of proposed methodologies for delimiting true science. "They tend to be self-serving," Hull writes, "designed to put one's opponents at a disadvantage while shoring up one's own position."[52]

If Laudan and Hull are right, what can we say about definitions of science that exclude any theory referring to an intelligent cause of life? Do they simply reflect many scientists' philosophical opposition to the idea? It appears so. For when evaluated from a purely logical point of view, the case for design is identical to the case one might build for any other explanation of the past.

Historical science is guided by the principle of uniformity—that the present is a key to the past. We postulate causes for past events by seeking an analogy among present events. Similar events warrant the assumption of similar causes. For example, when we observe the effects of water erosion in the present, we conclude that the same process explains the cutting of a river bed in the past. The surface of Mars has long, narrow trenches or rills, yet the planet has no water. Reasoning by analogy to phenomena observed on earth, scientists have concluded that at some time in the past there must have been running water on the surface of Mars.

The principle of uniformity is open to either natural or intelligent causes. As philosopher David Hume wrote in 1748, "from causes which appear similar we expect similar effects." And later: "The same rule holds whether the cause assigned be brute unconscious matter or a rational intelligent being."[53] In other words, the principle of uniformity is neutral in regard to the kind of cause invoked.

Applied to the origin of life, the principle of uniformity requires us to find an analogy in the present to the creation of information-rich structures such as DNA molecules. As we have seen, there *are* no known examples of information-rich structures created by natural processes. However, experience gives us a wealth of examples created by intelligent agents—books, poems, musical scores, computer programs. Even houses and automobiles represent information. Hence, the principle of uniformity suggests that the origin of life may likewise be attributed to an intelligent agent. Rejecting that conclusion as beyond the bounds of science gives rise to the suspicion that the deck is already stacked in favor of mechanistic materialism—that one's definition of science is nothing more than a *machine de guerre* in defense of a materialist worldview.[54]

If our definition of science is informed by actual scientific practice, certainly it will not be so narrow. Throughout the history of science, from Copernicus to quantum mechanics, science has been deeply implicated in metaphysical and religious questions. For example, Newton argued explicitly for the validity of drawing religious implications from science (then called Natural Philosophy). In the *General Scholium,* Newton wrote: "And thus much concerning God, to discourse of whom from the appearance of things, does certainly belong to Natural Philosophy."[55]

A contemporary example, is the work of Francis Crick, who states explicitly that his DNA research was motivated by the goal of promoting the philosophy of reductionism. Crick was educated as a physicist but switched to biology. "An important reason Crick changed to biology," Horace Judson says, "was that he is an atheist, and was impatient to throw light into the remaining shadowy sanctuaries of vitalistic illusions." Then Crick's own words: "My own motives I never had any doubt about; . . . I looked around for fields which would illuminate this particular point of view, against vitalism."[56] Of course, Crick is mistaken if he sees a necessary connection between atheism and reductionism. Plenty of vitalists have been atheists, and plenty of theists have rejected vitalism. Nonetheless, Crick's words exemplify the philosophical and religious dimensions to all scientific research. No definition of science that ignores or denies those dimensions can claim a basis in the actual practice of science.

A historical overview of scientific practice such as we have offered in this book reveals clearly that science and scholarship are never carried out in a philosophical and religious vacuum. The Christian religion, hand in hand with various philosophical outlooks, has motivated, sanctioned, and shaped large portions of the Western scientific heritage. Modern Christians ought to drink deeply at the well of historical precedent. If we do, we will never feel intimidated by positivists and others who deny that religion has any role in genuine scholarship.

In the broad scope of history, that claim is itself a temporary aberration—a mere blip on the screen, already beginning to fade.

N O T E S

CHAPTER ONE: *An Invented Institution*

1. Loren Eiseley, "Francis Bacon," in *The Horizon Book of Makers of Modern Thought*, intro. Bruce Mazlish (New York: American Heritage Publishing, 1972), pp. 95-96, emphasis in original.
2. Loren Eiseley, *Darwin's Century* (Garden City, NY: Doubleday, 1958, Doubleday Anchor Books, 1961), p. 62.
3. David C. Lindberg, "Conceptions of the Scientific Revolution," in *Reappraisals of the Scientific Revolution*, ed. David C. Lindberg and Robert S. Westman (Cambridge: Cambridge University Press, 1990), p. 14. Similarly, R. N. D. Martin says there is no evidence to show that Duhem's historical work was motivated by a desire to defend scholasticism. See *Pierre Duhem: Philosophy and History in the Work of a Believing Physicist* (La Salle, IL: Open Court, 1991).
4. Colin Russell, *Cross-Currents: Interactions Between Science and Faith* (Grand Rapids: Eerdmans, 1985), pp. 190-96.
5. John William Draper, *History of the Conflict Between Religion and Science* (New York: D. Appleton, 1875), pp. vi, xi, 364, 365.
6. The lesson of White's book, Sarton says, is that theologians who "were indiscreet enough to interfere" with science always ended up supporting the wrong theories. "I wonder," Sarton muses, "whether they were not the victims of a sly devil who wanted to make fun of them." There's no doubt that Sarton himself was making fun of them. He goes on to praise theologians who know better than to "tamper" with scientific controversies. George Sarton, "Introductory Essay," in *Science, Religion, and Reality*, ed. Joseph Needham (New York: George Braziller, 1955), pp. 14-15.
7. Bruce Mazlish, preface to Andrew Dickson White, *A History of the Warfare of Science with Theology*, abridged ed. (New York: Free Press, 1965), p. 13.
8. Andrew Dickson White, *A History of the Warfare of Science with Theology*, 2 vols. (New York: Dover Publications, 1960, reprint of an 1896 edition), 1:viii.

9. The term "scientific revolution" covers roughly the period between Copernicus and Newton. It became common usage after Butterfield's lectures, published as *The Origins of Modern Science* (1948), and A. R. Hall's book *The Scientific Revolution, 1500-1800* (1954). Some historians object to the term "revolution" to describe the beginnings of modern science, since the process was neither sudden nor violent. We will use the term only in the sense that certain philosophical concepts (e.g., Aristotelian cosmology) were overthrown and replaced.

10. M. B. Foster, "The Christian Doctrine of Creation and the Rise of Modern Natural Science," *Mind* 43 (1934), reprinted in *Science and Religious Belief: A Selection of Recent Historical Studies*, ed. C. A. Russell (London: University of London Press, 1973). Also reprinted in *Creation: The Impact of an Idea*, ed. Daniel O'Connor and Francis Oakley (New York: Charles Scribner's Sons, 1969).

11. Alfred North Whitehead, *Science and the Modern World* (New York: Macmillan, Free Press, 1925), pp. 12-13.

12. Langdon Gilkey, *Maker of Heaven and Earth: The Christian Doctrine of Creation in the Light of Modern Knowledge* (New York: University Press of America, 1959), p. 132.

13. Thomas Torrance writes that the "Christian belief in the goodness and integrity of the physical universe . . . played an incalculable part in transforming the ancient worldview. It destroyed the Platonic and Aristotelian idea that matter is, if not evil, the raw material of corruption and unreality and the source of disorder in the universe, and it also ruled entirely out of consideration the pessimistic views of nature that emanated from the dualist sects such as the Manichaeans and Gnostics, thereby emancipating the material reality of the universe for serious scientific attention." From *Divine and Contingent Order* (Oxford: Oxford University Press, 1981), p. 67.

14. Mary Hesse, *Science and the Human Imagination: Aspects of the History and Logic of Physical Science* (New York: Philosophical Library, 1955), pp. 42-43. See also Harvey Cox, "The Christian in a World of Technology," in *Science and Religion: New Perspectives on the Dialogue*, ed. Ian G. Barbour (New York: Harper and Row, 1968), p. 263.

15. Ian Barbour, *Issues in Science and Religion* (New York: Harper and Row, Harper Torchbooks, 1966), pp. 48-49. This is not to overlook the fact that the monks did engage in labor, regarding it as one way to glorify God. Nevertheless, many historians have noted the distinctive emphasis in Protestantism on the moral and spiritual value of all labor. See, for example, Max Weber in *The Protestant Ethic and the Spirit of Capitalism* (New York: Charles Scribner's Sons, 1958). For Luther, Weber says (p. 81), "every legitimate calling has exactly the same worth in the sight of God."

16. Cited in Eugene M. Klaaren, *Religious Origins of Modern Science: Belief in Creation in Seventeenth-Century Thought* (Grand Rapids: Eerdmans, 1977), p. 41.

17. Cited in Christopher Kaiser, *Creation and the History of Science* (Grand Rapids: Eerdmans, 1991), p. 127.

18. Harvey Cox, *The Secular City*, rev. ed. (Toronto: Macmillan, 1966), pp. 19-21. Similar themes can be found in Arend van Leeuwen, *Christianity in World History* (Edinburgh: Edinburgh House Press, 1964).

19. R. Hooykaas, *Religion and the Rise of Modern Science* (Grand Rapids: Eerdmans, 1972), p. 17.

20. The full quotation from Boyle, given in Klaaren p. 150, is as follows:

> The veneration, wherewith men are imbued for what they call nature, has been a discouraging impediment to the empire of man over the inferior creatures of God: for many have not only looked upon it, as an impossible thing to compass, but as something *impious to attempt*, the removing of those boundaries which nature seems to have put and settled among her productions; and whilst they look upon her as such a venerable thing, some make a kind of *scruple of conscience* to endeavor so to emulate any of her works, as to excel them. (emphasis added)

21. Cox, *Secular City*, p. 21. As Forbes observes, it was "Christianity, by its opposition to animism, [that] opened the door to a rational use of the forces of nature." R. J. Forbes, "Power," in *A History of Technology*, vol. 2, ed. Charles Singer (Oxford: Clarendon Press, 1956), p. 606.

22. Thomas Sieger Derr, *Ecology and Human Need*, originally published in 1973 under the title *Ecology and Human Liberation* (Philadelphia: Westminster Press, 1975), p. 20.

23. Melvin Calvin, *Chemical Evolution* (Oxford: Clarendon Press, 1969), p. 258.

24. Derr, *Ecology and Human Need*, p. 26. Derr goes on: "Many scientists, philosophers, and historians . . . have remarked that modern science owes much to the Christian faith in the dependability of the creator God."

25. Kaiser, *Creation and the History of Science*, p. 109.

26. Ernst Mayr, *The Growth of Biological Thought* (Cambridge: Harvard University Press, 1982), p. 199. The quotations here may appear to identify Mayr as a proponent of natural theology. He is not; his own position is a completely materialistic form of evolution.

27. A. R. Hall, *The Scientific Revolution, 1500-1800: The Formation of the Modern Scientific Attitude* (Boston: Beacon Press, 1954), pp. 171-72. As historian John Randall explains, "Natural laws were regarded as real laws or commands, decrees of the Almighty, literally obeyed without a single act of rebellion." John Herman Randall, *The Making of the Modern Mind* (New York: Columbia University Press, 1926, 1940), p. 274. See also Stephen F. Mason, *A History of the Sciences*, originally published under the title *Main Currents of Scientific Thought* (New York: Collier Books, 1962), pp. 173, 182.

28. Carl Becker, *The Heavenly City of the Eighteenth-Century Philosophers* (New Haven: Yale University Press, 1932), p. 55. By the eighteenth century, however, the logic of the argument began to be reversed, taking on the form familiar to us today. As science progressively revealed the marvelous order of nature, people began to argue not from God to order but from order to God. This is the classic argument from design.

  For example, in Hume's *Dialogues Concerning Natural Religion*, the character Cleanthes does not argue that God is eternal reason, and therefore nature must be rational; instead he argues that nature is a lawful machine, and therefore God must be a rational engineer. Natural law had ceased to be an article of faith and had become identified with the observed behavior of objects. (Becker, pp. 56-57.)

In other words, whereas formerly the existence of God was regarded as so certain that it could serve as the starting point for argument, now it was the orderliness of nature, discovered by science, that was regarded as more certain. Order in nature became the starting point of argument, and the existence of God became an inference from it. This is not to deny the importance or validity of design arguments but only to point out the massive intellectual shift that has taken place.

29. Hooykaas, *Religion and the Rise of Modern Science*, pp. 3-4.
30. Dudley Shapere, *Galileo: A Philosophical Study* (Chicago: University of Chicago Press, 1974), pp. 134-36, emphasis in original.
31. C. F. von Weizsacker, *The Relevance of Science* (New York: Harper and Row, 1964), p. 163. See also George Herbert Mead, *Movements of Thought in the Nineteenth Century*, Works of George Herbert Mead, vol. 2, ed. and intro. Merritt H. Moore (Chicago: University of Chicago Press), pp. 1, 5-8. Mead writes that science rests on the "confident faith" that every detail in nature can be rationally understood. The source of that faith, he says, is the theological doctrine that the world

> was created by a God who was infinitely intelligent and who had infinite power. Everything that such a deity created . . . must be the expression of that intelligence, and nothing could resist its expression. . . . There could be nothing accidental or irrational in such a world.

To speak of the rationality of creation is not to deny the Biblical teaching of the Fall, which states that since the original creation the world has been marred by sin, death, and disharmony. Yet the Fall does not completely destroy the inherent character of creation. It represents a temporary disfigurement of that character—a disfigurement that can be reversed in redemption. This is quite different from the Greek view where matter is intrinsically opposed to reason, order, and goodness.

32. R. G. Collingwood, *An Essay on Metaphysics* (Chicago: Henry Regnery, Gateway Editions, 1972; originally published by London: Oxford University Press, 1940), pp. 253-57.
33. Eiseley, *Darwin's Century*, p. 62.
34. Joseph Needham, *The Grand Titration: Science and Society in East and West* (Toronto: University of Toronto Press, 1969), p. 327.
35. Kaiser, *Creation and the History of Science*, pp. 10, 121. Similarly, historian Robert Cohen notes that the rise of science required a belief in a "rational creator of all things," with its corollary that "we lesser rational beings might, by virtue of that Godlike rationality, be able to decipher the laws of nature." Robert Cohen, "Alternative Interpretations of the History of Science," in *The Validation of Scientific Theories*, ed. Philipp G. Frank (Boston: Beacon Press, 1956), p. 227.
36. Paul Kocher, *Science and Religion in Elizabethan England* (San Marino, CA: Huntington Library, 1953), p. 32.
37. Hesse, *Science and the Human Imagination*, pp. 44-45. See also Gilkey, *Maker of Heaven and Earth*, pp. 123-25; O'Connor and Oakley, *Creation: The Impact of an Idea*, General Introduction, p. 18. It is important to keep in mind that, for Aristotle, Form does not mean shape but essential purpose.
38. Gary Deason, "Reformation Theology and the Mechanistic Conception of

Nature," in *God and Nature: Historical Essays on the Encounter Between Christianity and Science*, ed. David C. Lindberg and Ronald L. Numbers (Berkeley: University of California Press, 1986).

39. A. C. Crombie, *Medieval and Early Modern Science*, vol. 2 (Cambridge, MA: Harvard University Press, 1963), p. 315, emphasis added.

40. Cited in Kaiser, *Creation and the History of Science*, p. 154.

41. A thorough discussion of Boyle can be found in Klaaren, *Religious Origins of Modern Science*, from which these quotations were taken (pp. 135, 139, 151).

42. Cited in Edward B. Davis, "Newton's Rejection of the 'Newtonian World View': The Role of Divine Will in Newton's Natural Philosophy," in *Science and Christian Belief*, 3, no. 1, p. 117.

43. Barbour, *Issues in Science and Religion*, p. 379.

44. Kaiser, *Creation and the History of Science*, p. 110, emphasis added. Similarly, Marin Mersenne (1588-1648) criticized Kepler's early attempts to force the solar system into a geometrical pattern—his argument being that it is wrong to cherish any preconceived pattern for the structure of the solar system since it is only one of infinitely numerous possibilities and therefore ultimately dependent on the choice of the deity. See John Hedley Brooke, *Science and Religion: Some Historical Perspectives* (Cambridge: Cambridge University Press, 1991), p. 26.

45. Roger Cotes, preface to the second edition of Newton's *Principia*, in *Newton's Philosophy of Nature: Selections from His Writings*, ed. H. S. Thayer (New York: Hafner, 1953), emphasis added.

46. Brooke, *Science and Religion*, pp. 139-40, emphasis in original. This interpretation of the condemnation of 1277, as fostering experimental methodology in science, was first advanced by Pierre Duhem. It can also be found in Foster and Hooykaas.

Yet we need to be cautious about drawing a direct causal connection. Historian David Lindberg argues that the immediate effect of the condemnation was to throw a tighter theological rein around the neck of philosophical inquiry. See *The Beginnings of Western Science* (Chicago: University of Chicago Press, 1992), pp. 234-44.

Edward Grant maintains that the condemnation contributed initially to skepticism by eroding confidence in the capacity of human reason to arrive at demonstrated truth, whether in theology or in natural philosophy. For if there are no necessary rational connections in creation, how can reason penetrate its structure? See "Science and Theology in the Middle Ages," *God and Nature*, pp. 54-58. It took centuries before science came to be defined as a process not of deducing necessary connections but of describing contingent regularities.

47. Torrance, *Divine and Contingent Order*, p. 109. Similarly, Anglican theologian E. L. Mascall writes, "The Christian God is not only a God of omnipotence and freedom, He is also a God of rationality and order." From *Christian Theology and Natural Science* (New York: Longmans, Green, 1956), pp. 93-94. See also Francis Oakley, "Christian Theology and the Newtonian Science: The Rise of the Concept of the Laws of Nature," in *Creation: The Impact of an Idea*.

48. John Baillie, "Christianity in an Age of Science," in *Science and Faith Today* by John Baillie, Robert Boyd, Donald Mackay, Douglas Spanner (London: Lutterworth Press, 1953), p. 17, emphasis added.

49. Some historians have argued that the story of Galileo and the leaning tower of Pisa is apocryphal, or that it was merely a "thought experiment" carried out theoretically. Other historians are more inclined to accept the story as genuine. Either way the point still stands: Galileo argued explicitly that we cannot rationally intuit the ways God created objects to behave; instead, we must observe their actual behavior.

50. Klaaren, *Religious Origins of Modern Science*, p. 15. See also Paul Liben, "Science Within the Limits of Truth," *First Things*, no. 18, (December 1991), pp. 29-32.

51. Cited in Mason, *A History of the Sciences*, pp. 177, 178. See also Kocher, *Science and Religion*, pp. 24-28.

52. R. K. Merton, "Puritanism, Pietism, and Science," *Sociological Review*, 28, pt. 1, (January 1936). Reprinted in *Science and Ideas*, ed. Arnold B. Arons and Alfred M. Bork (Englewood Cliffs, NJ: Prentice-Hall, 1964).

53. P. M. Rattansi, "The Social Interpretation of Science in the Seventeenth Century," in *Science and Society*, ed. Peter Mathias (Cambridge: Cambridge University Press, 1972), pp. 2-3.

54. Lynn White, "What Accelerated Technological Progress in the Western Middle Ages?" in *Scientific Change*, ed. A. C. Crombie (New York: Basic Books), pp. 290-91.

55. Cox, "The Christian in a World of Technology," in *Science and Religion: New Perspectives on the Dialogue*, p. 264.

56. Brooke, *Science and Religion*, pp. 19-33. Brooke also mentions a fifth way Christianity has influenced science—by playing a *constitutive* role in theory formation (e.g., Ray and Linnaeus invoked the language of Genesis 1 in their definitions of species). This will be discussed in chapter 5.

57. White, *A History of the Warfare*, 1:126.

58. Russell, *Cross-Currents*, p. 42.

59. Randall, *Making of the Modern Mind*, p. 226.

60. Brooke, *Science and Religion*, p. 88. See also Russell, *Cross-Currents*, pp. 50-51. Arthur O. Lovejoy notes that modern writers often speak as though medieval cosmology, by assigning mankind the central place in the universe, gave "man a high sense of his own importance and dignity." But in fact the opposite is true. "For the medieval mind . . . the centre of the world was not a position of honor; it was rather the place farthest removed from the Empyrean, the bottom of the creation, to which its dregs and baser elements sank. . . . The geocentric cosmography served rather for man's humiliation than for his exaltation." Copernicanism was opposed in part precisely because the theory assigned too lofty a position to the earth by removing it from the center. From *The Great Chain of Being: A Study in the History of an Idea* (Cambridge: Harvard University Press, 1936, 1964), pp. 101-02.

61. Martin Rudwick, "Senses of the natural world and senses of God," in *The Sciences and Theology in the Twentieth Century*, ed. A. R. Peacocke (Notre Dame: University of Notre Dame Press, 1981, paperback ed., 1986), p. 242. For a detailed account of the Galileo controversy, see *The Galileo Connection* by Charles E. Hummel (Downers Grove: InterVarsity Press, 1986).

62. The Pope had even celebrated Galileo's telescopic discoveries in Latin verse. Giorgio de Santillana, *The Crime of Galileo* (New York: Time

Reading Program Special Edition, originally published by Chicago: University of Chicago Press, 1955), pp. xx, 165n.

63. Philipp Frank, *Philosophy of Science: The Link Between Science and Philosophy* (Englewood Cliffs, NJ: Prentice-Hall, Spectrum Books, 1957), p. 144.

64. It was for precisely the same reason that many Christians opposed Darwin's theory of evolution centuries later. Long after Aristotelianism had lost credibility in physics, it remained strong in biology. Darwin's completely materialistic account of life finally broke the Aristotelian connection between physical order and moral order. Adam Sedgwick (1785-1873), Darwin's former teacher, saw exactly what was happening and wrote to him saying,

> 'Tis the crown and glory of organic science that it *does*, through *final cause*, link material to moral. . . . You have ignored this link; and, if I do not mistake your meaning, you have done your best in one or two pregnant cases to break it.

Sedgwick went on the predict that if the link between the material and the moral order were ever broken (which he did not believe could happen), the human race would be morally brutalized and degraded. Cited in Charles Coulston Gillispie in *The Edge of Objectivity* (Princeton, NJ: Princeton University Press, 1960), p. 350, emphasis in original.

65. Hesse, *Science and the Human Imagination*, pp. 34-35.

66. Jerome Ravetz, "Tragedy in the History of Science," in *Changing Perspectives in the History of Science: Essays in Honour of Joseph Needham*, ed. Mikulás Teich and Robert Young (London: Heinemann, 1973), p. 212-14.

67. Herbert Butterfield, *The Origins of Modern Science: 1300-1800*, rev. ed. (New York: Free Press, 1957, 1965), pp. 178-81.

68. Russell, *Cross-Currents*, p. 44.

69. Rudwick, in *The Sciences and Theology*, pp. 256-57. Brooke (*Science and Religion*, pp. 98-99) conjectures that the "fateful urgency" with which Galileo sought to convert the Catholic hierarchy to Copernicanism may have reflected a genuine desire to uphold the reputation of Catholic scholarship, to spare it the ignominy of holding a faulty cosmology.

70. John Dillenberger, *Protestant Thought and Natural Science* (Notre Dame: University of Notre Dame Press, 1960), p. 29. If we truly want to understand the Reformers (and not merely castigate them), Dillenberger says, we must look at their generally positive views of science and not merely their reactions to individual theories.

71. B. A. Gerrish, "The Reformation and the Rise of Modern Science," in *The Impact of the Church Upon Its Culture*, ed. Jerald C. Brauer (Chicago: University of Chicago Press, 1968), p. 264n.

72. Mark Graubard, introduction, William Harvey, *On the Motion of the Heart and Blood in Animals*, trans. R. Willis, rev. and ed. Alex. Bowie (Chicago: Henry Regnery, Gateway Editions, 1962), p. 13.

73. P. M. Rattansi, "Science and Religion in the Seventeenth Century," in *The Emergence of Science in Western Europe*, ed. Maurice Crosland (London: Macmillan, 1975), pp. 81-82.

74. Eiseley, *Darwin's Century*, p. 62.

75. Surely a "strange contradiction in scientific thought," Whitehead comments. Whitehead, *Science and the Modern World*, p. 4.

CHAPTER TWO: The History of Science and the Science of History

1. Francis A. Yates, *Giordano Bruno and the Hermetic Tradition* (New York: Random House Vintage Books, 1964).
2. John Herman Randall, *The Making of the Modern Mind* (New York: Columbia University Press, 1926, 1940), p. 242.
3. Bernard Elevitch, "Bruno, Giordano," *The Encyclopedia of Philosophy*, vol. 1, Paul Edwards, editor in chief (New York: Macmillan and Free Press, 1967), p. 407.
4. Hugh Kearney, *Science and Change, 1500-1700* (New York: McGraw-Hill, World University Library, 1971), p. 106.
5. Yates, *Giordano Bruno*, pp. ix-x.
6. Sir James Jeans, *Physics and Philosophy* (New York: Dover Publications, 1982, republication of a work co-published by Cambridge University Press and Macmillan, 1943), p. 19.
7. Yates, *Giordano Bruno*, pp. 447-48, emphasis in original.
8. Charles Webster, *From Paracelsus to Newton: Magic and the Making of Modern Science* (Cambridge: Cambridge University Press, 1982), p. 12. See also Robert S. Westman and J. E. McGuire, *Hermeticism and the Scientific Revolution* (Los Angeles: William Andrews Clark Memorial Library, 1977), and Brian P. Copenhaver, "Natural Magic, Hermeticism, and Occultism," in *Reappraisals of the Scientific Revolution*, ed. David C. Lindberg and Robert S. Westman (Cambridge: Cambridge University Press, 1990), pp. 262, 264.
9. For a comprehensive introduction to the history of science as an academic discipline, see Helge Kragh, *An Introduction to the Historiography of Science* (Cambridge: Cambridge University Press, 1987).
   Another approach to the history of science, becoming increasingly popular today, comes from the field of sociology. Inspired by Marxism and by Karl Mannheim's sociology of knowledge, this approach is often called the sociology of science. Like all Marxist theories, the sociology of science tends to stress interests. It assumes that the source of ideas can be traced by asking: Whose interests does it serve?
   Some historians within this tradition are concerned with the *internal* sociology of science—how science is affected by institutionalization, patterns of education, organs of communication, changing values, and so on. See John Ziman, *Public Knowledge: The Social Dimension of Science* (London: Cambridge University Press, 1968).
   Others are concerned with the *external* sociology of science, with the interaction between the scientific community and the surrounding socioeconomic, political, and religious milieu. Two historical works within this tradition are Steven Shapin and Simon Schaffer, *Leviathan and the Air-Pump: Hobbes, Boyle, and the Experimental Life* (Princeton: Princeton University Press, 1985) and Margaret C. Jacob, *The Cultural Meaning of the Scientific Revolution* (New York: Knopf, 1988).
10. Ironically, the Enlightenment belief in progress was itself a secularization of the Christian belief in providence. As David C. Lindberg explains:

Secularization during the Enlightenment eroded belief in divine providence as a moving force in history and discredited Christian teleology as a theme by which to structure the course of historical change. The historiographic void was filled by the idea of progress, based on faith in the development and application of human reason.

From "Conceptions of the Scientific Revolution," in *Reappraisals of the Scientific Revolution*, p. 6.

11. Carl Becker, *The Heavenly City of the Eighteenth-Century Philosophers* (New Haven: Yale University Press, 1932), pp. 105, 108.

12. Thomas Kuhn, "The Relations Between History and History of Science," in *Historical Studies Today*, ed. Felix Gilbert and Stephen R. Graubard (New York: W. W. Norton, 1972, 1971). See also Thomas Kuhn, "The History of Science," in *The Essential Tension* (Chicago: University of Chicago Press, 1977).

13. Andrew Dickson White, *A History of the Warfare of Science with Theology* (New York: Dover Publications, 1960, republication of the 1896 edition).

14. Mary Hesse, *Science and the Human Imagination: Aspects of the History and Logic of Physical Science* (New York: Philosophical Library, 1955), p. 10.

15. Robert Westman, "Proofs, Poetics, and Patronage," *Reappraisals of the Scientific Revolution*, p. 169. A highly readable description of the positivist approach to the history of science can be found in Joseph Agassi, *Towards a Historiography of Science* (The Hague, Netherlands: Mouton, 1963), pp. 1-20.

16. Thomas Kuhn, "History and the History of Science," in *The Essential Tensions*, p. 140.

17. Antony Flew, *Darwinian Evolution* (London: Granada Publishing, Paladin Books, 1984), p. 47. Flew goes on to explain (pp. 47, 48, 50) what that everyday experience is: "Almost every animal or plant which forces itself on the attention of the biological layperson belongs to some commonly named kind very obviously and very widely different from every other ordinary familiar kind. Who would ever mistake a cat for a dog, a cow for a horse, or—come to think of it—a hawk for a handsaw? The same, of course, applies to specimens of all the kinds actually listed in Genesis. This first impression of the absolute distinctiveness of natural kinds is reinforced by the recognition that couples from all these kinds normally reproduce, as Genesis has it, after their own kind." These are the "inescapably familiar everyday realities which make that Genesis view so plausible."

18. For a detailed analysis of the history of the phrase "unity of knowledge," see Robert McRae, *The Problem of the Unity of the Sciences: Bacon to Kant* (Toronto: University of Toronto Press, 1961).

19. Wilhelm Dilthey, *Pattern and Meaning in History*, ed. and intro. H. P. Rickman (New York: Harper and Row, Harper Torchbooks, The Academy Library, 1961).

20. Hayden V. White, "Wilhelm Windelband," *The Encyclopedia of Philosophy*, vol. 8 (New York: Macmillan and Free Press), p. 321.

21. Bertrand Russell, *A History of Western Philosophy* (New York: Simon and Schuster, Clarion Books, 1945), p. 39.

22. Thomas Kuhn, *The Essential Tension* (Chicago: University of Chicago Press, 1977), pp. xi-xiii. Kuhn refers to what we are calling the idealist method as the "hermeneutic" method.

23. Marx W. Wartofsky, "The Relation Between Philosophy of Science and History of Science," in *Essays in Memory of Imre Lakatos*, Boston Studies in the Philosophy of Science, vol. 39, ed. R. S. Cohen, P. K. Feyerabend, and M. W. Wartofsky (Boston: D. Reidel Publishing, 1976), p. 728.

Idealist historians have not only revived study of the intellectual context of science, they have also rehabilitated the role of ideas *within* science—the theoretical side of science. Scientific controversies do not rage merely over empirical facts but over conceptual disagreements. Mass, force, action-at-a-distance, electron—these are all theoretical concepts. Progress in science often consists not in the discovery of new facts but in the clarification or redefinition of concepts. See Larry Laudan, *Progress and Its Problems: Towards a Theory of Scientific Growth* (Berkeley: University of California Press, 1977).

24. Cited in Lindberg, *Reappraisals of the Scientific Revolution*, p. 14.

25. Lynn Thorndike, *A History of Magic and Experimental Science*, 8 vols. (New York: Columbia Univ. Press, 1923-1958); Brian Vickers, ed., *Occult and Scientific Mentalities in the Renaissance* (Cambridge, England: Cambridge University Press, 1984); J. L. Righini Bonelli and William R. Shea, eds., *Reason, Experiment, and Mysticism in the Scientific Revolution* (New York: Macmillan, 1975); Margaret J. Osler and Paul Lawrence Barber, eds., *Religion, Science, and Worldview: Essays in Honor of Richard S. Westfall* (Cambridge, England: Cambridge University Press, 1985).

26. Alexandre Koyré, "Commentary" in *Scientific Change*, ed. A.C. Crombie (New York: Basic Books, 1963), p. 850.

27. Feyerabend argues that things such as myths and witchcraft are as well confirmed by experience as are scientific theories. See *Knowledge Without Foundations* (Oberlin, OH: Oberlin College, 1962), pp. 23, 27, 28. See also "Problems of Empiricism," in *Beyond the Edge of Certainty: Essays in Contemporary Science and Philosophy*, ed. Robert F. Colodny (Englewood Cliffs, NJ: Prentice-Hall, 1965), pp. 146, 225-26, n. 9.

Feyerabend argues that in a free society, "all traditions are given equal rights, equal access to education and other positions of power." Scientists, he says, represent merely one tradition and should have to compete for a hearing with Christians, Taoists, cannibals, Black Muslims, and Native Americans. "If the taxpayers of California want their state universities to teach Voodoo, folk medicine, astrology, rain-dance ceremonies, then this is what the universities will have to teach." From *Science in a Free Society* (London: NLB Publishers, 1978), pp. 30, 87.

28. R. G. Collingwood argued explicitly that all knowledge should be recast in the mold of history. (Recall that for the idealists, "history" meant what we call the humanities.) "I conclude that natural science as a form of thought exists and always has existed in a context of history. . . . From this I venture to infer that no one can understand natural science unless he understands history." From *The Idea of Nature* (Westport, CT: Greenwood Press, 1986; reprint of London: Oxford University Press, 1944), pp. 176-77.

29. Paolo Rossi, "Hermeticism and Rationality," in *Reason, Experiment, and Mysticism in the Scientific Revolution*, pp. 257ff.
30. *Ibid.*, p. 271, emphasis in original.

CHAPTER THREE: *A New "Thinking Cap"*

1. Herbert Butterfield, *The Origins of Modern Science, 1300-1800*, rev. ed. (New York: Free Press, 1957), p. 13.
2. Hugh Kearney labels them the organic, the magical, and the mechanistic worldviews. See *Science and Change: 1500-1700* (New York: McGraw-Hill, World University Library, 1971). His book is a major source for the following section.

    Other historians delimit the same three streams of thought but use different labels. Eugene M. Klaaren, in *Religious Origins of Modern Science* (Grand Rapids: Eerdmans, 1977), characterizes the three approaches as the ontological, the spiritual, and the voluntarist. He links them to various religious traditions as follows:

    1. The ontological approach, following Aristotle, sees God as the highest Being in a hierarchy of being, in which each level strives to reach its full potential. Science is a process of rational deduction to determine a thing's "nature." Religion stresses God's rationality; the believer's major goal is being in God's presence. This approach has been found most congenial by Catholicism.
    2. The spiritual approach sees God as a universal, indwelling Spirit and the creation as His body. Science is a process of gaining mystical insight into the spirits that animate the creation. Religion stresses God as the "Father of lights" (van Helmont's favorite phrase), i.e., the bestower of immediate, intuitive insight. The believer's major goal is dwelling in the spirit. This approach has been found congenial by Anabaptism and (later) pietism.
    3. The voluntarist approach sees God as an author or craftsman and the creation as His workmanship—like a clockmaker and his clock. Science is experimental, searching out the mechanical laws by which the clockwork operates. Religion stresses God's power and His will; the believer's major duty is to do His will. This approach has been most congenial to Reformation Protestantism, particularly Calvinism.

3. Mark Graubard, introduction, William Harvey, *On the Motion of the Heart and Blood in Animals* trans. R. Willis, rev. and ed. Alex Bowie (Chicago: Henry Regnery, Gateway Editions, 1962), pp. 5, 13.
4. *Ibid.*, pp. 16, 19. Of course, among the founders of modern science many *did* pride themselves on rejecting Aristotelianism, just as positivist historians say. Yet even these figures generally continued to think and work within an Aristotelian conceptual universe. After all, it was the universe they had been brought up in, the one they knew best, the one that formed their unconscious assumptions.

    For example, Jean-Baptiste van Helmont (1579-1644), credited with the discovery of gas, is generally included in the neo-Platonic tradition. He directed harsh, even abusive, criticisms against Aristotle and claimed that his own scientific concepts were distinctively Christian as opposed to

Aristotelian. Yet, says historian Walter Pagel, van Helmont's concept of gas continued to bear many of the marks of Aristotelianism. Gas represented for him a spiritual impulse within a material object—in Pagel's words, that which "makes the object tick and reach its destined end." In short, van Helmont's gas was a chemical version of an Aristotelian Form or final cause. From "The Spectre of Van Helmont," in *Changing Perspectives in the History of Science: Essays in Honour of Joseph Needham*, ed. Mikulás Teich and Robert Young (London: Heinemann, 1973), pp. 101-03.

5. Harvey, *On the Motion of the Heart*, p. 84, emphasis in original.

6. Kearney, *Science and Change*, p. 86. Even the notion that nature at its best moves in circular (or cyclical) motions is Aristotelian.

7. Harvey, *On the Motion of the Heart*, p. 85.

8. Kearney, *Science and Change*, pp. 86-87.

9. William B. Ashworth, Jr., "Natural History and the Emblematic World View," in *Reappraisals of the Scientific Revolution*, ed. David C. Lindberg and Robert S. Westman (Cambridge: Cambridge University Press, 1990), p. 305.

10. Kearney, *Science and Change*, p. 40.

11. *Ibid.*, p. 98.

12. Cited in Thomas Kuhn, *The Copernican Revolution: Planetary Astronomy in the Development of Western Thought*, foreword James B. Conant (New York: Random House, Vintage Books, 1957, 1959), p. 131. Kuhn notes that "neo-Platonism is explicit in Copernicus's attitude toward both the sun and mathematical simplicity. It is an essential element in the intellectual climate that gave birth to his vision of the universe."

13. Butterfield, *The Origins of Modern Science*, pp. 70-71; Colin Russell, *Cross-Currents: Interactions Between Science and Faith* (Grand Rapids: Eerdmans, 1985), p. 39. For several additional arguments raised at the time against heliocentrism, see Morris Kline, *Mathematics: The Loss of Certainty* (New York: Oxford University Press, 1980), p. 39.

14. A. R. Hall, *The Scientific Revolution, 1500-1800: The Formation of the Modern Scientific Attitude* (Boston: Beacon Press, 1954), p. 36.

15. Kearney, *Science and Change*, p. 104.

16. *Ibid.*, p. 134.

17. Cited in Kuhn, *The Copernican Revolution*, p. 131.

18. Gerald Holton, *Thematic Origins of Scientific Thought: Kepler to Einstein*, rev. ed. (Cambridge, MA: Harvard University Press, 1973, 1988), pp. 65, 70.

19. Richard S. Westfall, *The Construction of Modern Science: Mechanisms and Mechanics* (New York: John Wiley, 1971; Cambridge, England: Cambridge University Press, 1977), pp. 25-28.

20. Cited in John Hedley Brooke, *Science and Religion: Some Historical Perspectives* (Cambridge, England: Cambridge University Press, 1991), p. 119.

21. Kearney, *Science and Change*, p. 112.

22. Butterfield, *The Origins of Modern Science*, p. 47.

23. Allen G. Debus, "The Medico-Chemical World of the Paracelsians," in *Changing Perspectives*, pp. 86-87. For a discussion of Paracelsus from a Christian point of view, see Christopher Kaiser, *Creation and the History of Science* (Grand Rapids: Eerdmans, 1991), pp. 116-20.

24. Augustine may in turn have picked up the concept from the Greek philosopher Anaxagoras, who believed that there were "panspermia," or germs of life, scattered among the other "seeds" that make up the universe. Anaxagoras taught that where the seeds of life combined in sufficient quantity with seeds of other matter, organisms formed. See Hilde Hein, *On the Nature and Origin of Life* (New York: McGraw-Hill, 1971), p. 111.

25. Pagel, in *Changing Perspectives*, pp. 101-03.

26. R. G. Collingwood, *The Idea of Nature* (Westport, CT: Greenwood Press, 1986, reprint; originally published by London: Oxford University Press, 1944), p. 111. The ancient Greek philosophers essentially secularized pagan animism. They turned it into the principle that the world of nature is saturated or permeated by mind. They based their reasoning on the observation that nature is a world of bodies in motion (which they regarded as a characteristic of life) and that these motions are orderly (which they regarded as a sign of a mind). Thus the Greeks concluded that, as Collingwood puts it (pp. 3-4), "the world of nature is not only alive but intelligent; not only a vast animal with a 'soul' or life of its own, but a rational animal with a 'mind' of its own." Individual plants and animals, in Greek thought, represented "a localization of this all-pervading vitality and rationality."

27. Blaise Pascal (1623-1662) was one of the few mechanists who declined to argue from the order in the universe to the existence of God. God is known not through the lawful patterns of nature, he held, but through miraculous intervention in those patterns. The world of matter follows mechanical laws; the world of the spirit breaks into that pattern according to the inexplicable will of God.

28. John Maynard Keynes, "Newton, the Man," in *Essays in Biography*, 2d ed., ed. Geoffrey Keynes (London: Rupert Hart-Davis, 1951), p. 310.

29. Roger Cotes, preface to the second edition of Newton's *Principia*, in *Newton's Philosophy of Nature: Selections from his Writings*, ed. H. S. Thayer (New York: Hafner, 1953), p. 134.

30. Keynes, in *Essays in Biography*, pp. 311, 313-14, emphasis in original.

31. P. M. Rattansi, "Reason in Sixteenth- and Seventeenth-Century Natural Philosophy," in *Changing Perspectives*, p. 159.

32. Richard Westfall argues that Newton's concept of gravitational force derived from the alchemical notion of active principles in nature. See "The Role of Alchemy in Newton's Career," in *Reason, Experiment, and Mysticism in the Scientific Revolution*, ed. M. L. Righini Bonelli and William R. Shea (London: Macmillan, 1975). See two responses to Westfall within the same volume: Paolo Casini, "Newton—A Skeptical Alchemist?" and Marie Boas Hall, "Newton's Voyage in the Strange Seas of Alchemy." For a more recent statement of Westfall's position, see Richard Westfall, "Newton and Alchemy," in Brian Vickers, *Occult and Scientific Mentalities in the Renaissance* (Cambridge, England: Cambridge University Press, 1984).

33. E. A. Burtt, *The Metaphysical Foundations of Modern Science*, rev. ed. (New York: Doubleday Anchor Books, 1932, 1954), pp. 256-64.

34. Philipp Frank, *Philosophy of Science: The Link Between Science and Philosophy* (Englewood Cliffs, NJ: Prentice-Hall, Spectrum Books, 1957), p. 24.

35. Kuhn, *The Copernican Revolution*, p. 132, emphasis added.

36. Burtt, *Metaphysical Foundations*, pp. 36, 52-53.
37. Kearney, *Science and Change*, p. 138.
38. Burtt, *Metaphysical Foundations*, p. 284.
39. Allen Debus, *Man and Nature in the Renaissance* (New York: Cambridge University Press, 1978), p. 11.
40. John Dillenberger, *Protestant Thought and Natural Science* (Notre Dame: University of Notre Dame Press, 1960), p. 27.
41. B. A. Gerrish, "The Reformation and the Rise of Modern Science," in *The Impact of the Church upon Its Culture*, ed. Jerald D. Brauer (Chicago: University of Chicago Press, 1968), p. 248.
42. Kearney, *Science and Change*, p. 149. For a more detailed discussion of Galileo's clash with the church, see chapter 1.
43. Gary Hatfield, "Metaphysics and the New Science," in *Reappraisals of the Scientific Revolution*.
44. William Shea, Introduction, *Reason, Experiment, and Mysticism*, p. 15.
45. Paolo Rossi, "Hermeticism and Rationality," in *Reason, Experiment, and Mysticism*, p. 260; Debus, *Man and Nature*, p. 134.
46. Mary Hesse, "Reasons and Evaluations in the History of Science," in *Changing Perspectives*, pp. 143-44.
47. Robert Westman, "Proofs, Poetics, and Patronage: Copernicus's Preface to *De revolutionibus*," in *Reappraisals of the Scientific Revolution*.

CHAPTER FOUR: *The Newtonian World Machine*

1. Samuel Clarke, a friend and disciple of Newton's who acted as his spokesman, wrote:

> The Notion of the world's being a great Machine, going on without the Interposition of God, as a Clock continues to go without the Assistance of a Clockmaker; is the Notion of Materialism and Fate, and tends, (under pretence of making God a Supra-mundane Intelligence,) to exclude Providence and God's Government in reality out of the World.

Cited in Edward B. Davis "Newton's Rejection of the 'Newtonian World View': The Role of Divine Will in Newton's Natural Philosophy," in *Science and Christian Belief*, 3, no. 1, (1991), p. 113. As Davis notes, since Clarke consulted with Newton on his writings, these words undoubtedly represent Newton's own view.

2. For a list of the discoveries Galileo made and how they overturned Aristotle's physics, see John Herman Randall, *The Making of the Modern Mind* (New York: Columbia University Press, 1926, 1940), pp. 232-33. Aristotelian concepts continued to exert a great influence in biology, however, as we shall see in the next chapter.

3. E. L. Mascall, *Christian Theology and Natural Science* (Hamden, CT: Archon Books, 1965), p. 198.

4. T. F. Torrance, "Divine and Contingent Order," in *The Sciences and Theology in the Twentieth Century*, ed. A. R. Peacocke (Notre Dame: University of Notre Dame Press, 1981). Christopher Kaiser uses the phrase "relative autonomy" to mean the same thing. See *Creation and the History of Science* (Grand Rapids: Eerdmans, 1991), pp. 15, 131.

5. Kaiser, *Creation and the History of Science*, p. 16.

6. *Ibid.*, p. 93.
7. Richard S. Westfall, *The Construction of Modern Science: Mechanisms and Mechanics* (New York: John Wiley, 1971; Cambridge: Cambridge University Press, 1977), p. 29.
8. Cited in Kaiser, *Creation and the History of Science*, p. 154.
9. "Leibniz," in *Eighteenth-Century Philosophy: Readings in the History of Philosophy*, ed. Lewis White Beck, general editors, Paul Edwards and Richard Popkin (New York: Free Press, 1966), p. 192.
10. Kaiser, *Creation and the History of Science*, pp. 158-61.
11. Alexandre Koyré, *From the Closed World to the Infinite Universe* (Baltimore: Johns Hopkins University Press, 1957, paperback edition, 1968), p. 273.
12. As Marvin Olasky puts it, "If God is everywhere . . . God is nowhere. Theoretical pantheism could merge nicely with practical materialism." From *Prodigal Press* (Wheaton, IL: Crossway Books, 1988), p. 24.
13. Westfall, *Construction of Modern Science*, pp. 69-72.
14. Kaiser, *Creation and the History of Science*, p. 163. The mechanistic worldview in science correlated in theology with the doctrine of salvation preached by Martin Luther and John Calvin, in which human beings can do nothing to effect their own salvation. They are passive; God alone saves and justifies. See Jacques Roger, "The Mechanistic Conception of Life," in *God and Nature: Historical Essays on the Encounter between Christianity and Science*, ed. David C. Lindberg and Ronald L. Numbers (Berkeley: University of California Press, 1986), p. 279.
15. Kaiser, *Creation and the History of Science*, pp. 163-64.
16. Herbert Butterfield, *The Origins of Modern Science, 1300-1800*, rev. ed. (New York: Free Press, 1957), p. 137. The "successors" of whom Butterfield speaks are Boyle and Newton. For a detailed account of the tensions felt by Christians who adopted the mechanistic philosophy, see Richard Westfall, *Science and Religion in Seventeenth-Century England* (New Haven, CT: Yale University Press, 1958; Hamden, CT: Archon Books, 1970).
17. For additional parallels between Boyle's scientific concepts and the neo-Platonic worldview, see Westfall, *Construction of Modern Science*, pp. 76-80.
18. For more on the Cambridge Platonists, see Koyré, *From the Closed World*.
19. Kaiser, *Creation and the History of Science*, p. 189.
20. See Koyré, *From the Closed World*, chapter 5. For the theological implications of Newton's view of space, see Charles Thaxton, "A Dialogue with 'Prof' on Christianity and Science," in *God and Culture*, ed., D. A. Carson and John D. Woodbridge (Grand Rapids: Eerdmans, 1993), pp. 293-97.
21. Randall, *Making of the Modern Mind*, p. 276. By contrast, Randall goes on to say, "the very form of nineteenth-century evolutionary science has made that idea [of an external Creator] all but impossible, and substituted for it the notion of God as immanent, as a soul or spirit dwelling within the universe and developing it through long ages."
22. As Leibniz wrote, Newton and his followers taught that "God Almighty wants to *wind up* his Watch from Time to Time: Otherwise it would cease to move. He had not, it seems, sufficient Foresight to make it a perpetual Motion. Nay, the Machine of God's making, is so imperfect, according to these Gentlemen, that he is obliged to *clean* it now and then by an extra-

ordinary Concourse, and even to *mend* it, as a Clockmaker mends his Work; who must consequently be so much the more unskillful a Workman, as he is often obliged to mend his Work and to set it Right." Cited in Koyré, *From the Closed World*, p. 236, emphasis in original.

23. E. A. Burtt, *The Metaphysical Foundations of Modern Science*, rev. ed. (New York: Doubleday Anchor Books, 1932, 1954), p. 298.

24. Mechanistic explanations of light and other electromagnetic phenomena were not entirely successful, however, which opened the door to the new physics of relativity and quantum mechanics (see chapter 8). Life remained problematic as well (see chapter 5).

25. Burtt, *Metaphysical Foundations*, pp. 238-39.

26. Butterfield, *Origins of Modern Science*, chapter 9. See also Randall, *Making of the Modern Mind*, p. 264.

27. For a detailed account, see John Dillenberger, *Protestant Thought and Natural Science* (Notre Dame: University of Notre Dame Press, 1960), chapters 5 and 6.

28. Cited in Randall, *Making of the Modern Mind*, p. 287.

29. For a detailed account, see *ibid.*, chapters 12-15.

30. The tendency of each party to define itself in exclusion to the other led to a distortion of the full-bodied Biblical tradition—a distortion that continues to plague modern Christians. Today in the creation/evolution debate, for example, theistic evolutionists tend to stress God's working through processes immanent in creation, while creationists tend to stress God's transcendent power to create structures *de novo*.

CHAPTER FIVE: *The Belated Revolution in Biology*

1. William Coleman, *Biology in the Nineteenth Century: Problems of Form, Function, and Transformation* (New York: John Wiley, 1971; Cambridge, England: Cambridge University Press, 1977), p. 12.

2. For an excellent though brief description of the three worldviews in biology, see John C. Greene, *Science, Ideology, and World View: Essays in the History of Evolutionary Ideas* (Berkeley: University of California, 1981), chapter 3. A fuller description is found in Charles Coulston Gillispie, *The Edge of Objectivity* (Princeton, NJ: Princeton University Press, 1960). James R. Moore describes the three worldviews as they divided Christians at the time of Darwin in *The Post-Darwinian Controversies* (Cambridge, England: Cambridge University Press, 1979).

   Coleman likewise outlines three approaches in the history of biology, though he delineates them somewhat differently, as does E. S. Russell in *Form and Function: A Contribution to the History of Animal Morphology* (London: John Murray, 1916; Chicago: University of Chicago Press, 1982).

3. Arthur O. Lovejoy, *The Great Chain of Being: A Study in the History of an Idea* (Cambridge, MA: Harvard University Press, 1936, 1964), pp. 273-74. For example, on p. 273, Lovejoy quotes the French *philosophe* J. B. Robinet as saying, "Arts and sciences, laws, the diversity of the forms of government, war and commerce—everything, in short, is only a development. The seeds of all were latent in Nature; they have unfolded, each in its own time."

4. A. R. Hall, *The Scientific Revolution 1500-1800: The Formation of the Modern Scientific Attitude* (Boston: Beacon Press, 1954), p. 281.

5. Ernst Mayr, *The Growth of Biological Thought: Diversity, Evolution, and Inheritance* (Cambridge, MA: Harvard University Press, 1982), p. 102.

6. Interestingly, however, natural theology was popular with these two groups for opposing reasons. Christians saw in natural theology useful arguments against unbelief. Deists saw in it useful arguments against orthodox Christianity and in favor of a "natural" religion that rejected special revelation and proclaimed that knowledge of God is accessible to all rational minds from natural phenomena alone. See John Hedley Brooke, *Science and Religion: Some Historical Perspectives* (Cambridge, England: Cambridge University Press, 1991), p. 193.

7. Mayr, *Growth of Biological Thought,* pp. 103, 104.

8. Marjorie Grene, *A Portrait of Aristotle* (Chicago: University of Chicago Press, Phoenix Books, 1963). See especially pp. 60-62.

9. Interestingly, Aristotle did not teach that species are immutable, a position often attributed to him. The Forms are eternal; but since in his philosophy the material world always falls short of the eternal Forms, Aristotle expected actual biological organisms to exhibit a wide range of irregularity—to be erratic, unstable, variable. But there can be no science of biology if organisms are erratic and unstable. Hence, a scientific approach to biology was first made possible by a Christian adaptation of Aristotelianism, which taught that God created not only eternal Forms but also actual biological species and that these were therefore objective and constant. See Conway Zirkle, "Species Before Darwin," *Proceedings of the American Philosophical Society* 103, no. 5, (October 1959), pp. 636-44.

10. Cited in Richard S. Westfall, *The Construction of Modern Science: Mechanisms and Mechanics* (New York: John Wiley, 1971; Cambridge, England: Cambridge University Press, 1977), pp. 91-92.

11. Mayr, *Growth of Biological Thought,* p. 256-57.

12. Erik Nordenskiöld, *The History of Biology: A Survey,* originally published in Swedish in three volumes in 1920-24 (New York: Alfred A. Knopf, 1928; St. Clair Shores, MI: Scholarly Press, 1976), p. 200.

13. This form of the natural theology was sometimes called physico-theology, to emphasize that its starting point was evidence for design in the physical universe.

14. James L. Larson, *Reason and Experience: The Representation of Natural Order in the Work of Carl von Linné* (Berkeley: University of California Press, 1971), pp. 149-51.

15. William Coleman, *Georges Cuvier, Zoologist: A Study in the History of Evolution Theory* (Cambridge, MA: Harvard University Press, 1964), pp. 144-60; E. S. Russell, *Form and Function,* pp. 35-42.

For modern evolutionists, one of the most salient arguments in favor of evolution comes from the fossil record, which shows that many organisms living in the past differed from modern forms. Cuvier was well aware of the fossils; as noted, he established the science of paleontology. But he did not feel that the order of the fossils required an evolutionary explanation. Instead, to account for the succession of fossils in the rock strata, he proposed a theory of successive catastrophes, such as floods and volcanic activity, each cutting a huge swath in the biosphere. After every catastrophe, Cuvier proposed, a new population of organisms migrated in, which

explains why a different group of organisms dominated each successive era of geological history. This was a catastrophist theory of earth's history.
16. Coleman, *Georges Cuvier*, p. 26.
17. Cited in *ibid.*, p. 28.
18. As Jacques Roger explains, the Reformation led to an overall worldview that stressed the distinction between God and His creation. In theology it led to the doctrine of salvation preached by Martin Luther and John Calvin, in which sinners are incapable of effecting their own salvation. In science it led to the mechanistic concept of matter as passive and inert, incapable of creating anything on its own. Positively, that meant, in Roger's words, that "God, being the only source of grace and salvation in the spiritual world, was the sole origin of motion and activity in nature." From "The Mechanistic Conception of Life," in *God and Nature: Historical Essays on the Encounter between Christianity and Science*, ed. David C. Lindberg and Ronald L. Numbers (Berkeley: University of California Press, 1986), p. 279. See also Gary B. Deason, "Reformation Theology and the Mechanistic Conception of Nature" in the same volume.
19. Expressions in literature, philosophy, and politics are merely "the fruits of romanticism," says Gillispie, *The Edge of Objectivity*, p. 179. "Its roots go deeper into man's consciousness of nature."
20. Coleman, *Biology in the Nineteenth Century*, p. 121.
21. Mayr, *Growth of Biological Thought*, p. 97.
22. Lovejoy, *Great Chain of Being*, p. 297.
23. R. G. Collingwood, *The Idea of Nature* (Westport, CT: Greenwood Press, 1986; reprint of London: Oxford University Press, 1944), p. 110.
24. On Maupertuis, see Mayr, *Growth of Biological Thought*, p. 328; on Buffon, see Mayr, p. 41. Buffon's *Histoire naturelle* "decisively influenced Herder and through him the Romantics and *Naturphilosophie.*"
25. Cited in Dietrich von Engelhardt, "Historical Consciousness in the German Romantic *Naturforschung*," in *Romanticism and the Sciences*, ed. Andrew Cunningham and Nicholas Jardine (Cambridge, England: Cambridge University Press, 1990), p. 58.
   In another essay in the same book, Evelleen Richards discusses in detail the romantic "metaphor of gestation." She cites Lorenz Oken's concept of a "perfect parallelism" between the forms assumed by the developing human embryo and the ascending sequence of mature forms constituting the animal series. See "'Metaphorical Mystifications': The Romantic Gestation of Nature in British Biology."
26. See, for example, Lovejoy, *Great Chain of Being* (pp. 281-83). Robinet was "one of the earlier prophets" of an active principle permeating nature (a "*puissance active*"). A succinct introduction to German romanticism and its influence on biology can be found in Peter Bowler, *Evolution, the History of an Idea* (Berkeley: University of California, 1984), pp. 99-102. Aristotelian biology was often vitalistic as well, but the Aristotelian concept of Form emphasized an intelligible pattern in contrast to an active force.
27. For a detailed account of this transformation, see Lovejoy, *Great Chain of Being*.
28. Ian G. Barbour, *Issues in Science and Religion* (New York: Harper and Row, Harper Torchbooks, 1966, 1972), p. 67.

29. John H. Randall, *The Making of the Modern Mind* (New York: Columbia University Press, 1926, 1940), p. 419.
30. Lovejoy, *Great Chain of Being*, pp. 317, 322.
31. Greene, *Science, Ideology, and World View*, pp. 34-35.
32. Coleman, *Biology in the Nineteenth Century*, p. 121.
33. Roger, in *God and Nature*, p. 289. Buffon's predecessor, Maupertuis, likewise assumed that elementary particles of matter are endowed with something like will, memory, and perception. For a helpful essay on various forms of panpsychism see "Panpsychism," by Paul Edwards, *The Encyclopedia of Philosophy*, vol. 6, Paul Edwards, editor-in-chief (New York: Macmillan and the Free Press, 1967), pp. 22-31.
34. *Ibid.*, p. 289.
35. Nordenskiöld, *History of Biology*, p. 323, emphasis added.
36. *Ibid.*, pp. 327-30. Interestingly, even after citing these passages that clearly reveal Lamarck's neo-Platonic leanings, Nordenskiöld continues to refer to his conception of life as "mechanical" and "materialistic" and describes his evolutionary theory as having "a purely physical character."
37. Russell, *Form and Function*, pp. 218ff.
38. Gillispie, *The Edge of Objectivity*, p. 276.
39. Roger, in *God and Nature*, pp. 288-89.
40. *Ibid.*, pp. 287, 289.
41. Mayr, *Growth of Biological Thought*, p. 389. Similarly, Coleman (*Biology in the Nineteenth Century*, p. 153) explains that "the reductionists were inspired by abhorrence of their predecessors' speculative excesses."
42. Roger, in *God and Nature*, p. 291.
43. Coleman, *Biology in the Nineteenth Century*, p. 150.
44. Roger, in *God and Nature*, p. 292.
45. Coleman, *Biology in the Nineteenth Century*, p. 152.
46. *Ibid.* Coleman writes: "The reductionists' terms remain, however, merely premises and are not to be considered necessary conclusions drawn from organic . . . phenomena."
47. Cited in Gertrude Himmelfarb, *Darwin and the Darwinian Revolution* (Garden City, NY: Doubleday Anchor Books, 1959), pp. 329-30.
48. Thomas Paul Thigpen, "On the Origin of Theses: An Exploration of Horace Bushnell's Rejection of Darwinism," *Church History* 57, no. 4, (December 1988), pp. 499-513.
49. Jacques Barzun, *Darwin, Marx, Wagner: Critique of a Heritage*, 2d ed. (Chicago: University of Chicago Press, 1941, 1958, 1981), pp. 11, 36.
50. Gillispie, *The Edge of Objectivity*, p. 317.
51. Russell, *Form and Function*, p. 309. See also pp. xxxii, 204, 235.
52. Neal C. Gillespie, *Charles Darwin and the Problem of Creation* (Chicago: University of Chicago Press, 1979), p. 19.
53. Charles Darwin, *On the Origin of Species*, a facsimile of the First Edition, intro. Ernst Mayr (Cambridge, MA: Harvard University Press, 1964), p. 482. For a response to the charge that the concept of creation is not scientific, see J. P. Moreland, *Christianity and the Nature of Science: A Philosophical Investigation* (Grand Rapids: Baker Book House, 1989), chapter 6.
54. Carl Becker, *The Heavenly City of the Eighteenth-Century Philosophers* (New Haven, CT: Yale University Press, 1932), pp. 161-62.
55. Cited in Randall, *Making of the Modern Mind*, pp. 581-82.

56. Philip F. Rehbock, "Transcendental Anatomy," in *Romanticism and the Sciences*, p. 153. In the same volume, Evelleen Richards ("The Romantic Gestation of Nature," p. 136) speaks of "Owen's formal synthesis of Geoffroyan morphology and Cuvierian teleology."

57. Bowler, *Evolution, the History*, p. 120.

58. In the colorful description given by Gillispie (*The Edge of Objectivity*, p. 321), Haeckel "worked a syncretism between the Goethean sense of unity in nature and the Darwinian proof of organic evolution. Haeckel's were the voice of Jacob and the hands of Esau, the historicist spirit of romantic idealism and the hairy philosophy of monistic materialism."

59. There were two forms of emboitement theory. One stressed the role of the sperm and was called animaculism. It held that an entire miniature human being (a homunculus) was curled up inside the head of each spermatozoon. The other form of emboitement stressed the role of the egg and was called ovism. It held that the entire human race was present already in Eve. See Westfall, *Construction of Modern Science*, pp. 97-104.

60. Mayr, *Growth of Biological Thought*, pp. 88-89.

61. Coleman, *Biology in the Nineteenth Century*, p. 144.

62. Douglas Futuyma, *Science on Trial: The Case for Evolution* (New York: Pantheon, 1983), pp. 12-13; Richard Dawkins, *The Blind Watchmaker: Why the Evidence of Evolution Reveals a Universe Without Design* (New York: W. W. Norton, 1986, 1987).

63. Howard J. Van Till, Davis A. Young, Clarence Menninga, *Science Held Hostage: What's Wrong with Creation Science and Evolutionism* (Downers Grove, IL: InterVarsity Press, 1988).

64. Frank L. Marsh, *Variation and Fixity in Nature: The Meaning of Diversity and Discontinuity in the World of Living Things, and Their Bearing on Creation and Evolution* (Mountain View, CA: Pacific Press, 1976), p. 87; Lane P. Lester and Raymond G. Bohlin, *The Natural Limits to Biological Change* (Grand Rapids: Zondervan/Probe, 1984), p. 162. Michael Denton, *Evolution: A Theory in Crisis* (Bethesda, MD: Adler and Adler, 1986).

65. Barbour, *Issues in Science & Religion*.

66. E. J. Ambrose, *The Nature and Origin of the Biological World* (Chichester, England: Ellis Horwood Ltd., 1982).

Interestingly, the same theological fault lines split Christians in Darwin's day. Christian Aristotelians and Christian mechanists disagreed over Darwinism (the former rejecting it, the latter accepting it), while largely remaining theologically orthodox. But Christians with romantic leanings were attracted to non-Darwinian forms of evolution (Larmarckianism, etc.) and embraced theological liberalism. See Moore, *Post-Darwinian Controversies*.

CHAPTER SIX: *Math in the Past*

1. Cited in Philipp Frank, *Philosophy of Science: The Link Between Science and Philosophy* (Englewood Cliffs, NJ: Prentice-Hall, Spectrum Books, 1957), p. 83.

2. Morris Kline, *Mathematics in Western Culture* (New York: Oxford University Press, 1953), p. 96.

3. Morris Kline, *Mathematics: The Loss of Certainty* (New York: Oxford University Press, 1980), p. 29.

4. *Ibid.*, pp. 34-35.
5. Cited in *ibid.*, p. 31.
6. A. R. Hall, *The Scientific Revolution, 1500-1800* (Boston: Beacon Press, 1954), p. 36.
7. E. A. Burtt, *The Metaphysical Foundations of Modern Science*, rev. ed. (New York: Doubleday Anchor Books, 1932, 1954), pp. 38, 52.
8. John H. Randall, *The Making of the Modern Mind*, (New York: Columbia University Press, 1926, 1940), p. 220.
9. R. G. Collingwood, *An Essay on Metaphysics* (Chicago: Henry Regnery, Gateway Edition, 1972; originally published by London: Oxford University Press, 1940), p. 250.
10. Richard S. Westfall, *The Construction of Modern Science: Mechanisms and Mechanics* (New York: John Wiley, 1971; Cambridge, England: Cambridge University Press, 1977), pp. 21-22. See also Herbert Butterfield, *The Origins of Modern Science, 1300-1800*, rev. ed. (New York: Free Press, 1957), pp. 17, 25, 96-97. As A. R. Hall puts it (*The Scientific Revolution*, pp. 170-71), the world of Galileo's theories was an "ideal world of abstraction without resistance or friction, in which bodies were perfectly smooth and planes infinite, where gravity was always a strictly perpendicular force, and projectiles described the most exquisitely exact parabolas." To apply to the real world, of course, at some point Galileo had to add friction, air resistance, and everything else back in.
11. Kline, *Mathematics: The Loss of Certainty*, p. 52.
12. Randall, *Making of the Modern Mind*, p. 258.
13. Cited in Kline, *Mathematics: The Loss of Certainty*, p. 36.
14. Burtt, *Metaphysical Foundations*, pp. 63, 64.
15. Cited in *ibid.*, p. 75.
16. Hans Reichenbach, *The Rise of Scientific Philosophy* (Berkeley: University of California Press, 1954), p. 103.
17. Cited in Robert McRae, *The Problem of the Unity of the Sciences: Bacon to Kant* (Toronto: University of Toronto Press, 1961), pp. 59-60.
18. Randall, *Making of the Modern Mind*, p. 267.
19. Karl Popper, *Conjectures and Refutations* (New York: Basic Books, 1962), pp. 15-16.
20. Randall, *Making of the Modern Mind*, p. 268.
21. Burtt, *Metaphysical Foundations*, p. 123. "How, indeed, do we know that there is any such world?" (p. 185). See also his discussion of epistemology on pp. 300ff.

CHAPTER SEVEN: *The Idol Falls*

1. Rudolph Weingartner, "Historical Explanation," *The Encyclopedia of Philosophy*, vol. 4, Paul Edwards, editor-in-chief (New York: Macmillan and Free Press), p. 7.
2. Morris Kline, *Mathematics: The Loss of Certainty* (New York: Oxford University Press, 1980), p. 74, emphasis added.
3. John Hedley Brooke, *Science and Religion: Some Historical Perspectives* (Cambridge, England: Cambridge University Press, 1991), p. 186.
4. John H. Randall, *The Making of the Modern Mind* (New York: Columbia University Press, 1926, 1940), p. 271.

5. Eric Temple Bell, *The Magic of Numbers* (New York: Dover Books, 1946), pp. 373-76.
6. Kline, *Mathematics: The Loss of Certainty*, p. 88.
7. Hans Reichenbach, *The Rise of Scientific Philosophy* (Berkeley: University of California Press, 1954), p. 142. See also Loren Graham, *Science in Russia and the Soviet Union* (Cambridge: Cambridge University Press, 1993), p. 119.
8. Arthur Lovejoy, *The Great Chain of Being: A Study of the History of an Idea* (Cambridge, MA: Harvard University Press, 1936, 1964), p. 66. The Greeks had what Lovejoy calls "an aesthetic aversion" to the notion of infinity, which they equated with indefiniteness. To say of something that it is infinite is to say that it "has no clear-cut arithmetical character at all." An infinite number is therefore, in the words of Plotinus, "contrary to the very nature of Number."
9. Quoted in Kline, *Mathematics: The Loss of Certainty*, p. 151.
10. Philipp Frank, *Philosophy of Science: The Link Between Science and Philosophy* (Englewood Cliffs, NJ: Prentice-Hall, Spectrum Books, 1957), pp. 59, 72, 75.
11. Vern S. Poythress, "A Biblical View of Mathematics," in *Foundations of Christian Scholarship* (Vallecito, CA: Ross House Books, 1979), p. 169.
12. See Benacerraf and Putnam, "Introduction," *Philosophy of Mathematics*, p. 18.
13. Intuitionist L. E. J. Brouwer acknowledges his philosophical debt to Kant in "Intuitionism and Formalism," in *Philosophy of Mathematics*, 2d ed., ed. Paul Benacerraf and Hilary Putnam (Cambridge, England: Cambridge University Press, 1983), pp. 77ff.
14. Arend Heyting, "The Intuitionist Foundations of Mathematics," in *Philosophy of Mathematics*, p. 52. A more moderate form of intuitionism acknowledged some elements of mathematics as "given," a view expressed by Leopold Kronecker when he said, "God created the natural numbers, the rest is the work of man."
15. Frank, *Philosophy of Science*, pp. 70, 73.
16. Stephen Barker, "Non-Euclidean Geometry," in *Mathematics: People, Problems, Results*, vol. 2, ed. Douglas M. Campbell and John C. Higgins (Belmont, CA: Wadsworth International, Brigham Young University, 1984), pp. 117-21.
17. John Passmore, *A Hundred Years of Philosophy* (Baltimore, MD: Penguin Books, 1957, 1966), p. 395.
18. Kline, *Mathematics: The Loss of Certainty*, p. 264. Gödel's paper also contained his famous incompleteness theorem, demonstrating that no system can ever prove every true statement contained in the system.
19. Cited in *ibid.*, p. 394.
20. Georg Cantor, a devout Lutheran, worked out his mathematical theories under the direct inspiration of what he called "Christian philosophy." Bruce Hedman argues that Cantor's set theory rests on the distinction between God's absolute rationality and the created and contingent nature of human rationality. See "Cantor's Concept of Infinity: Implications of Infinity for Contingence," *Perspectives on Science and Christian Faith* 45, no. 1, (March 1993).
21. Cited in Kline, *Mathematics: The Loss of Certainty*, p. 257.
22. *Ibid.*, p. 316.

23. *Ibid.*, p. 97.
24. Cited in Frank, *Philosophy of Science*, p. 48.
25. Bell, *The Magic of Numbers*, pp. 331, 355.
26. Edward A. Purcell, *The Crisis of Democratic Theory: Scientific Naturalism and the Problem of Value* (Lexington, KY: University Press of Kentucky, 1973), p. 53. Quotations in the following section are all cited in chapter 4 of Purcell's book.
27. Michael Guillen, *Bridges to Infinity* (Los Angeles: Jeremy Tarcher, 1983), p. 62.
28. Carl Hempel, "On the Nature of Mathematical Truth," in *The World of Mathematics*, vol. 3, ed. James R. Newman (New York: Simon and Schuster, 1956), pp. 1619ff. See also Douglas Gasking, "Mathematics and the World," in *ibid.*, pp. 1708ff.
29. Poythress, in *Foundations*, p. 170.
30. Peter Bowler, *Evolution, the History of an Idea* (Berkeley: University of California Press, 1984), pp. 25-26.
31. Peggy Marchi, "Mathematics as a Critical Enterprise," in *Essays in Memory of Imre Lakatos*, ed. R. S. Cohen, R. K. Feyerabend, M. W. Wartofsky, Boston Studies in the Philosophy of Science, vol. 39 (Boston: D. Reidel Publishing, 1976), p. 382.
32. Eugene P. Wigner, "The Unreasonable Effectiveness of Mathematics in the Natural Sciences," in *Mathematics: People, Problems, Results*, pp. 117, 120, 122, 124.
33. Kline, *Mathematics: The Loss of Certainty*, pp. 335, 340, 348.
34. Gasking, in *World of Mathematics*, pp. 1708ff.
35. Guillen, *Bridges to Infinity*, p. 71.
36. For a recent restatement of Dooyeweerdian thought, see Roy A. Clouser, *The Myth of Religious Neutrality* (Notre Dame, IN: University of Notre Dame Press, 1991). Chapter 4 treats mathematics. Other Christians who have written on the subject of mathematics are listed in Gene Chase and Calvin Jongsma, *Bibliography of Christianity and Mathematics* (Sioux Center, IA: Dordt College Press).

CHAPTER EIGHT: *Is Everything Relative?*

1. Paul Johnson, *Modern Times: The World from the Twenties to the Eighties* (New York: Harper and Row, 1983), pp. 1, 4-5.
2. Among the best popularizations of Einstein's theories are his own book, *Relativity: The Special and the General Theory*, trans. Robert W. Lawson (New York: Crown Publishers, 1961) and Lincoln Barnett, *The Universe and Dr. Einstein*, rev. ed., foreword, Albert Einstein (Mattituck, NY: American Reprint Co., 1948, 1950). For a simple textbook approach see Sung Kyu Kim, *Physics: The Fabric of Reality* (New York: Macmillan, 1975) and Walter Fuchs, *Physics for the Modern Mind*, foreword, Max Born, trans. Dr. M. Wilson and M. Wheaton (New York: Macmillan, 1965, 1967). For a very brief but readable introduction, see Robert M. Hazen and James Trefil, *Science Matters: Achieving Scientific Literacy* (New York: Doubleday, Anchor Books, 1991).
3. Eric Chaisson, *Relatively Speaking* (New York: W. W. Norton, 1988), pp. 42-44.
4. Dudley Shapere, *Galileo: A Philosophical Study* (Chicago: University of

Chicago Press, 1974), pp. 99-100; Richard Westfall, *The Construction of Modern Science: Mechanisms and Mechanics* (New York: John Wiley, 1971; Cambridge, England: Cambridge University Press, 1977), p. 17; E. J. Dijksterhuis, *The Mechanization of the World Picture* (Princeton, NJ: Princeton University Press, 1950, translated 1961), pp. 352-57. Actually, Aristotle's experiment would have worked if he had had better instruments. Galileo's relativity principle applies only to uniform linear motion. Since the earth rotates on its axis, its surface is not an inertial frame. This produces what is known as the Coriolis force, which is demonstrated by the Foucault pendulum.

5. This has nothing to do with the Doppler effect, which applies to the frequency of sound waves, not to their velocity.

6. Chaisson, *Relatively Speaking*, p. 56. Eric Chaisson notes that scientists have hypothesized the existence of particles that move *faster* than the speed of light but can never move any more *slowly*. They have dubbed these hypothetical particles "tachyons" (after the Greek word *taxio*, meaning swift). If tachyons exist, then what relativity excludes is crossing of the light barrier.

7. Albert Einstein and Leopold Infeld, *The Evolution of Physics* (New York: Simon and Schuster, Touchstone Book, 1938, 1966), p. 197.

8. *Ibid.*, p. 221.

9. Hans Reichenbach, *From Copernicus to Einstein* (New York: Wisdom Library, division of Philosophical Library, n.d.), chapter 4.

10. Chaisson, *Relatively Speaking*, p. 81.

11. Obviously we are not talking about Euclidean geometry here, where space is always flat and lines always straight. In his concept of curved space, Einstein was the first to apply non-Euclidean forms of geometry to physical theories.

   Hence an indirect consequence of relativity theory was that it popularized non-Euclidean geometry. As discussed in chapter 7, the development of non-Euclidean geometry had a devastating impact on the academic world, where it became a powerful metaphor for the overthrow of accepted truths and authoritative systems of thought. But its destructive effects did not find their way into popular culture until Einstein put forth his notion of curved space, which made use of non-Euclidean geometry.

12. For a brief list of dissenters from Einsteinian theory, see Petr Beckman, *Einstein Plus Two* (Boulder, CO: Golem Press, 1987), pp. 20-21. Among Christians, physicist Thomas Barnes offers a critique of relativity in *Physics of the Future* (El Cajon, CA: Institute for Creation Research, 1983), and offers his alternative using concepts of classical physics in *Space Medium* (El Paso, TX: Geo/Space Research Foundation, 1986).

13. Herbert Dingle, letter to the editor, *The Economist*, March 5, 1977. For a full treatment, see Dingle's book, *Science at the Crossroads* (London: Brian and O'Keefe, 1972).

14. P. A. M. Dirac, "The Early Years of Relativity," in *Albert Einstein: Historical and Cultural Perspectives*, ed. Gerald Holton and Yehuda Elkana (Princeton, NJ: Princeton University Press, 1982), pp. 79-80.

15. An excellent account of the way relativity and quantum theory were taken up by artists and writers can be found in Alan J. Friedman and Carol C. Donley, *Einstein as Myth and Muse* (New York: Cambridge University Press, 1985).

16. Gerald Holton, "Einstein and the Shaping of Our Imagination," in *Albert Einstein: Historical and Cultural Perspectives*, pp. xiv-xvii. See also Friedman and Donley, *Einstein as Myth*.

17. Dirac, in *Albert Einstein: Historical and Cultural Perspectives*, pp. 79-80.

18. Newspaper quotations are from Friedman and Donley, *Einstein as Myth*, pp. 10-11.

19. Loren R. Graham, "The Reception of Einstein's Ideas," in *Albert Einstein: Historical and Cultural Perspectives*, p. 119.

20. Ian Barbour, *Issues in Science and Religion* (New York: Harper and Row, Harper Torchbooks, 1966), pp. 28, 285.

    Moreover, since relativity theory is so difficult to understand, it encouraged radical skepticism—doubt in the ability of human reason to know truth. If Einstein is right, then many of our common-sense notions about such fundamental things as time and space are wrong. How then can the average person trust his reason as a guide to truth? Yaron Ezrahi, "Einstein and the Light of Reason," in *Albert Einstein: Historical and Cultural Perspectives*.

21. Cited by Graham, in *Albert Einstein: Historical and Cultural Perspectives*, p. 107.

22. Holton, in *ibid.*, p. xv.

23. Francis Schaeffer, *How Should We Then Live?* (Old Tappan, NJ: Fleming H. Revell, 1976), p. 138.

24. Cited in Gerald Holton, *Thematic Origins of Scientific Thought*, rev. ed. (Cambridge, MA: Harvard University Press, 1988), pp. 250-64, emphasis added.

25. Cited in *ibid.*, pp. 254-55, emphasis in original.

26. Cited in Steven Weinberg, *Dreams of a Final Theory: The Search for the Fundamental Laws of Nature* (New York: Random House, Pantheon Books, 1992), pp. 242, 245, emphasis added.

27. Friedman and Donley, *Einstein as Myth*, p. 111.

28. E. L. Mascall, *Christian Theology and Natural Science* (Hamden, CT: Archon Books, 1965), p. 169.

29. Stanley Jaki, *The Origin of Science and the Science of Its Origin* (South Bend, IN: Regnery Gateway, 1978), p. 98.

30. Nick Herbert, *Quantum Reality: Beyond the New Physics* (New York: Doubleday Anchor Books, 1985), p. 36.

31. J. C. Polkinghorne, *The Quantum World* (Princeton, NJ: Princeton University Press, 1984), p. ix.

CHAPTER NINE: *Quantum Mysteries*

1. It is important to distinguish relativity theory from quantum mechanics. As we saw in the last chapter, relativity theory remains as objective and deterministic as classical physics was. Yet since both relativity and quantum mechanics rejected central concepts of Newtonian physics, and since they appeared at about the same time, the two are generally lumped together under the rubric of the "new physics."

2. John Gribbin, *In Search of Schrödinger's Cat: Quantum Physics and Reality* (New York: Bantam Books, 1984), p. 2. A little later (p. 4), we find another sweeping statement: ". . . experiments prove that there is no underlying reality to the world."

3. J. C. Polkinghorne, *The Quantum World* (Princeton, NJ: Princeton University Press, 1984), p. 1.
4. Quoted in Tony Hey and Patrick Walters, *The Quantum Universe* (Cambridge, England: Cambridge University Press, 1987), p. 46.
5. Cited in Alan J. Friedman and Carol C. Donley, *Einstein as Myth and Muse* (New York: Cambridge University Press, 1985), p. 114.
6. To understand what an interference pattern is, imagine two water waves colliding. Where a crest of one wave meets a trough of the other, the two cancel each other out. (This corresponds to the areas where the photographic screen remains blank.) Where two crests meet, they reinforce each other and form a composite crest of combined height. (This corresponds to the areas where electrons hit the screen, creating dark stripes.)
7. Nick Herbert, *Quantum Reality: Beyond the New Physics* (New York: Doubleday Anchor Books, 1985), pp. 65-66.
8. P. C. W. Davies and J. R. Brown, eds., *The Ghost in the Atom* (Cambridge, England: Cambridge University Press, 1986), p. 8. Actually, even with one slit open, the electrons show some wavelike behavior (e.g., they form a diffraction pattern). But they do not form an interference pattern.
9. Herbert, *Quantum Reality*, p. 38.
10. Friedman and Donley, *Einstein as Myth*, p. 117.
11. Sir George Thomson, *The Inspiration of Science* (London: Oxford University Press, 1961), p. 117.
12. Ian G. Barbour, *Issues in Science and Religion* (New York: Harper and Row, Harper Torchbooks, 1966), p. 293. See also Polkinghorne, *Quantum World*, pp. 7-8.
13. Friedman and Donley, *Einstein as Myth*, p. 118.
14. Fritjof Capra, *Turning Point* (New York: Simon and Schuster, 1982), p. 87.
15. Interview with John Wheeler in *Ghost in the Atom*, p. 60.
16. The Uncertainty Principle should not be interpreted to mean a psychological uncertainty on the part of the atomic physicist. It can be quantified in a precise mathematical formula:

$$\Delta p \, \Delta x \geq h$$

where Δp is the uncertainty in momentum, Δx is the uncertainty in position, and h is Planck's constant. Operationally this means that as we determine the position of an atomic entity more precisely (as Δp decreases), the momentum becomes less precise (Δx increases).

The quantities in the formula are determined by the experimental setup. Take, for example, the classic two-slit experiment in which a stream of electrons passes through two parallel slits and hits a photographic screen on the other side. If the distance between the two slits is a, then the uncertainty in the position is a. Hence the uncertainties we are talking about do not refer to some state in the physicist's mind; they are determined by the design of the experiment. Philipp Frank, *Philosophy of Science: The Link Between Science and Philosophy* (Englewood Cliffs, NJ: Prentice-Hall, Spectrum Books, 1957), pp, 207-10. See also Herbert, *Quantum Reality*, pp. 67-70.
17. Roy A. Clouser, *The Myth of Religious Neutrality* (Notre Dame: University of Notre Dame Press, 1991), p. 136.

18. Hugh Ross, *The Fingerprint of God* (Orange, CA: Promise Publishing, 1989), p. 134.
19. Frank, *Philosophy of Science*, chapter 9.
20. Werner Heisenberg, *Physics and Philosophy: The Revolution in Modern Science* (New York: Harper and Row, Harper Torchbooks, 1958), p. 54.
21. Gary Zukav, *The Dancing Wu Li Masters* (New York: Bantam Books, 1979), p. 28, emphasis in original.
22. Michael Talbot, *Mysticism and the New Physics* (New York: Bantam Books, 1981), p. 34.
23. P. C. W. Davies and J. R. Brown, *Ghost in the Atom*, pp. 1, 4.
24. Herbert, *Quantum Reality*, p. 157.
25. *Ibid.*, pp. 46, 99.
26. Heisenberg, *Physics and Philosophy*, pp. 58, 81.
27. Herbert, *Quantum Reality*, p. 141, 148.
28. Interview with David Bohm in *Ghost in the Atom*, pp. 118-19.
29. See John D. Barrow and Frank J. Tipler, *The Anthropic Cosmological Principle* (Oxford: Oxford University Press, 1988).
30. Polkinghorne, *Quantum World*, p. 65. See also Ian Barbour, *Religion in an Age of Science* (New York: HarperCollins, HarperSanFrancisco, 1990), p. 113.
31. Cited in Herbert, *Quantum Reality*, p. 18, emphasis in original.
32. Fritjof Capra, *The Tao of Physics* (London: Fontana Paperbacks, Flamingo edition, 1975, 1983), p. 150.
33. Cited in Marilyn Ferguson, *The Aquarian Conspiracy: Personal and Social Transformation in the 1980s* (Los Angeles: J. P. Tarcher, 1980), p. 172.
34. Barbour, *Issues in Science and Religion*, p. 119.
35. Davies and Brown, *Ghost in the Atom*, p. 37.
36. Interview with Rudolf Peierls in *ibid.*, p. 81.
37. Interview with David Deutsch in *ibid.*, p. 90.
38. Here we are talking about ontological realism (what sort of world exists) not epistemological realism (whether theories can be true), which is discussed later.
39. Polkinghorne, *Quantum World*, p. 33.
40. A comparison of positivism with other philosophies of science, presented in the form of a debate, can be found in Larry Laudan, *Science and Relativism: Some Key Controversies in the Philosophy of Science* (Chicago: University of Chicago Press, 1990).
41. Davies and Brown, *Ghost in the Atom*, pp. 24-26.
42. From a personal letter, cited in Polkinghorne, *Quantum World*, p. 79.
43. Interview with David Bohm in *Ghost in the Atom*, p. 124.
44. Polkinghorne, *Quantum World*, p. 79.
45. Del Ratzsch, *Philosophy of Science: The Natural Sciences in Christian Perspective* (Downers Grove, IL: InterVarsity Press, 1986), pp. 36, 84, emphases in original. Later Ratzsch notes that "realism has the advantage of conforming to what most practicing scientists have believed they were doing" (p. 90).
46. A prominent proponent of instrumentalism is Larry Laudan. See *Progress and Its Problems: Towards a Theory of Scientific Growth* (Berkeley: University of California Press, 1977).
47. Herbert, *Quantum Reality*, p. 4.

48. Frederick Suppe, *The Structure of Scientific Theories*, 2d ed. (Chicago: University of Illinois Press, 1977), p. 135.

49. For a defense of realism, see W. H. Newton-Smith, *The Rationality of Science* (London: Routledge, 1981).

50. Barbour, *Issues in Science and Religion*, p. 171, emphasis in original.

51. Clouser, *Myth of Religious Neutrality*, p. 137.

52. For some of the other reasons, see Ratzsch, *Philosophy of Science*, pp. 80-85. See also Suppe, *Structure of Scientific Theories*, pp. 651-728, who says the emerging trend in philosophy of science today is "historical realism."

53. E. L. Mascall, *Christian Theology and Natural Science* (Hamden, CT: Archon Books, 1965), pp. 174-75.

54. Ratzsch, *Philosophy of Science*, pp. 85ff. Presenting similar arguments, J. P. Moreland, who teaches philosophy of religion at Talbot Seminary of Biola University, urges Christians to adopt selective ("eclectic") realism. See *Christianity and the Nature of Science* (Grand Rapids: Baker Book House, 1989).

55. Arthur Eddington, *The Nature of the Physical World* (Ann Arbor, MI: University of Michigan Press, Ann Arbor Paperbacks, 1958).

56. In academic circles, idealist interpretations of the new physics lost credibility after being skillfully debunked by L. Susan Stebbing in *Philosophy and the Physicists* (London: Methuen and Company, [1937], New York: Dover Publications, 1958).

57. Zukav, *Dancing Wu Li Masters*, p. 28, emphases in original.

58. See Israel Scheffler, *Science and Subjectivity* (Indianapolis, IN: Hackett Publishing, 1982).

59. Stebbing, *Philosophy and the Physicists*, pp. 145, 149. Of course, not everyone who accepts evolution gives it a materialistic interpretation (see chapter 5).

60. Floyd Matson, *The Broken Image* (New York: George Braziller, 1964), p. 130.

61. Pascual Jordan, *Science and the Course of History* (New Haven, CT: Yale University Press, 1955), p. 113.

62. James Jeans, *Physics and Philosophy* (Cambridge, England: Cambridge University Press and Macmillan, 1943, New York: Dover Publications, 1981), p. 216.

63. Michael Polanyi, *Personal Knowledge* (Chicago: University of Chicago Press, 1962), p. 390n.

64. Barbour, *Issues in Science and Religion*, p. 309.

65. *Ibid.*, p. 313.

66. See the writings of Hermann Dooyeweerd, who proposed an entire Christian philosophy based on anti-reductionism. His most comprehensive work is *A New Critique of Theoretical Thought* (Jordan Station, Ontario: Paideia Press, 1984).

67. Richard Bube, *The Encounter Between Christianity and Science* (Grand Rapids: Eerdmans, 1968), p. 184.

68. Rudolf Bultmann, *Jesus Christ and Mythology* (New York: Charles Scribner's Sons, 1958), pp. 37-38.

69. Colin Brown, *Miracles and the Critical Mind* (Grand Rapids: Eerdmans, 1984), pp. 223-24, 232, 291-92.

70. C. S. Lewis, *Miracles: A Preliminary Study* (New York: Macmillan, 1947).

71. Arthur Koestler, *Arrow in the Blue* (London: Hamish Hamilton, 1952), p. 258.
72. Percy Bridgman, *Reflections of a Physicist* (New York: Philosophical Library, 1950), p. 93.
73. Bertrand Russell, *Religion and Science* (Home University Library, 1935, London: Oxford University Press, 1961), pp. 160-61.
74. Matson, *Broken Image*, p. 146, emphasis added.
75. From *Too True to Be Good*, cited in Frank, *Philosophy of Science*, pp. 232-33.
76. Koestler, *Arrow in the Blue*, p. 258.
77. Gordon Clark, *The Philosophy of Science and Belief in God* (Nutley, NJ: Craig Press, 1964), pp. 66, 91-95. Clark embraces an operationalist view of science.
78. Mary Hesse, *Science and the Human Imagination* (New York: Philosophical Library, 1955), p. 90.
79. Carl Becker, *The Heavenly City of the Eighteenth-Century Philosophers* (New Haven, CT: Yale University Press, 1932), p. 24.

CHAPTER TEN: *A Chemical Code*

1. Michael Denton, *Evolution: A Theory in Crisis* (Bethesda, MD: Adler and Adler, 1986), p. 329.
2. Good historical accounts can be found in Horace Freeland Judson in *The Eighth Day of Creation* (New York: Simon and Schuster, Touchstone Book, 1979) and John Gribbin, *In Search of the Double Helix* (New York: Bantam Books, 1987).
3. Jacques Monod, *Chance and Necessity* (New York: Random House, Vintage Books, 1971, 1972), pp. 95-97.
4. Today biologists have discovered some regularities in amino acid sequences, so that one can predict certain secondary and tertiary structures such as alpha helices and hydrophobic domains, etc., with fair accuracy. The implications, however, remain essentially the same. See footnote 26.
5. Interview with Jacques Monod in Judson, *Eighth Day*, p. 213.
6. George W. Beadle, "The Language of the Gene," in *The Languages of Science*, intro. Philippe Le Corbeiller (New York: Basic Books, 1963), p. 62.
7. Interview with Max Delbrück in Judson, *Eighth Day*, p. 59, emphasis in original.
8. Erwin Schrödinger, *What Is Life?* (Cambridge, England: Cambridge University Press, 1944, 1967), p. 61.
9. Judson, *Eighth Day*, pp. 228-29, 250ff.
10. Michael A. Simon, *The Matter of Life: Philosophical Problems of Biology* (New Haven, CT: Yale University Press, 1971), p. 138.
11. F. Sanger, G. M. Air, B. G. Barrell, et al., "Nucleotide Sequence of Bacteriophage Phi-X-174," *Nature* 265 (1977), p. 687.
12. Robert Shapiro, *Origins: A Skeptic's Guide to the Creation of Life on Earth* (New York: Simon and Schuster, Summit Books, 1986), p. 76.
13. Lila Gatlin, *Information Theory and the Living System* (New York: Columbia University Press, 1972), p. 1.
14. Jeremy Campbell, *Grammatical Man: Information, Entropy, Language, and Life* (New York: Simon and Schuster, 1982), p. 16.

15. Bernd-Olaf Kuppers, *Information and the Origin of Life* (Cambridge, MA: MIT Press, 1990), pp. 170-72.
16. Francis Crick, *Of Molecules and Men* (Seattle: University of Washington Press, 1966), p. 11.
17. J. D. Watson, *The Molecular Biology of the Gene* (New York: W. A. Benjamin, 1965), p. 67.
18. Crick, *Of Molecules and Men*, p. 10, emphasis in original.
19. P. S. Moorhead and M. M. Kaplan, eds., *Mathematical Challenges to the Neo-Darwinian Interpretation of Evolution* (Philadelphia: Wistar Institute, 1967).
20. Interview with Cyril Ponnamperuma in Shapiro, *Origins: A Skeptic's Guide*, pp. 186-87.
21. D. H. Kenyon and G. Steinman, *Biochemical Predestination* (New York: McGraw-Hill, 1969).
22. R. A. Kok, J. A. Taylor, and W. L. Bradley, "A Statistical Examination of Self-Ordering of Amino Acids in Proteins," *Origins of Life and Evolution of the Biosphere* 18 (1988), p. 135.
23. Interview in the *Bible Science Newsletter*, September 1989. After rejecting his own earlier theory, Kenyon has now become a creationist.
    Of course, even if the predestinist theory were right, that still would not explain the ultimate source of the ordered sequence of bases in DNA. Instead, it would only push the question back a step. If the simple chemicals that compose life contain all the instructions needed to construct living things from scratch, then these chemicals are not simple at all but veritable mines of information. Where did all this information come from? Why are chemicals "programmed" to create life? See A. E. Wilder-Smith, *The Creation of Life* (Wheaton, IL: Harold Shaw Publishers, 1970), pp. 116, 121, 132.
24. Shapiro, *Origins: A Skeptic's Guide*, p. 116. Claims about the results of origin-of-life experiments are often exaggerated, even in the scientific literature, Shapiro says. "I have seen several statements in scientific sources which claim that proteins and nucleic acids themselves have been prepared" in simulation experiments. But such statements are not true. These complex molecules have *not* formed. All that has appeared are their simplest building blocks, and these are not in the right forms for life. See p. 108.
    Moreover, even these skimpy results can be obtained only by nurturing the experiment along in such a way that conditions are completely unlike anything that would occur naturally. (pp. 177-89, 204.)
    For a discussion of the various ways the investigator intervenes in origin-of-life experiments, and the impact of that intervention on the plausibility of the experiment, see Charles Thaxton, Walter Bradley, and Roger Olsen, *The Mystery of Life's Origin: Reassessing Current Theories* (New York: Philosophical Library, 1984; Dallas: Lewis and Stanley, 1993), chapter 6.
25. Comprehensive critiques of origin-of-life theories can be found in Shapiro, *Origins: A Skeptic's Guide*, and in Thaxton, Bradley, and Olsen, *Mystery of Life's Origin*. See also Walter Bradley and Charles Thaxton, "Information and the Origin of Life," in *The Creation Hypothesis*, ed. J. P. Moreland (Downers Grove, IL: InterVarsity Press, 1994).
26. Today molecular biologists have mapped hundreds of protein sequences,

and some regularities have in fact emerged. Amino acids do exhibit some stable preferences. But that does not change the basic argument presented here. In fact, it strengthens the argument. It means that the analogy between protein structure and a language is even closer than was previously thought.

No language allows letters and words to be combined completely randomly. Rules of grammar and composition restrict what combinations are allowable. These constraints, which produce certain regularities within a language, are analogous to the constraints that produce regularities in amino acid combinations.

The constraints imposed by rules of grammar and composition do not, however, dictate actual content. They cannot produce, say, Shakespeare's *Hamlet*. By the same token, the minor constraints in amino acid sequences do not account for a protein's overall sequence. See Klaus Dose, "The Origin of Life: More Questions Than Answers," *Interdisciplinary Science Reviews* 13, no. 4 (1988), p. 354. Discussing differences in relative reactivities among amino acids, Dose says:

> These differences in relative activities are obviously too small to allow sufficient sequence selection to produce, for example, prebiotic polypeptides of specific structures and functions as required for protoenzymes.

27. Shapiro, *Origins: A Skeptic's Guide*, p. 170. Some scientists, such as Manfred Eigen in Göttingen, have devised RNA theories that do not rely on chance. They hope to increase the odds of RNA formation by assuming that all its energy-rich precursors (e.g., nucleotides) were readily available in the primordial soup.

But, of course, that begs a very large question: Is it reasonable to assume that precursors such as nucleotides were all present in large amounts, just waiting to assemble into RNA? There is no experimental evidence that nucleotides would form from the starting materials available on the early earth. Certainly, none have formed in simulation experiments.

In experimental situations only the simplest building blocks of nucleotides have formed. And even these minor successes took place through highly artificial laboratory manipulations, not under conditions that would have held in a natural setting on the early earth. (See Shapiro, pp. 171-89.)

28. We will not take the space here to indicate all the elements that modern organicism retains from nineteenth-century romantic biology. Suffice it to point out a few similarities (see chapter 5 for comparison).

Like their nineteenth-century predecessors, organicists generally see evolution as progressive—advancing toward some goal—an idea rejected by mechanistic evolutionists. To support progressivism, organicists often draw a parallel between the evolution of life and individual development from a fertilized egg. As Michael Polanyi writes, "Evolution may be seen then as a progressive intensification of the higher principles of life. This is what we witness in the development of the embryo and of the growing child, processes akin to evolution." From "Life's Irreducible Structure," in *Knowing and Being: Essays by Michael Polanyi*, ed. Marjorie Grene (Chicago: University of Chicago Press, 1969), p. 234.

The progressive nature of evolution is described by organicists as

ascent up a hierarchy of levels of complexity—a modernized version of the
great chain of being or ladder of life. E. J. Ambrose describes it as a "ladder of complexity." See *The Nature and Origin of the Biological World*
(Chichester, England: Ellis Horwood Ltd., 1982), p. 117.

New levels of complexity are attributed to a process described as
"emergent." That is, at each stage of evolution novel and more complex
properties are said to appear from inherently simpler starting materials.
The term is borrowed from the nineteenth-century epigeneticists, who were
also called emergentists.

29. The discussion that follows is based on several works by Polanyi: "Life's
    Irreducible Structure" in *Knowing and Being*; *Personal Knowledge:
    Towards a Post-Critical Philosophy* (Chicago: University of Chicago Press,
    1958, 1962), pp. 328-31; *The Tacit Dimension* (New York: Doubleday,
    1966); "Life Transcending Physics and Chemistry," *Chemical and
    Engineering News* (August 21, 1967), pp. 54-65; Michael Polanyi and
    Harry Prosch, *Meaning* (Chicago: University of Chicago Press, 1975),
    chapter 11.

30. Polanyi, "Life's Irreducible Structure," in *Knowing and Being*, pp. 229,
    230.

31. Max Delbrück, "How Aristotle Discovered DNA," in *Physics and Our
    World: A Symposium in Honor of Victor F. Weisskopf*, ed. Kerson Huang
    (New York: American Institute of Physics, 1976).

32. B. C. Goodwin, "Biology and Meaning," in *Towards a Theoretical Biology*
    vol. 4, ed. C. H. Waddington (Edinburgh: Edinburgh University Press,
    1972). Goodwin goes on to say (p. 269): "Aristotle was correct to insist
    that something like formative 'ideas,' different in some sense from ordinary
    physical matter, must guide the intricate and extraordinarily varied for-
    mative processes of organic nature."

33. Ernst Mayr, *The Growth of Biological Thought: Diversity, Evolution, and
    Inheritance* (Cambridge, MA: Harvard University Press, 1982), pp. 88-90.
    Mayr says that Aristotle's *eidos* was "conceptually virtually identical" with
    the genetic program in DNA.

34. Campbell, *Grammatical Man*, p. 270.

35. Richard Dawkins, *The Blind Watchmaker: Why the Evidence of Evolution
    Reveals a Universe Without Design* (New York: W. W. Norton, 1986,
    1987), p. 150.

36. A. G. Cairns-Smith, *Seven Clues to the Origin of Life* (New York:
    Cambridge University Press, 1985). See also Dawkins, *Blind Watchmaker*,
    pp. 148-58.

37. L. E. Orgel, *The Origins of Life* (New York: John Wiley and Sons, 1973),
    p. 190.

38. *Ibid.*, p. 190.

39. For a more technical description of these distinctions, see Hubert P.
    Yockey, "A Calculation of the Probability of Spontaneous Biogenesis by
    Information Theory," *Journal of Theoretical Biology* 67 (1977), p. 345-
    76.

40. Hubert Yockey, *Information Theory and Molecular Biology* (Cambridge,
    England: Cambridge University Press, 1992), p. 262-63. "The clay sce-
    nario," Yockey writes, "is one of the attempts to use the 'order' that is
    characteristic of a crystal as an analogue of the 'order' that is supposed to
    characterize information biomolecules." But the two kinds of order are not

analogous. Hence, the "transfer of information from clay surfaces to organic macromolecules . . . is mathematically *impossible*, not just unlikely."

41. This argument is presented in A. E. Wilder-Smith, *The Natural Sciences Know Nothing of Evolution* (San Diego, CA: CLP Publishers, Master Books, 1981), pp. 77-87. See also the works by Polanyi cited in note 29.

42. H. H. Pattee, "Laws and Constraints, Symbols and Languages," in *Towards a Theoretical Biology*, p. 249.

43. Henry Quastler, *The Emergence of Biological Organization* (New Haven, CT: Yale University Press, 1964), pp. 15-17.

44. Pattee, "Laws and Constraints," in *Towards a Theoretical Biology*, p. 252.

45. Monod, *Chance and Necessity*, p. 108.

46. Peter Calow, *Biological Machines: A Cybernetic Approach to Life* (New York: Crane Russak, 1976), p. 112.

47. As C. S. Lewis argued, the laws of nature do not make events occur. They are conditional: They tell us what pattern events must take once they are initiated, but they have no power to initiate anything in themselves. A natural law tells us that "If A, then B," but it has no power to make A happen. See *Miracles* (New York: Macmillan, 1947).

48. Frederick Ferré, "Design Argument," *Dictionary of the History of Ideas*, vol. 1 (New York: Charles Scribner's Sons, 1973), p. 673.

As critics have pointed out, the label "argument *from* design" is not quite accurate. More accurate is the "argument *to* design." Proponents start by considering some structure or process in the natural world and argue *to* the conclusion that it exhibits the characteristics of intelligent design.

49. Francis Crick, *What Mad Pursuit* (New York: Basic Books, 1988), p. 138.

50. Paul Nelson, "Concluding Remarks," Sources of Information Content in DNA: An International Conference, held June 23-26, 1988, in Tacoma, Washington.

51. Larry Laudan, "The Demise of the Demarcation Problem," *Physics, Philosophy, and Psychoanalysis*, ed. Robert S. Cohen and Larry Laudan (Dordrecht, Holland: D. Reidel, 1983), pp. 119.

52. David Hull, "The Limits of Cladism," *Systematic Zoology* 28 (1979), p. 419.

53. David Hume, *An Inquiry Concerning Human Understanding* (New York: Bobbs-Merrill, 1955 [1748]), Section IV, Part II, p. 50; Section XI, p. 146.

54. For a penetrating analysis of the way science has been defined to allow only philosophical naturalism, see the works of Phillip Johnson: *Darwin on Trial* (Washington, DC: Regnery Gateway, 1991); "Evolution As Dogma," *First Things*, no. 6, (October 1990); "Creator or Blind Watchmaker?" *First Things*, no. 29, (January 1993); "God and Evolution: An Exchange," with Howard Van Till, *First Things*, no. 34, (June/July 1993).

See also J. P. Moreland, "Must Natural Science Presuppose Methodological Naturalism?" in *The Creation Hypothesis*, ed. J. P. Moreland (Downers Grove, IL: InterVarsity Press, 1994).

55. For philosophical arguments that creation cannot be disqualified from science, see two books by J. P. Moreland: *Scaling the Secular City* (Grand Rapids: Baker Book House, 1987), chapter 7; *Christianity and the Nature of Science: A Philosophical Investigation* (Grand Rapids: Baker Book House, 1989), chapter 6.

56. Judson, *Eighth Day*, p. 109.

SUGGESTED READING

Barbour, Ian. *Issues in Science and Religion*. New York: Harper and Row, Harper Torchbooks, 1966.

Barzun, Jacques. *Darwin, Marx, Wagner: Critique of a Heritage*, 2nd ed. Chicago: University of Chicago Press, 1941, 1958, 1981.

Becker, Carl. *The Heavenly City of the Eighteenth-Century Philosophers*. New Haven, CT: Yale University Press, 1932.

Bell, Eric Temple. *The Magic of Numbers*. New York: Dover Books, 1946.

Benacerraf, Paul, and Putnam, Hilary, eds. *Philosophy of Mathematics*, 2nd ed. Cambridge: Cambridge University Press, 1983.

Campbell, Douglas M., and Higgins, John C., eds. *Mathematics: People, Problems, Results*. Belmont, CA: Wadsworth International, Brigham Young University, 1984.

Brooke, John Hedley. *Science and Religion: Some Historical Perspectives*. Cambridge: Cambridge University Press, 1991.

Burtt, E. A. *The Metaphysical Foundations of Modern Science*, rev. ed. New York: Doubleday Anchor Books, 1932, 1954.

Butterfield, Herbert. *The Origins of Modern Science: 1300-1800*, rev. ed. New York: The Free Press, 1957, 1965.

Clouser, Roy A. *The Myth of Religious Neutrality*. Notre Dame, IN: University of Notre Dame Press, 1991.

Coleman, William. *Biology in the Nineteenth Century: Problems of Form, Function, and Transformation*. New York: John Wiley and Sons, 1971; Cambridge: Cambridge University Press, 1977.

Collingwood, R. G. *An Essay on Metaphysics*. Chicago: Henry Regnery, Gateway Edition, 1972; originally published by London: Oxford University Press, 1940.

_____. *The Idea of Nature*. Westport, CT: Greenwood Press, 1986; reprint of London: Oxford University Press, 1944.

Cunningham, Andrew, and Jardine, Nicholas, eds. *Romanticism in the Sciences*. Cambridge: Cambridge University Press, 1990.

Davies, P. C. W., and Brown, J. R., eds. *Ghost in the Atom*. Cambridge: Cambridge University Press, 1986.

Dillenberger, John. *Protestant Thought and Natural Science*. Notre Dame, IN: University of Notre Dame Press, 1960.

Einstein, Albert, and Infeld, Leopold. *The Evolution of Physics*. New York: Simon and Schuster, Touchstone Book, 1938, 1966.

Frank, Philipp. *Philosophy of Science: The Link Between Science and Philosophy*. Englewood Cliffs, NJ: Prentice-Hall, Spectrum Books, 1957.

Friedman, Alan J., and Donley, Carol C. *Einstein as Myth and Muse*. New York: Cambridge University Press, 1985.

Gillespie, Neal C. *Charles Darwin and the Problem of Creation*. Chicago: University of Chicago Press, 1979.

Gillispie, Charles Coulston. *The Edge of Objectivity*. Princeton, NJ: Princeton University Press, 1960.

Greene, John C. *Science, Ideology, and World View: Essays in the History of Evolutionary Ideas*. Berkeley: University of California Press, 1981.

Gregory, Frederick. *Scientific Materialism in Nineteenth-Century Germany*. Boston: D. Reidel, 1977.

Hall, A. R. *The Scientific Revolution, 1500-1800: The Formation of the Modern Scientific Attitude*. Boston: The Beacon Press, 1954.

Herbert, Nick. *Quantum Reality: Beyond the New Physics*. New York: Doubleday Anchor Books, 1985.

Hesse, Mary. *Science and the Human Imagination: Aspects of the History and Logic of Physical Science*. New York: Philosophical Library, 1955.

Holton, Gerald, and Elkana, Yehuda, eds. *Albert Einstein: Historical and Cultural Perspectives*. Princeton, NJ: Princeton University Press, 1982.

Hooykaas, R. *Religion and the Rise of Modern Science*. Grand Rapids: Eerdmans, 1972.

Jaki, Stanley L. *The Road of Science and the Ways to God*. Chicago: University of Chicago Press, 1978.

Judson, Horace Freeland. *The Eighth Day of Creation*. New York: Simon and Schuster, Touchstone Book, 1979.

Kaiser, Christopher. *Creation and the History of Science*. Grand Rapids: Eerdmans, 1991.

Kearney, Hugh. *Science and Change, 1500-1700*. New York: McGraw-Hill, World University Library, 1971.

Klaaren, Eugene M. *Religious Origins of Modern Science: Belief in Creation in Seventeenth-Century Thought*. Grand Rapids: Eerdmans, 1977.

Kline, Morris. *Mathematics: The Loss of Certainty*. New York: Oxford University Press, 1980.

Koyré, Alexandre. *From the Closed World to the Infinite Universe*. Baltimore: The Johns Hopkins University Press, 1957, paperback edition, 1968.

Kuhn, Thomas. *The Essential Tension*. Chicago: University of Chicago Press, 1977.

Lindberg, David C., and Numbers, Ronald L., eds. *God and Nature: Historical Essays on the Encounter between Christianity and Science*. Berkeley: University of California Press, 1986.

Lindberg, David C., and Westman, Robert S., eds. *Reappraisals of the Scientific Revolution*. Cambridge: Cambridge University Press, 1990.

Lovejoy, Arthur O. *The Great Chain of Being: A Study in the History of an Idea*. Cambridge: Harvard University Press, 1936, 1964.

Mascall, E. L. *Christian Theology and Natural Science*. Hamden, CT: Archon Books, 1965.

Mayr, Ernst. *The Growth of Biological Thought*. Cambridge: Harvard University Press, 1982.

Monod, Jacques. *Chance and Necessity*. New York: Random House, Vintage Books, 1971, 1972.

Moore, James R. *The Post-Darwinian Controversies*. Cambridge: Cambridge University Press, 1979.

Moreland, J. P. *Christianity and the Nature of Science: A Philosophical Investigation*. Grand Rapids: Baker Book House, 1989.

Newman, James R., ed. *The World of Mathematics*. New York: Simon and Schuster, 1956.

Nordenskiöld, Erik. *The History of Biology: A Survey*, originally published in Swedish in three volumes in 1920-24. New York: translated and published by Alfred A. Knopf, 1928; St. Clair Shores, MI: Scholarly Press, 1976.

O'Connor, Daniel, and Oakley, Francis, eds. *Creation: The Impact of an Idea*. New York: Charles Scribner's Sons, 1969.

Polanyi, Michael. *Knowing and Being: Essays by Michael Polanyi*, ed. Marjorie Grene. Chicago: University of Chicago Press, 1969.

_____. *The Tacit Dimension*. New York: Doubleday, 1966.

Polkinghorne, J. C. *The Quantum World*. Princeton, NJ: Princeton University Press, 1984.

Purcell, Edward A. *The Crisis of Democratic Theory*. Lexington, KY: University Press of Kentucky, 1973.

Randall, John Herman. *The Making of the Modern Mind*. New York: Columbia University Press, 1926, 1940.

Ratzsch, Del. *Philosophy of Science: The Natural Sciences in Christian Perspective*. Downers Grove, IL: InterVarsity Press, 1986.

Reichenbach, Hans. *From Copernicus to Einstein*. New York: Wisdom Library, division of Philosophical Library, n.d..

_____. *The Rise of Scientific Philosophy*. Berkeley: University of California Press, 1954.

Russell, Colin. *Cross-Currents: Interactions Between Science and Faith*. Grand Rapids: Eerdmans, 1985.

Shapiro, Robert. *Origins: A Skeptic's Guide to the Creation of Life on Earth*. New York: Simon and Schuster, Summit Books, 1986.

Stebbing, L. Susan. *Philosophy and the Physicists*. London: Methuen and Company, [1937]; New York: Dover Publications, 1958.

Teich, Mikuláš, and Young, Robert, eds. *Changing Perspectives in the History of Science: Essays in Honour of Joseph Needham*. London: Heinemann, 1973.

Thaxton, Charles; Bradley, Walter; and Olsen, Roger. *The Mystery of Life's Origin: Reassessing Current Theories*. New York: Philosophical Library, 1984; Dallas: Lewis and Stanley, 1993.

Torrance, Thomas. *Divine and Contingent Order*. Oxford: Oxford University Press, 1981.

Westfall, Richard S. *Science and Religion in Seventeenth-Century England*. New Haven, CT: Yale University Press, 1958; Hamden, CT: Archon Books, 1970.

_____. *The Construction of Modern Science: Mechanisms and Mechanics*. New York: John Wiley and Sons, 1971; Cambridge: Cambridge University Press, 1977.

Wilder-Smith, A. E. *The Creation of Life.* Wheaton, IL: Harold Shaw Publishers, 1970.

_____. *The Natural Sciences Know Nothing of Evolution.* San Diego, CA: CLP Publishers, Master Books, 1981.

INDEX